Please Make This Look Nice

WHEN?

Screen print make-ready

dedicated to

Mom & Dad
Meredith
Joanna
Olivia & Iris

and every failure
and every rare success

and everything and everyone else
yesterday, today, and tomorrow

Please
Make
This L
ook Ni
ce

The G
raphic
Desig
n Proc
ess

Peter Ahlberg

Skira Rizzoli
New York

Fore word

Brett Littman

Over the last eight years at The Drawing Center, we've taken an approach to drawing that considers it analogous to thinking—the visualization of thinking. We are looking at sketches, notational work, doodles—things that don't necessarily rise to the "fully rendered" concept of what we typically think of as a drawing. One of the great values of the medium of drawing is its demonstration of the human mind at work. This is why I believe in celebrating a drawing's unfinished quality—the shakiness, the in-between-ness, the place where we're on the way to something else.

In the case of graphic design, I would guess that many people aren't even aware that there is a process—drawing or otherwise. They think that Helvetica just appears on their computer and don't understand that the letterforms were actually created by someone—or many people, as the case may be.

Embedded in that discussion too is the complicated and under-studied role that digital tools play within drawing today—an issue relevant to graphic design as well as architecture. I view all of those practices—old and new—as interlinked exploration for this institution. This project—and its focus on drawing within a different discipline—will build on a series of previous shows we've mounted, like those of Frederick Kiesler, Lebbeus Woods, and Ferran Adria, because it's in line with that very expansive notion of where drawing is occurring.

It's interesting to me that no one has ever said that drawing is dead—unlike painting and sculpture, whose efficacy has been much debated in the twenty-first century. If you want to talk about drawing you're usually talking about line, whereas if you're talking about painting you're talking about history. The issues are different, as is what's at stake.

Drawing is something that practitioners of every discipline engage in. It doesn't matter whether or not you're a good renderer. Everyone has the capability to draw—whether it's a stick figure or much more. It is a base, human activity, very close to consciousness. It can be seen as the idea of simply putting "a pencil to paper" in order to think. A scientist doesn't learn how to paint, but he or she can surely draw. App developers might not know how to draw but they definitely know how to make a flow chart. I've spoken to engineers, architects, graphic designers, musicians, and choreographers. They're all approaching drawing in the same way and it's not far from what visual artists are doing. Today I very rarely visit a studio where anyone pulls out a work on paper and says, "This is my drawing." They're showing me an algorithm on a computer, an animation, they're singing to me, they're talking about archival material and collage.

At The Drawing Center, we take drawing as a kind of metaphor, or metaphorical activity, rather than just a discipline. Surely we're not defining drawing as pencil on paper, or for that matter anything having to do with the substrate. It can occur on a canvas, it can occur in space, on a computer screen, and it can occur in the body. The question is, "What is the limit of drawing?" and also, "Is this thing a drawing?" We're often led to that question by the work that we're looking at. Drawing can be something that is tangential and non-linear but it always has a certain set of parameters. Pat Steir gave a great lecture here called "Everything I Do Is Drawing." She showed her paintings and murals and of course a lot of her drawing work, and she said that when she approaches painting, her concerns are not painterly—they are the concerns of someone who draws. For me, that was a very important moment.

Within the context of this project, I've been giving a lot of thought to the idea of what museums might look like in the twenty-first century. We're not doing a relational aesthetic exhibition here with *Please Make This Look Nice*, even though we're inviting people to work here at The Drawing Center. But maybe, with the right institutional culture, we could be inviting architects, graphic designers, scientists, and so on, to talk with us and work alongside us as we develop our ideas.

I find those types of conversations to be the most stimulating ones I'm having today. I guess I'm a little bit of a romantic in the sense that I don't know why all of the arts—and I'm going to put architecture and graphic design in there as art forms—are so divided. I don't get it. I think the beauty of The Drawing Center is that its umbrella is big enough to capture all of it.

PETER AHLBERG Sony digital voice recorder used for all interviews

Introduction

Peter Ahlberg

In May of 2013 I proposed an exhibition at The Drawing Center that would look at the role of drawing within the graphic design process. A series of meetings with the institution's curatorial team ensued, productive discussions during which they pressed me with questions about what constituted a "process drawing" and framing my subject (with chronology, technology, and so forth) to determine what exactly would be shown and why. But with each new definition and set of parameters, I felt increasingly certain that more was being lost than gained, and that the graphic design process was actually more varied and less quantifiable than I first thought. As Ivan Chermayeff would say to me later, "Not *the* graphic design process, *a* graphic design process."

Eventually, rather than seeking individual acts of "traditional" drawing within the process, I concluded that the whole design process is itself an act of drawing. Indeed, lines are drawn throughout the design process—intentionally and fortuitously—albeit not in the traditional sense (although that is certainly part of it). A very broad definition of drawing allows for the inclusion of techniques as seemingly disparate as iterative sketching in Adobe Illustrator, collecting antique books, meandering around the Internet, applying paint to canvas, taking notes at a meeting, and preparing mechanicals for print production. These directly and indirectly related activities collectively result in finished work. Seeing the process in this holistic way resonated deeply with my own experiences (both first-hand and observational) and brought clarity to something that had long struck me as flawed within the typical dialogue of graphic design—the implicit or explicit "right" or "best" ways of working that often describe the process as logical, linear, and objective. The imagining of the process as a tunnel-like experience without diversion from the path of idea to execution might be a powerful tool when used to teach, talk about, and present work to a client, but ultimately it is not a universal standard.

One of the most illuminating conversations I had about graphic design and drawing was with Carin Goldberg. She pointed out that considering the graphic design process through the lens of drawing allows you to see it as a practice, a way of training your mind and muscles to gain strength, knowledge, and clarity. One doesn't draw just in order to become a better renderer, but rather to become a better seer, a better thinker, and as Milton Glaser eloquently put it, "to understand what is real." Drawing encourages things to happen through the physicality of the tool—whatever that tool is—things that might not happen just in your head. Tying that understanding to the graphic design process can invigorate and reinvigorate because the process then becomes about the gesture, the mark, the movement, the dialogue, and so on, ultimately expanding and enriching the way people approach the making of work.

It is notable that this book accompanies an exhibition at The Drawing Center specifically, as opposed to a design-focused venue or institution. As Brett Littman notes in his Foreword, drawing is so directly aligned with consciousness and the action of thinking that it can really be seen as a "base, human activity"—one that is practiced regardless of age, profession, or even one's ability to render. Experimental Jetset brilliantly suggests that because drawing and writing are inseparable activities, graphic design is, in many ways, the manifestation of this confluence or intertwining, the indistinguishable relationship "between the verbal and the visual." By removing graphic design from the bubble of "design for designers," and placing it in this much broader context of drawing, we are able to gain deeper insight to, new perspectives on, and greater appreciation for both practices. The making of graphic design becomes more relevant to the culture.

All of the texts included in this book are condensed and edited transcriptions of interviews I conducted over the course of about a year beginning in October of 2014. The majority of the interviews were recorded with an old digital voice recorder, save for a few that were conducted by e-mail. There were about twelve basic questions/topics I tried to address in each interview—with some slight variation for each interviewee:

1. **Background (childhood/education, introduction to design, career beginnings)**
2. **Moment of realization/turning point related to design work and/or process**
3. **Role of collaboration and trust within your process**
4. **Role of doubt within your process**
5. **Role of time within your process**
6. **Most valued/gratifying aspect or phase of your process**
7. **Technology's impact on your process**
8. **Disconnect between the "real" process and the "presented" process**
9. **How the intended medium of a project changes your process**
10. **Creative practices outside of the studio**
11. **Interests outside of design**
12. **Importance/use of drawing as related to design work and/or process**

Conversations did not always proceed in this order and of course there were many additional follow-up and improvised questions, but it is important for the reader to be aware of the prompts above because the final texts included in this volume intentionally hide the interviewer (me) to allow each designer's voice to be heard in a continuum. Additionally, the thematic sub-headings throughout each interview are derived from the content of the answers that follow, as opposed to standing in for the question that was asked.

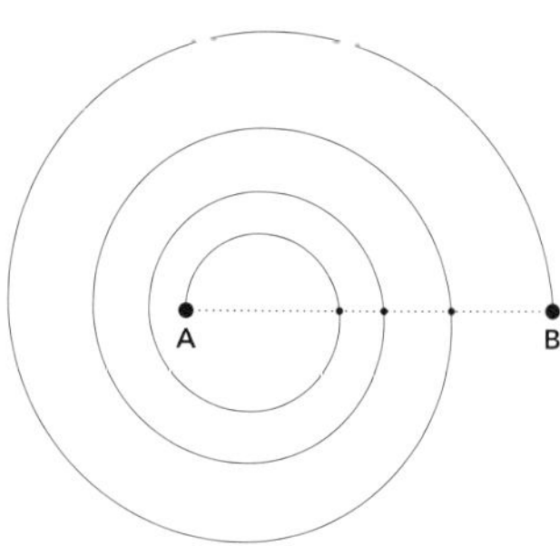

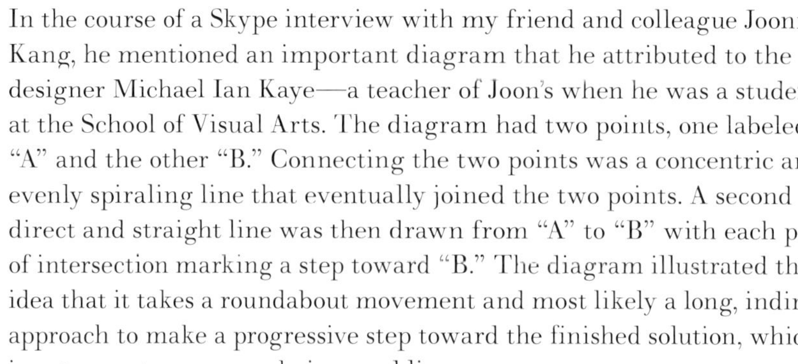

In the course of a Skype interview with my friend and colleague Joonmo Kang, he mentioned an important diagram that he attributed to the designer Michael Ian Kaye—a teacher of Joon's when he was a student at the School of Visual Arts. The diagram had two points, one labeled "A" and the other "B." Connecting the two points was a concentric and evenly spiraling line that eventually joined the two points. A second direct and straight line was then drawn from "A" to "B" with each point of intersection marking a step toward "B." The diagram illustrated the idea that it takes a roundabout movement and most likely a long, indirect approach to make a progressive step toward the finished solution, which in retrospect can seem obvious and linear.

This idea of a designer drawing the way in which he or she understands the process so perfectly captured the essence of this project and distilled seemingly disparate questions into such a simple framework that I used it as a "final question" for nearly all the interviews that followed.

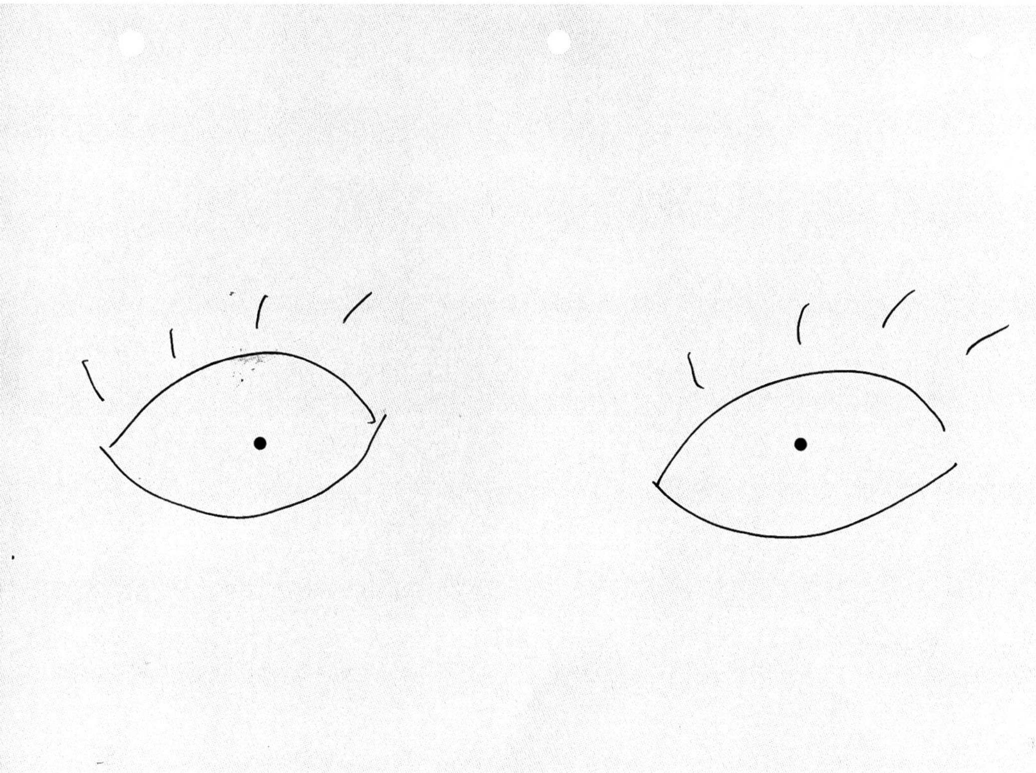

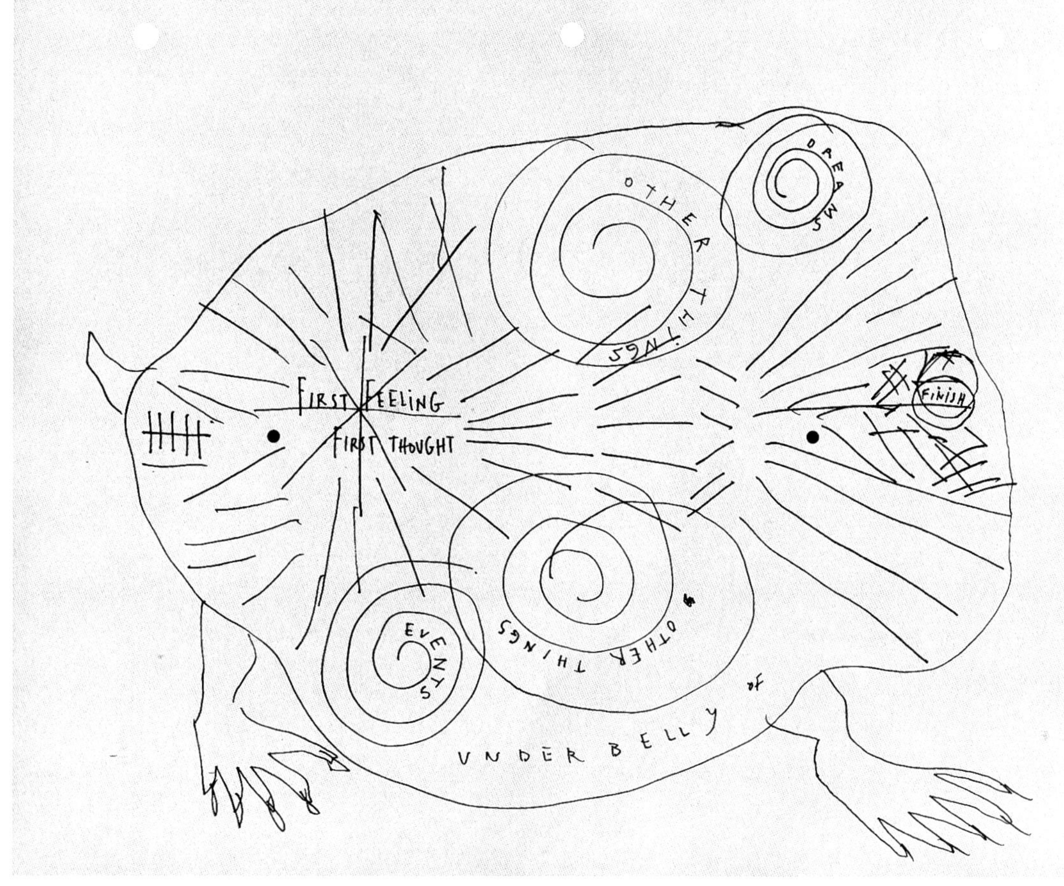

 [top] CARIN GOLDBERG [bottom] MAIRA KALMAN

At the start of this project I anticipated a clear ideological divide among designers, perhaps a few opposing camps, rooted mainly in the historical concerns and battles (see, for example, "Confusion and Chaos: The Seduction of Contemporary Graphic Design" by Paul Rand) that have played out in the field over the last fifty or so years—along with a handful of young, rebellious outliers. But based on my own observational experiences, few designers today can be categorized in the way they once were. In fact, as Michael Bierut also points out, a designer's methodology stems ultimately from his or her "personal idiosyncrasies and temperament." Looking back on the several dozen interviews conducted during the research for this book, I was surprised at how diverse the responses were and how different people's interests and priorities laid.

Still, there are unexpected parallels and shared similarities between those who I might otherwise consider very different designers. For example, Maira Kalman and Stefan Sagmeister both use note/index cards as part of their process. Whereas Maira uses cards to impose a sort of malleable order, Stefan seems to use them as a tool for abstracting ideas and then seeing if those tangential ideas have any relationships. I also see a connection between Elliott Earls, Milton Glaser, and Karlssonwilker in their emphasis on the act of making over having a strong idea: Elliott experiments with a variety of tools and media, Milton celebrates the spontaneous and serendipitous, and Karlssonwilker prioritizes playfulness throughout the design process. In looking at the role of collage within the design process, such luminaries as Alan Fletcher and Ivan Chermayeff are trying to discover relationships between seemingly unrelated forms whereas John Gall makes collage work emphasizing the differentness of forms, testing their interactions in a shared space. Stephen Doyle and Nolen Strals from Post Typography both address their respective religious family upbringings and how this background plays out in their work today.

Visually, I am in awe of the materials in this book not least because they were only intended to live for a moment, ephemeral documents created as a means of understanding or making something else. Nearly all of them were made privately, never meant for public viewing or distribution, and yet they are still utterly compelling and dynamic in every respect. For projects such as Milton Glaser's poster for the 1976 Montreaux Jazz Festival we are able to see directly how photographic reference material translated into a sketch, which then translated into a finished work. Other work is more mysterious. In Paul Sahre's silkscreen make-readys we see evidence of the making of six different posters—separated by many years—unintentionally composited on two sides of the same sheet of paper. Dress Code's photography, taken on the set of a commercial for Google, is as much about documentation as it is a collection of evocative and alluring images. Ellen Lupton and Abbott Miller's poster paste-up and Rubylith mechanicals are as much a time capsule of a specific moment in graphic design history as they are stand-alone objects of material beauty. Paula Scher's work, in its staggering variety, is a demonstration of what exploring typographic form—in two- and three-dimensions—can look like in the twenty-first century.

I recently spoke to a colleague who claimed that there are over three-thousand design studios, agencies, and creative departments in New York alone—a statistic I can't confirm but one that nonetheless illustrates an important point

• GETTING TO THE POINT •

[top] STEPHEN DOYLE [bottom] ABBOTT MILLER

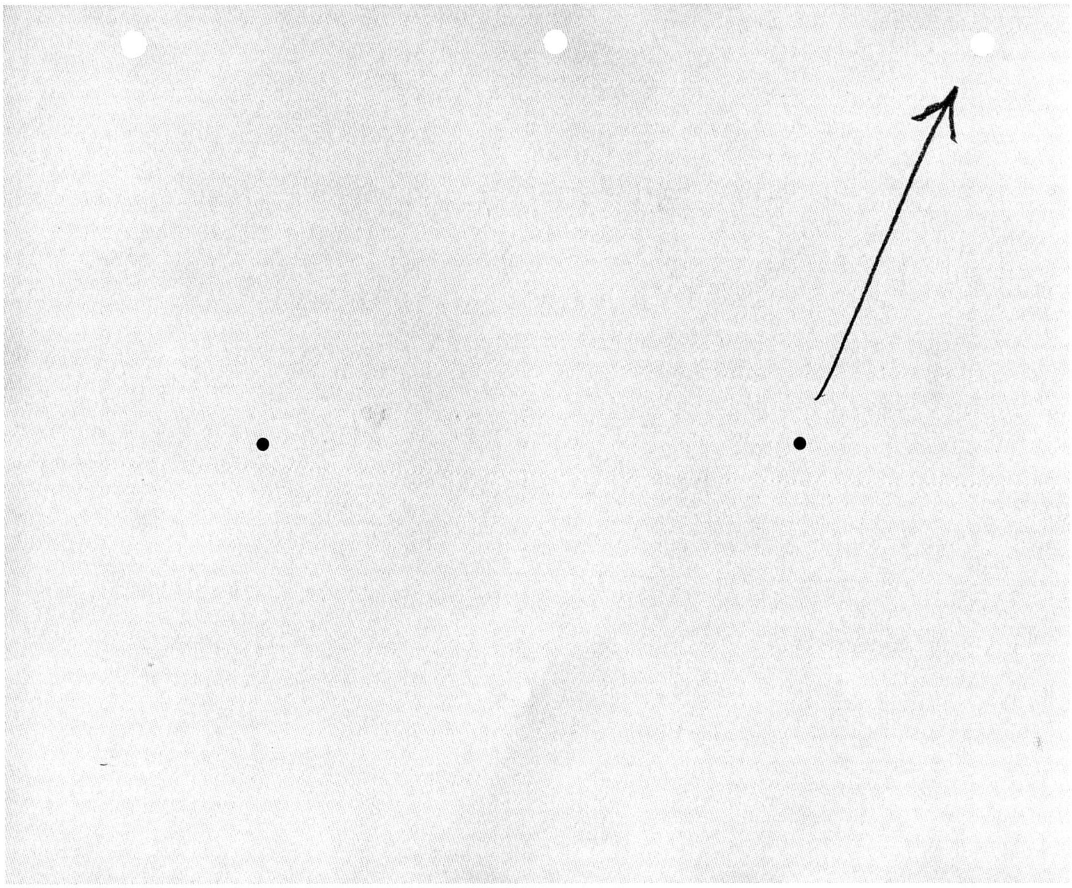

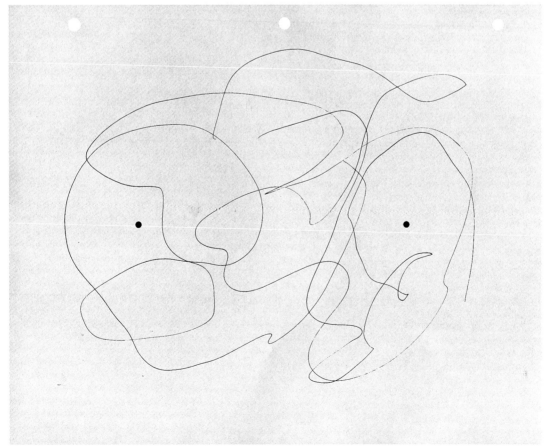

[top] **IVAN CHERMAYEFF** [bottom] **NATASHA JEN**

about this book. The work presented and conversations included in this book are archetypal, representational—a thorough cross-sampling of the different points of view that comprise the landscape of graphic design, but are by no means meant to be comprehensive. In a field so nebulous, approximate in its definition, and one that includes a vast number of sub-disciplines and specializations—the process is so deeply and specifically personal that if a book were to address and include the unique point of view of each working designer it would become an infinite and ever-expanding project like the fabled map in Jorge Luis Borges's "On Exactitude in Science"—a map so detailed it becomes as large as the very territory it represents.

So while this book is a collection of remarkable conversations, I am also hopeful that it is part of a much larger conversation and investigation into the nature of creativity—within the practice of graphic design and beyond.

Signs and Me
in the Cinema

Peter Wollen

Indian
Bloom

revered for throughout mill
music, ancient, remote and
not simply a new art; it is
porates others, which opera
channels, using different c
in the most acute form th
the different arts, their simi
of translation and transcript … esthetics
by the Wagnerian notion of … rechtian
critique of Wagner, questic … heory of
synesthesia, to Lessing's *L* … *ndances.*
Yet the impact of the ci … most nil.
Universities still continue … f aesthetics, robbed of immediacy … d by the
enormity of the challenge … . Many
writers on aesthetics have … ema any
status whatever; they have … to their
customary pursuits. Variou … renovate
aesthetics, but these have … th other
academic disciplines—psyc … ciology,
linguistic philosophy—rath … the arts
themselves. It is incredib … ave not
seized on the cinema with e … udovkin,
Eisenstein or Welles may be mentioned but, on the whole, there is
a depressing ignorance, even unconcern.

In the 1920s the Russians—Kuleshov, Pudovkin, Eisenstein—managed to force themselves on the attention. The situation in which they worked, of course, was unique. The Bolshevik Revolution had swept away and destroyed the old order in education as in

gest a numbe
ilm aesthetic
ciple has be
take place i
erse of disc
expelled. T
onsive to c
other arts, c
ch too long
countries a
in which t
ly, irrespective of what
iters about the cinema
as if linguistics did not
of montage in blissful
ic.
t because, by right, film
study of aesthetics in

in par
enthus
interim
It is
him fo
the wr
quite
circum
probab
The m
them
proble
sions.
in alm
Eisens
directo
concept of montage. There are
tions of Eisenstein's views abou
current has reacted against this
instead of the shot and the movin
It seems to me that what is neede
of Eisenstein's theories but a c

Detail of paste-up for poster for Cooper Union School of Art Visiting Artist Lecture Series, 1985

g

nd enlarged

Contents

The Cinema One series is published by
Indiana University Press
in association with the British Film Institute

third edition, revised and enlarged, 1972

Library of Congress catalog card number: 72-82722
ISBN 0-253-18141-0

7 8 9 10 82 81 80

America

last. And, of course, it will take even longer before all
l has been studied in depth and the findings published.
the 1920s in the Soviet Union is an extraordinarily
riod—not only complex but startlingly and breath-
ginal. The huge political and social upheavals of the
uced an unprecedented situation in the arts, in culture
n the movement of thought and ideology. In the section on Eisenstein in this book, I have tried to shift the terrain of discussion and to indicate, in broad outlines, what I take to be the main drift of Eisenstein's thought and to locate it in its setting. All this is necessarily very provisional; I look forward eagerly to a new epoch in the historiography of the Soviet Union, the arts in the 1920s, in particular the cinema, and to the debate which is bound to follow.

or film aesthetics, however, has not
d. Eisenstein, as we have seen, was
nt which included not only film
ers and architects. It is relatively
inema of the 1920s into the normal
. Hollywood, on the other hand, is
henomenon, much more forbidding,
e is no difficulty in talking about
s a poet like Mayakovsky, a painter like Malevich, or a theatre director like Stanislavsky. But John Ford or Raoul Walsh? The initial reaction, as we well know, was to damn Hollywood completely, to see it as a threat to civilised values and sensibilities. The extent of the panic can be seen by the way in which the most bourgeois critics and theorists manage to find *Battleship Potemkin* far preferable to any Metro-Goldwyn-Mayer

r of pedestrian exposi-
, of course, a counter-
stressing the sequence
t the stationary camera.
ot an outright rejection
vestigation of them, a

Michael Bierut

January 29, 2015

"Process" vs Process

A lot of us are required to talk about the process because we have agreements with our clients. Typically, part of that agreement is describing, in advance, the steps that we'll take to get them from nothing to whatever it is that they want. Those steps are predictable and they follow a sequence.The challenge is that so often, the actual work doesn't have anything to do with the way that the process is described. I wrote an essay about this. It acknowledged that what actually happens is very unpredictable.

If I'm working on a big project that has complexity, I'll include a "discovery orientation" phase as a beginning step in the proposal. Sometimes I call it "analysis." Often, I think other designers will have a step that comes after that where you take that analysis and translate it into some sort of form—you could call it a "creative brief development" or something. I'm not a big believer in that. You get people to nod their heads at a workshop where the whole team with the Post-it notes and white boards arrives at the five attributes of whatever their thing is, and then everyone's in agreement about that. I think that might have the function of getting people used to thinking about the problem and acquainting them with the idea of reaching a consensus as a social exercise but I assume those five attribute words are almost always meaningless because you still have to translate them into some physical form. If "authentic" is one of those words, there's no such thing as an "authentic" typeface. The power that designers have to actually make things can help jump-start the process.

I'm content just to talk to people, listen to them, then come back and show them something, and say, "One way to interpret what you said is something that looks like this. What do you think?" I might guess right, and I win. Or I might guess completely wrong the next twenty times. That's what makes actually writing out the phases of a project and costing them such a funny exercise, like a delusion for everyone, because I don't let them pay me less if they decide faster. And to tell you the truth, I don't make them pay me more if it takes them longer. I say, "I will keep working against the brief until you have something you're satisfied with." If for some reason the brief changes, I have the right to charge more. If for some reason I just don't seem to be able to get the job done, they have the right to fire me. But aside from that, let's just assume that I'm going to stick to this goddamn thing until we have it. So then, in theory, if all goes really smoothly, you go through an iterative design process, you come to some agreement about what the thing is that you're designing and then you implement or execute it. Sometimes, if it's complicated, there are stages that go after that or in between, where you're testing it to make sure it works or coming up with operating instructions so that other people can do it.

I don't have much cause to actually think in an organized way about the process other than that.

Personality

All designers I know and admire—the work that they do and the way that they do that work is the product of personal idiosyncrasies and what kind of temperament they have as a human being. So I can't work the way that some other designers work. It would drive me crazy. Even the thought of it gives me the heebie-jeebies because I'm so impatient. I have a really short attention span. My way of working is to lunge as fast as possible toward the finish line and sometimes I completely miss, or head in the wrong direction, or cross the finish line of someone else's race. This idea of willfully suspending my goal-oriented predilections so I can just experiment is something I've tried to do and that I associate with failure. I feel like I'm wasting time, I'm messing around, I have no idea what I'm doing. I don't find that a pleasing thing. I know there are a lot of designers who valorize that willful ignorance, not knowing what you're doing and the kinds of discoveries you make when you're just experimenting. I know all that stuff, and I also know that that stuff is just not the way I do it.

Massimo Vignelli

Massimo was interesting because he really did have a methodology. He worked across so many disciplines and thought much more like an architect. Architecture requires patience because of the nature of the time frame and the scale—the fact that projects will take years to realize and that what you're building is probably going to have some permanence in the world. As a graphic designer you can be in the mood to try this, you can feel that the situation is exactly right for that, you can think there's this thing that you always wanted to do and now here's your chance, and you say, "I'll try this, no one will notice." You might not get paid that much, so why not? You can take risks—do it one way on Monday, another way on Tuesday, and then it is all in the recycling bin on Thursday. With architects, I think there's a reason why Richard Meier buildings look alike. Because he feels a responsibility to his clients, of course, and to the overall body of work he's creating.

Massimo carried this through to the world of graphic design as well. You wouldn't go to him for a zany book. You knew the kind of book he designed. You knew the kind of identity he designed. His way of doing an identity was to pick a really classic typeface and come up with some characteristic way of organizing it graphically. I'm not even sure that's a method because that was just his way. It was a Vignelli solution to something. One of the reasons I prospered there was that I thought that way of working was congenial and it was interesting. I liked doing it and I was learning something as I was doing it. At the same time, I would go off the clock at the end of the day and do a freelance job. I would do something that had nothing to do with anything, because I didn't think there was a moral imperative to do it that way. Massimo actually thought that somehow there was some ideal that all those things were contributing to, which is what gave his work such force and made him such a powerful person and powerfully persuasive with clients. I think it makes his work, compared to a lot of other modernists, much more grounded and passionate. He really did feel deeply about all that stuff and he was great at it. I think that if he took a step back he could actually see that passion in other people, even if he disagreed with the output. He could see it was the same thing.

He was one of those designers—who again, I am not like—where the minute the client left the room he could say, "It should be like this" and do a drawing of it.

Notebooks

My favorite thing to do is to be on the intake as long as possible and not think about solutions. I would love to not think about what the solution will be.

The secret indulgence that I have in my job is that some projects permit me to go to school on someone else's dime. I've been to amazing places, talked to amazing people, been in really remarkable situations, and the fact that I can design something because of all that is great. As a result my notebooks are typically not filled with drawings. They're filled with notes on conversations.

Occasionally I'll make a little drawing of what it could be and what it could look like.

This is notebook 106 or so. I always carry the one before around with me too in case I want to look up something. They go back to 1982, I think, and I have them all by my desk except for two that I lost along the way. None of them are lined, a few of them of them were gridded, but then I abandoned that, and now they are all plain white paper. They're just these humble things filled mostly with notes on meetings. I'm in my intake mode. Sometimes I never look at the notes afterwards. Sometimes I'll circle certain things that strike me in the conversation. A lot of times people say something that will start something in my head. The first thing that will happen a lot of times has less to do with a visual aha moment. It's just a sense of, "This should be this sort of thing."

The Nature of Graphic Design

I think a lot about the differences between all these things that are called "design," which tend to be lumped together a bit more than I think they should be. Graphic design, product design, architecture, fashion design, interior design—I think that people love the idea that "design is one big thing"—as Massimo used to say. I actually think that graphic design has particular characteristics that make it very different from other kinds of design. Every one of those other disciplines has its own particular characteristics but one that is shared is the requirement of functionality. However, the functional requirements of graphic design are often so minimal that they can't really dictate form the way function can dictate form in product design or the way the program can dictate form in architecture.

Also, I think one of the challenges of graphic design, because it's a communicative tool, is that it's inherently social. It's not a private thing. It doesn't work if no one can understand it. Not everyone has to understand it and not everyone has to understand it immediately, but you're doing it because someone out there is supposed to be receiving a message, some sort of transaction is happening. Those transactions are predicated on conventions and what we've all agreed things represent.

A Designer's Evolution

When you're first starting out—let's take designing a logo as a problem—it's always the same problem. It doesn't matter what the company is or what they do. You approach it as the same project. Along the way, as you get more experienced, you realize that there's a difference between doing a logo for a really big ubiquitous company versus a small one, and certain things just look too small or too big or they don't have the right tone or this has a degree of cleverness that makes it not seem right. All of a sudden you have this navigational mechanism that is pointing you in the right direction. I didn't have that when I was younger. I've gotten that through experience.

When I look at a lot of my earliest projects, they were either timidly imitative or else they were kooky self-indulgent gambles with no relationship to actually doing the job they were meant to do. I was just too careless with the connotations that were part of the formal choices I was making.

There are so many variables that come into design. I'm always the same person, except I'm more experienced now than I was last year and the year before that and before that. More experience means that I'm better at some things and worse at other things. There's something nice about being ignorant and having the freedom of not knowing what you're doing. Knowing too clearly what works and doesn't work—that's the downside of experience.

Even though I'm the same person, the nature of the project itself is different. Most important the mixture of people I'm working with are different. The client will be different. Even the designers on my team might be different. So every time you exchange one of the players, the nature of the game changes.

Starting Point

A lot of times I'll be sitting with one of my designers and I'll say, "Let's get all the obvious things out first. You could do this or that, you can do it upside down." Sometimes an obvious thing is the right answer. Sometimes when you're doing an obvious thing you make a mistake and the mistake actually leads you in a different direction. Sometimes I've gone into meetings just with obvious crap and I say, "These are all the obvious things and I don't think any of these are right, but I want to have a conversation in hopes that the conversation will take us to some new place."

Massimo wasn't like that at all. He would come out of a meeting and have a single idea of what should happen. It wasn't quite, "Take it or leave it," but it was, "Here's a solution for you, isn't it great?" Sometimes the client would agree and sometimes not. If not, he'd pivot and maneuver off of that to figure out how to get it exactly right. But I'll go into a client meeting with stuff that I don't even think is finished or fully realized because I want information from the client, not necessarily approval. I don't think if I get it absolutely right, they'll approve it. Because a lot of the time, all the stuff you're brooding about is not something they're going to notice anyway. I think some people would think this is shocking—going in with some half-baked piece of shit to a client—but I do it all the time.

Client Considerations

I believe that we're victims of our own temperament. I think Massimo was temperamentally predisposed to dominate when presenting to a client. I have partners here who have strong opinions from the get go, but I usually don't. There will be some horrible stupid idea that it definitely shouldn't be, but I always think the best idea I've got is just one option and someone else might have just as good of an idea or even a better idea. I'll say to a client, "Why do you want to redesign it, doesn't it work pretty well now?" I don't think other designers say that. I say, "That's not the way I would do it, but it seems to be making you a lot of money." People will tell you everything. They'll give it all away if you play it that way. I think most designers don't because they're so eager to establish their authority and expertise.

I'll tell almost any prospective client that I'm not an expert on what it is that they do. Even if they've seen work that I've done that makes them think I know what it is that they do, I'll warn them it was an accident or a one-time thing. I'm desperately trying to preserve my status as an outsider so I can ask questions that I wouldn't otherwise.

One of my predispositions is that as I'm working, I'll start thinking really early on about how I can explain this solution to the client. I will, as I'm making choices, almost edit the choices to things that I think can translate into a coherent story for the client or whoever has to approve the work.

Massimo never did that. His explanation was, "Isn't this fantastic?" I'm not kidding. He did it with such passion that it was irresistible. I can't simulate that. There are a lot of things I learned from him without actually being able to put them into practice.

Audience

When you're in school, you're just trying to please your teacher. When you get your first job, you're just trying to please your boss. Then you hit the big time and you actually have people who hire you and then you think you're supposed to be pleasing your client. I think the highest state of being is thinking about the real audience for the work and how you want them to perceive it. Part of the pleasure I take in doing graphic design is trying to assume the persona of the audience member. I was never a big sports fan and then I got the New York Jets as a client. I then became sincerely interested and enthusiastic about football. I wasn't pretending. No one is born interested in stamp collecting or bird watching. Somehow along the way, you learn to take pleasure in different kinds of bird calls and feathers. It's the same with football.

There are certain times when the idea of being in that audience is something that I find baffling. It's just unfathomable to me. For instance, I've never been a smoker. I just find cigarettes awful, so any projects that involve cigarettes and smoke and nicotine, I just can't do it. It's another world for me. I don't have the internal mechanisms to let me assume the persona of the person who's going to be on the other end. On the other hand, if I'm designing for the MIT Media Lab, while I'm not a PhD genius or scientist, I can get close enough to understanding what that world is that I can make a convincing offer.

Clients will give you a brief on a piece of paper and those are almost always so inadequate and thin and faltering that they never help. Likewise, dry recitations of who an audience is—"52 percent male 48 percent female, this income level, and so on"—is never as good as someone frankly laying it out for you, someone who actually knows something really well and can break it down for you. People like that can go on forever and my mind is just going bing bing bing.

Research and Technology

The ability to research things now is so much more robust than it used to be because of Wikipedia or Google. You can actually get a dossier on every single person that you go into a meeting with and you can make assumptions, often specious, about what role they're going to play. This technology comes into your life both gradually and quickly, and as it's happening you're obliterating your memory of what it was like before. I started in 1980 before FedEx and faxes. I had a client in San Francisco and I worked in New York. If I wanted to show them a design, I would send it in a package that would arrive three days later, and then they would call me on the telephone and react to it. I would have Xeroxes of it, and I'd look at my Xeroxes and make notes. I remember one time, the package had to be there the very next day, so someone had to drive to JFK and deal directly with someone from Lufthansa cargo. We paid them a lot of money. That's the obvious part that's different. You're also able to visualize solutions faster. But I don't think it has rewired my brain in any way. I'm too stubborn.

Rhythm

I'm a real voracious reader. I think reading makes you smart. People think I know a lot about stuff and it's because I've read about it. Likewise, listening to music like the *Goldberg Variations* by Bach, which is really a designed thing. If you layout a sixty-plus-page book, every one of the spreads has an underlying structure that connects it to the one before and the one after, but they each have to be unique and respond to what the elements on those few pages are. The *Goldberg Variations* is a theme at the beginning and then thirty-two variations on it and the whole theme repeated at the end. That idea that the theme always has the same number of measures and the same tonic structure, and yet, he works all these changes on it—that for me is the real lesson for design. This may be the essence of what design is.

Gratification

I take pleasure in the making of things, but it is really nice to finish. To have nothing before and then have something afterwards—that's great. Whether you're making a baby or a business card, right?

Experimental Jetset

May 3, 2015

Early Days

The three of us met when we were still students at the Gerrit Rietveld Academy in Amsterdam. In 1997, the editors of *Blvd*, a Dutch pop-culture magazine, asked Danny to redesign their publication. Danny actually wanted to turn down the assignment, as he was in his final year of school and wanted to concentrate on his graduation project. Linda van Deursen, who was our teacher around that time, advised Danny to take on the assignment, and let it count as a graduation project.

Danny realized the assignment was too vast for one person, so he asked Marieke to collaborate with him. They had also worked together on flyers and posters for the Amsterdam rock venue Paradiso and used to publish a small punkzine called *PHK*. All this took place between 1995 and 1997.

While Danny and Marieke were working on the redesign of *Blvd*, they realized they needed a third person. They really liked the work of Erwin, so Marieke and Danny asked Erwin to join them. Since then, we have been working together. We don't have any employees or interns—it's just the three of us.

Infinite Process

It's really interesting that you acknowledge us as "process-led" designers, as we don't think a lot of other people regard us as such. But we do see our work as process-led even though it's hard to define the notion of the process. The way we see it, process is something quite difficult to capture—it's the movement that exists in between certain steps. While it's easy to pinpoint the different steps—research, sketches, presentations, proofs, the actual result—the movement that happens between these steps is impossible to grasp.

In that sense, this whole notion of the process reminds us of one of those famous paradoxes by the Greek philosopher Zeno. In order for an arrow to go from one point to another, it first has to cross a point between. Or, to put it very simply: to fly from point A to point B, the arrow first has to cross point C. But in order to go from A to C, the arrow has to cross D. This goes on forever.

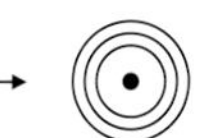

Each set of points will always have another point in the middle, and thus the arrow actually has to cross an infinite number of points, which would take an infinite amount of time. For Zeno, this shows the impossibility of movement. In a similar way, one could argue that pure process is an impossibility. Process, as a dynamic movement, can only be measured by showing the static steps in between. But the process itself will forever remain invisible—locked in a constant state of being in-between.

A different way of approaching the notion of process can be found in the way in which we regard our practice—as an ongoing body of work. In other words, we see our practice, as a whole, as a process in itself. Each of our projects is built atop the ones that we did earlier. In all our work we see traces of all the previous work that we did. It's a very "palimpsest" way of working. We never start with a completely clean slate, but always have the feeling that we're building upon a previous layer. We definitely see our whole body of work as a progression, as a slow movement. All our projects become part of the same narrative.

Within the field of graphic design, this goes completely against the preferred way of working. Most designers feel an obligation to start each project entirely new, "from zero," but for us, that's an impossible proposition. We cannot help but regard our practice as an ongoing development, a progressive accumulation, or, in other words, a process.

Working with People

Obviously, graphic design is an extremely collaborative practice. It consists of working with editors, curators, artists, writers, printers, binders, and so on. But we're always a bit wary of the word "collaboration" itself. Maybe that's because we do have a slightly anti-social streak, which is of course really strange, as we see our practice basically as a social, and also socialist, construct. Still, we have a slight sense of discomfort when it comes to the notion of collaboration. Maybe that's because we feel as if we're already fully collaborating within the studio with the three of us, so we feel less inclined to extend this collaboration outside of the studio.

Nowadays, a lot of graphic designers refer to their clients/commissioners as "partners" and they also prefer to say that they are working "with" people, instead of "for" people, which is all very understandable. We also regard some of the artists and curators we work with as partners and collaborators and sometimes even as friends, rather than as clients. We are specifically thinking of people such as Guus Beumer, Karina Bisch, and Johannes Schwartz.

On the other hand, we also find it a bit awkward, all this talk about "partners and collaborators." It conjures up images of designers sitting at their computers with the clients sitting right next to them, making all the decisions together. That seems like an absolute nightmare to us.

Despite the good working relationships we have with a lot of people, we always feel that within a collaboration, there should also be a tiny element of conflict. Or some sort of acknowledgment that the interests of all the parties involved in a design project aren't necessarily shared, not completely. There might be an overlap of interests, but they are never completely identical. Naturally this creates a certain amount of tension, of conflict, of distance—but that's what makes graphic design so interesting in the first place, we think.

That's why we usually prefer to talk about "working for," instead of "working with." We realize that the meaning of that phrase, "working for," is very much connected to the notion of design as a service, which is not necessarily a notion we're fond of, but paradoxically, it is exactly that phrase that gives us some sense of autonomy, of authorship. It gives us critical distance from the client. "Working with" sounds too much as if we're sitting on the client's lap, so to speak. Or that the client is sitting on our lap. It creeps us out. In order to design, we need some space to breath. That little word "for" gives us this space.

Cross-pollination

It's interesting to focus on something that we think is quite typical of our process—the fact that somehow, when we're working on several projects at the same time, these projects tend to influence each other. They almost blend into each other. We can't really avoid it and actually we wouldn't want to.

As an example, two projects that we were working on roughly in the same period are *Two or Three Things I Know About Provo*, a series of two exhibitions that we curated in 2011 and 2012, and the graphic identity of the Whitney Museum, which we developed between 2011 and 2013. In both projects, we focused on a certain city-specificity.

Two or Three Things was a project about Provo, an anarchist movement in the 1960s that was very much shaped by the city of Amsterdam. And the graphic identity of the Whitney was very much grounded in the city of New York in the sense that, during the design process, it became clear to us that the shape of the "zigzag" could refer to things such as the ziggurat-shape of the architecture of both the old and current building of the Whitney, or the iconic fire-escape stairs in the streets of New York, or the zigzag-like path of the Whitney Museum through Manhattan, from location to location, over the years. In both projects, we tried to emphasize the way in which both subjects (Provo and the Whitney) were and still are grounded in their specific locations—Amsterdam and New York, respectively.

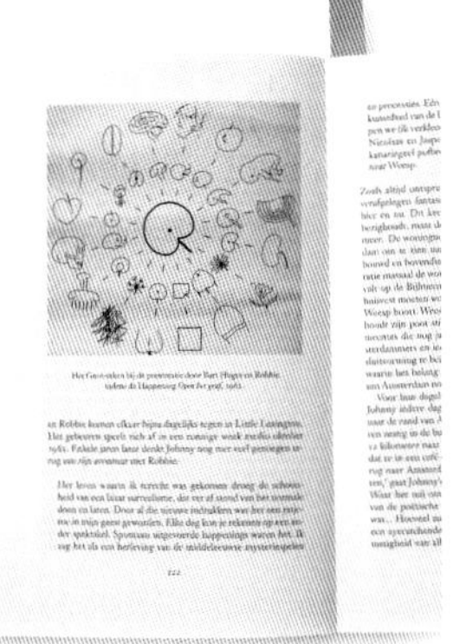

The projects are also related in the notion of the "open sign," for lack of a better term. We regard the "responsive W"—the mark we developed for the Whitney as a graphic structure that can contain several meanings. As well, the Provos used as their "logo" a symbol that could contain several meanings. This symbol was created by pre-Provo pioneers Bart Hughes and Robert Jasper Grootveld as a mark signifying a wide variety of things from a fetus to a brain to a skull. We've included a chart of the sign, as created in 1962 by Hughes and Grootveld.

While we were working on both projects, the two signs became inextricably linked to each other, in our own minds. Both are graphic structures open to several interpretations and both signs are rooted in particular cities—the Provo "apple" in Amsterdam, and the "W" in New York, which is, after all, New Amsterdam.

Confluence of Disciplines

Both writing and drawing play a very important role in our process. We would argue that writing and drawing are basically identical activities. Writing is a form of drawing and drawing is a form of writing. What's interesting about graphic design is exactly the fact that it is a field in which it is impossible to distinguish between writing and drawing, between the verbal and the visual.

This is already encapsulated in the etymology of the word "graphic." The word is derived from the Proto-Indo-European base word "grebh," which simply means "to carve" or "to scratch," but in Greek times, the word "graphikos" referred both to the act of drawing and writing. In a sense, we do believe that the current practice of graphic design still refers to this classic notion—the idea that writing is a form of drawing, and drawing is a form of writing.

Outside the Studio

Music plays a large role in our lives, and in our work. We have often mentioned the influence of punk rock. Though we were too young to actively participate in the original punk explosion of 1977, we could still hear the echoes throughout the 1980s, and it really inspired us. As teenagers, we were involved in all kinds of post-punk subcultures (two-tone ska, psychobilly, new wave, garage rock, mod, American hardcore), and all these movements shaped us in the most profound way. It was relics like record sleeves, buttons, patches, DIY fanzines, mix-tapes, t-shirts, and Xeroxed mini-comics that made us aware of graphic design in the first place.

Politics influence our work as well. A lot of people might be surprised to learn that we basically see ourselves as a Marxist design group. Our whole perception of design, of art, of modernism, of culture as a whole can be traced back to one single sentence, written by [Karl] Marx and [Friedrich] Engels in *The Holy Family* in 1844—"If humans are made by their environment, then this environment has to be made human." This is actually our own translation of the German, which is, "Wenn der Mensch von den Umständen gebildet wird, so muss man die Umstände menschlich bilden."

Our ideology is based on the idea that we, as humans, are shaped by our material surroundings, and that in return, we must shape these material surroundings ourselves. This is also how we interpret the whole notion of "dialectical materialism." But instead of expressing this ideology in an overt way—for example, with explicit slogans or messages, we have chosen to internalize these Marxist principles in a much more implicit manner. In our work, we try to explore possible ways to emphasize the materiality of the designed object through its aesthetic dimension. By referring to all sorts of possible material gestures—overprinting, folding, perforating, tearing—we try to make the viewer/reader aware that he or she is first of all looking at a printed, material object—an object that is made by humans, and thus that also can be changed by humans.

Issues of animal welfare, animal rights, vegetarianism, and veganism also play an important part in our lives. It's hard to explain exactly how vegetarianism informs our work—we haven't even figured that out ourselves, but we do think there is a connection between our work and our ethical views on animals. A lot of our work revolves around a critical, almost Brechtian examination of the illusory effect of images. We try to somehow go against the "spectacle." And the notion of meat is obviously one of the biggest spectacles of all—a concept that is completely dependent on illusions and images—tradition, taste, customs, habits, and rituals. In both our work and in our ethical outlook on animals, we try to break the illusory spell of the spectacle, and try to go against the alienation and sheer cruelty caused by this spectacle.

Somehow, we think there is a connection there, though it's not really something that clearly manifests itself in our work. As a subject, the suffering of animals is so extremely grave, and so extremely saddening, it's near impossible to deal with, at least for us. So it's not really a topic we would use in our work in a casual or light way. It's much too serious for that.

Paul Sahre

November 11, 2014

Ideas

As designers, we use problem solving, but that's not all design is. It's broader than that and it's more complicated than that. Design is about details and refinement—but that's not all it is either, despite the fact that some people are really drawn to those aspects as well.

I like to keep ideas just ideas in the beginning. Part of it is trying to figure out how to execute an idea so that it makes sense, or that it works given whatever the situation, and in a way that is more than what it is.

I don't use sketchbooks but I understand why people do. They can provide comfort in an otherwise chaotic process. It's easy to look at a sketchbook after the fact and say, "Oh! It was a clear plan from the very beginning." When in actuality everything was on the table until the last fucking second—that there's actually a funny, unexpected trail created over the course of a project.

If I'm designing a book cover, the initial ideas I write in the margins of whatever I'm reading, or maybe there isn't any sketching needed except the client needs to see something so that they can say, "Oh, ok." In other words, my notes and shitty sketches are a tool to give to an art director to take to his or her editor so he or she can see something and understand what I am proposing without getting hung up on the form the idea will take. The great thing about my bad sketches is that they don't get me too tied to how the thing is going to look in the end.

Usually having two or three ideas is also necessary for the client's process and the channels that they have to go through to get a thing approved. Starting with something formless is a way to get everyone invested in an idea before time and effort is invested in refinement and detail. It's just a way to get things jumpstarted and moving in a particular direction—and hopefully it's moving in a direction where you are still going to be nimble enough to change directions if you have to.

Early Days

When I was a junior at Kent State and was just sort of flailing around, I found Bob Gill's book *Forget All the Rules...[You Ever Learned About Graphic Design: Including the Ones in This Book]*. I remember thinking, "Yes! This I can totally get behind." There was just something objective about his approach and here I was drowning in a sea of subjectivity. I found his book incredibly liberating and it really changed the way I was thinking about and making work.

I think that those ideas and that way of thinking have so much traction now and are so accepted that you almost want to rebel against it all. When there's too much objectivity, you want there to be more subjectivity.

Silkscreening

When you're designing on a computer it's a very intellectual thing, it's all in your head. All you're doing is flicking your wrist, and occasionally typing. What you're doing and what you think you're doing are totally opposite. When you're designing on a computer you think you're leaping over tall buildings or pushing boulders up mountains but really you're just sitting there staring at a screen. So for me, silkscreening is great because I'm sore the next day—it's a great balance for the cerebral thing we do on the computer.

I got into silkscreen when I was in graduate school learning about the printing process—making paper, making plates, etchings, and other stuff that all fell under the heading of "printmaking." At the time I was sort of obsessed with the idea of multiple copies of something. I loved the idea that what I made would be replicated many, many, many times. There is a power in that which goes back to [Johannes] Gutenberg and the way printing and mass-production can spread ideas that I was just discovering.

I was once with a fellow grad student and it was about three in the morning and we were doing a poster for the Kent State University School of Art. Things weren't going well—it was late, the ink was all oil-based and toxic back then, and at one point he just snaps and yells, "What are we doing here? Why are we doing this to ourselves!?" And I just laughed and said, "Because it's fun." Silkscreening was something that I really enjoyed and also something I could have direct control over. I liked that you needed very little space to do it. Over the years—especially moving around in New York—I've been able to do lots of screen printing in the bathrooms of small studio apartments using the bathtub as a spray sink without the landlord ever knowing.

When I was in Baltimore starting my career, graphic designers didn't print their own work. I mean, absolutely nobody did. Silkscreen was dead and the computer was the new thing that everyone was preoccupied with. I had brought my supplies from school and set-up a crude silkscreen studio. I got a theater client and started doing screen printed posters for them. As the designer and the printer, I realized how many opportunities there were to make changes to what you were doing, even in the middle of the printing process—that the process could extend deep into production if you were controlling that too.

It was also interesting how the design responded to what screen printing could or couldn't do well. My work became much more simplified and graphic and that was something that people really responded to, which was great. But for me a lot of it came out of designing to the production. The design process was influenced by the production process.

I typically print at 13 1/2 x 20 inches vertical, which is an unusual dimension and one that I joke about owning. It comes from a compromise I struck with Fells Point Corner Theatre in Baltimore where the chairperson said, "We need small posters because we're just putting these on light poles and cigarette machines in and around the city. So maybe just 11 x 17 inches?" And I said, "11 x 17 is not a poster—18 x 24 is a poster!" 11 x 17 just wasn't satisfying for me but 18 x 24 was too big for them so 13 1/2 x 20 was a way of splitting the difference. But the size is also good because the smaller your print, the less paper you have to buy, the less ink you use, and so on. So this format ended up being ideal in terms of my ability to afford materials and execute the posters with a moderately high level of craftsmanship. Even after I stopped doing work for Fells Point I kept that size, which now gives a nice continuity to many of the posters I've printed over the years.

Gilligan's Island

I don't know where I read this but in the 1960s when Sherwood Schwartz was going to the networks with the show idea for *Gilligan's Island*, they kept rejecting it. They said, "You could maybe make one or two shows about a group of people stranded on an island, but you couldn't make a season-long series." So he came back with a scroll of forty different episode ideas, and I thought, "This is exactly the same as our design process. It's just a different medium." It was a terrible show, but I totally appreciate the way he convinced the suits to make the thing he wanted to make.

Even after Schwartz finally got them to green-light a pilot, they were like, "This is the worst fucking thing we've ever seen!" Schwartz reedited it and took it back to them. They still hated it, but he talked them into testing it, and an audience loved it. The TV executives thought there was something wrong so they got another audience and did another testing and they loved it. Even the critics hated it. They were like, "This isn't the worst television show this season, it's the worst show of all time." But Schwartz got his show made. The point I'm trying to make is that the client—or the audience—is the real random element in the process. These are the X factors because those things really drive how you sketch and how you develop a project, but you have so little control over them. The thing we can control as designers is our determination to get something made.

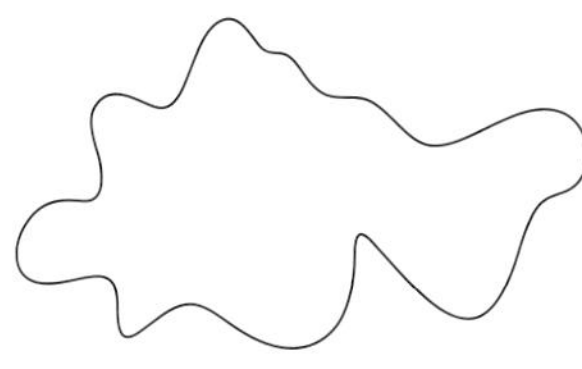

Too Many Cooks

I'm working on this book project where the client sent me a whole list of things to think about and pay attention to while I'm working. This is almost always problematic. It's part of a process that is supposed to help clarify a situation but almost always does the opposite. You have a situation where a team of thirty people "defines" the thing. If you actually delivered the thing that they're defining it would just be a brown blob because it has to be funny, but serious, and this, but that, and it should target these people, but not alienate these people, and also women should love it.

Advice for Young Designers

A lot of time thinking about process is something young designers constantly have to do. Partially because they are new at it, but also because of the situations they will find themselves in. Some are seemingly stupid, arbitrary, impossible situations. Sometimes you can jump up and down and scream and yell—and sometimes you need to—but usually you just have to accept that someone doesn't like the color blue and accept that you only have two days to do a thing. That is not an easy thing for most people to do.

The two most important qualities for a designer are curiosity and keeping an open mind to possibility. Having the guts to go somewhere that you might not even think is going to work, and committing even if you don't think a direction is going to work. Sometimes that is why you are being asked to work in a certain direction in the first place. To see if something won't work.

Gratification

I personally don't think there's ever a comfortable or pleasant stage in the process—not at any point. Even after you've climbed that mountain, planted your flag, and you've made it. Then you say, "Now what?" Then you're a little down because a project is done. That's all it is. There is no more potential.

If there is a gratifying part of the process it's the perpetual not-knowing—the potentiality of something. Doing something you're not sure you can do and then maybe surprising yourself when you actually do it. But during the process? It's uncomfortable. It's uncomfortable during and it's uncomfortable after. I lose sleep. I worry. I'm constantly thinking about it. I'm not eating well. I'm stressed out. I'm like, "Fuck! This thing is going to be a complete disaster!"

So no, there's not a pleasant part about it, but that is the fun part. That's what motivates me. The fun is the challenge and working through it. Maybe there are other designers out there who enjoy the process more than I do, but if I want to enjoy myself, I listen to music or go surfing. I don't design to enjoy myself. I do it because it is always a challenge.

Natasha Jen

May 15, 2015

Hindsight

I think for most people it's difficult to zoom out and look at yourself and your practice and your "career" in a third person way. As I get older—I'm 38 now—there is finally a history behind me. This history provides the space and distance to zoom out and see.

I got into design very accidentally. I always had artistic impulses as a child. I liked to draw, make a mess, make things. I never really knew, nor did my parents know how to channel that creative impulse. The most immediate conclusion was, "You're an artist," but that's a very large category.

Getting into graphic design was really a practical concern. You learn an identifiable skill. But the notion of design was a completely alien thing to me. I think it remained alien to me until probably five or six years ago. I began to have a little clarity and a little better understanding. I think that has to do with the type of education you receive. Design schools are all very different. Here in America, especially at undergraduate school, the focus is on applied design. You always get certain objects, or genres, or types of things to design. Within that framework it's difficult to think about design as a way of being, because you're always conditioned by the object or by the genre of things that you have to design, from signage to books to posters. That's how I understood design because that's what was taught to me.

Now that I'm getting older, I've begun to look at it as just a way of being. You have enough experience, you live through it. I lived through it. I'm just learning by doing. I've never had this larger framework that governed how I work. As I continue to work in a design practice, I'm able to build that framework for myself, and articulate it. And also think about it and constantly reconfigure it, because you're always in a form of adaptation. We're human beings, and we're changing every day. That influences how you work and the outcome of your work, which I find interesting because the design process in my mind has a lot to do with ways of being, the time we're in, the technology, and whatever world surrounds us. So for me, there's no such thing as the design process. It's just a form of being and it's always changing itself. But in a professional practice, businesses tend to concretize, to make something tangible and understandable in form in order to commoditize and sell it. The whole notion of how the design process informs businesses is a very trendy topic right now. You see that there are individuals and companies that really focus on developing that idea as a type of science or some kind of study. But for me, I find it not applicable.

What It Looks Like

Despite the diagrams that show this A to B linear progress, design is always clueless, multidirectional. You're always going all around the possibilities and always bouncing back and forth off many different walls. You head this way,

then you bounce back in the opposite direction until you finally figure out the space that can yield interesting, productive work. That process itself is actually a really painful process. But that painful bouncing around, that directionless-ness is interesting.

What It Feels Like

Being a designer is a very psychotic existence because the act of design as a commodity and as a way of being is a very vulnerable thing. Design is vulnerable because the process is uncertain and there's always an economic relationship. The applied design relationship or the client-designer power structure makes this whole thing—this act—very vulnerable. Everyday I struggle with that vulnerability. But you can never express it in your work or in how you present the work. You have to build a really strong, powerful wall around to defend it. I think that vulnerability is shared by everybody, whether you're the creative director or an intern. Everyone is uncertain because you're always doubting the thing that you just gave birth to. There is never a moment that you will say, "This is it." Rarely, for me. Even after it's done. It's difficult for me to actually look at the work that I've done. I know that some actors also share this kind of vulnerability and they refuse to see the films in which they play a major role.

Creativity vs Economy

To be able to find a new way to think about things—that is what excites me every day. By excitement, I mean a childlike impulse. That excites me because I have to emphasize the business aspects, which can become really formula-oriented, repetitive, and solution-focused. Again, it's always operating within an economic structure, and this business side of things can become exhausting. You're constantly struggling between the two ends of the spectrum. You need to exist as a creative being with impulses that are hard to manage, to explain, to control, yet you need to operate this whole practice as a business. For me, it's taking a very typical project or problem but trying to find a completely unexpected way to think about it and to look at it. That doesn't guarantee that the result is going to be a groundbreaking thing. It's just being able to push yourself into some other realm, completely unrelated, and use these two opposing points as the lens through which you think about this problem. That I find very interesting because your mind is traveling within this infinite space and within the entire history of mankind.

It's about how you find sources of—I hate the word inspiration—but in this case, sources of inspiration. How do you actually structure them? How do you blend them? How do you interlace things that are seemingly completely unrelated. That part of design is exciting. But then again, if you zoom out from the aspect of creation, from being a creative, and you actually inject this whole act of design into a client-designer relationship, for clients that is also a very scary process because there isn't a tangible form that they're commissioning. They don't know what they're getting yet, so that makes the whole process and relationship a psychotic one.

Time

First, I try to get as much slowness as possible. You negotiate. Again, this is a pragmatic part that comes in because I think that in order to create a level of freedom—freedom of time, freedom of space—you need to do a lot of negotiation, ironically. So you negotiate with the clients and with your team—you're always in the role of negotiator. Design itself, even the process of coming up with a form, that itself is a constant negotiation. You're negotiating with all kinds of forces and people around you, including people who work with you and work for you. So I always try to buy us a little more time, but we work incredibly productively and fast. I never had a plan to make this our way of working—reviewing every round within twenty-four hours—but I began to realize that this kind of rhythm is what I'm comfortable with. In a way, it's a really sneaky way of working. I am trying to work as fast as possible, yet I'm also trying to get as much time as possible, which I think all comes down to the very vulnerability and insecurity of design. You want to do as much as you can, explore as much as possible, but you're also working against limited time and human and economic resources. You begin to think like a really greedy omnivore—you want to just have everything. It all comes down to that insecurity.

Slow space only exists in my mind. It's a mental calculation and mental behavior. In actuality, here, in my practice and in my team, slowness is unthinkable. It's forbidden, slowness. It can only exist here, in this infinite space. I find myself sometimes a little confused by the overwhelming amount of things that need to be addressed and considered, and procrastination became a kind of self-defense mechanism—you just refuse to deal with it. I know it's really bad, but I began to notice certain procrastination tendencies that I've developed and they always have to do with the amount of work or responsibilities that I have.

Often everything shares the same priority. What do you do with that? You just walk away and say, "Fuck this, sorry, I don't know what to do. Let me just walk away for a moment. I'll come back." You still have to do it, you still have to prioritize things in a different way, but I find myself constantly confronted with situations in which everything is the top priority.

Building on History

You begin to understand the choices that you made in the past, which may not have been apparent at the time. Making certain career choices, even when I was in school making internship choices. At that time I had no idea, I did some things just because I thought, "The name sounds great, let me just try." But now, looking back, I begin to actually understand why I made those choices. I realize that the whole time I was following my intuition, despite that it was really blurry and vague for me at the time. I think having that moment of clarity now and realizing that I was actually following my intuition helps me to believe in the way that I think a little bit better. Not entirely, but I begin to see that that whole history, the past fifteen years, has been tested. Those decisions lead to the moment where I am right now. So those decisions accumulated in the current me. I think in terms of the trajectory of things so I can feel more confident about the decisions that I'm going to make. That's a kind of empowerment that I never really expected.

Wanderlust

I am a kind of aimless wanderer when it comes to visuals. It's actually a really bad habit because I tend to spend a lot of time wandering on the Internet, often just aimlessly poking around. I use Pinterest as part of my wandering. It's not practical until you begin to apply it to something, but the joy of that wandering is something that I enjoy tremendously.

Since I was a child, you could throw me into any room, any place, and I would always find my own interest. I would begin to look at everything, open every single book. I always have that tendency, so I'm never really bored. It's very dangerous with the Internet because there's basically an infinite space. The exciting thing about design, for me, is to find a very different way to think about things. I think that this kind of wandering actually allows me to do that because you run into different universes all the time, and you can probably bring something from there to here.

I wander around in the city too, going mostly to stores. I find going to stores incredibly inspiring just because of the visual stimulus. You're confronted all the time, and of course, sometimes this whole thing results in shopping, but I think I'm getting a little more cautious of that. For me, New York is really the best place to get inspiration, from every block, every moment.

An Outsider's Perspective

As an immigrant, it doesn't matter if you're naturalized or not. There's always this sense of alienation that is actually fundamental to my existence. Alienation, not necessarily in a bad sense, but this self-awareness of being an outsider makes you a little more sensitive about yourself in relationship to this space you're in, whether it's an actual space or a relationship kind of space. When you're put into any new environment, you're in a defense mode. You're just trying to cope with the differences and the newness and learn everything. To be able to work with it is the nature, for me, of being an immigrant here. I still feel an outsider in pretty much every situation that I'm in. Even where I am right now. You always have this detachment, it's a consciousness that is just there. You never feel really comfortable about anything.

Now that I've been here for almost half of my life, surprisingly, when I go back to Taiwan, I feel like an alien when I get there. It's always about a sense of placelessness. You feel that you're not here, nor are you there. I haven't talked to any therapist about this, but maybe I don't need to. I'm still functioning pretty happily.

Idea and Form

I probably need to frame this whole dichotomy between concept and form. For a lot of designers, it's a linear A to B—start with a concept and end up with a tangible form. Some start up with this, end up with that. Some jump into that right away. For me, I don't see it as linear, it's always omni-directional. You're constantly bouncing back and forth between the idea of it and the physical manifestation of it. How can you possibly divorce the two? Every object, everything we see, is a concept. That's really how I see it. The most beautiful design in my mind is one that you can look at the form and break down the thinking behind it. It's unpacking itself for you. That is the most beautiful form of design. The physical manifestation itself is the translation of the thinking. It can be a messy process, but the designer manages to distill it, clean it up, organize it, structure it in such a way that it is crystal clear. For me, that is the most compelling design. In architecture, you see that. In fashion, you see that. As well as in graphic design you can see the decisions being made behind the interplay between the visual and the words. That's how we work.

Milton Glaser

April 22, 2015

On Drawing

You begin to draw to acquire a connection between your brain and your hand. When you draw you have some difficulty because the path between the hand and the brain has to be clarified, or dug, or established. So for a long time you can't interpret what's in front of you because dimensionality can never be represented accurately. Once you change something from three into two dimensions, it isn't the same thing. Of course, historically, drawing was always a matter of replication. At a certain point the new development that was realized was that replication either wasn't possible or was not even desirable. Something else was important.

I started to learn to draw very early. I went to a life drawing class at the Art Students League and I drew for about ten years on a regular basis, all through high school and so on. One believes that the implicit character of drawing is to accurately represent what is in front of you. So you spend ten years to be able to do that and then discover that isn't the point. Learning how to draw accurately is the beginning of learning how to draw, but to some degree accuracy is an impediment to the experience of drawing and to the quality of what you produce. The real purpose of drawing is to understand what is real and in a sense, it's like a Buddhist's idea of accepting what is. So if I look at your ear and I try to draw it, I actually become observant for the first time because I will not notice your ear unless I have that intention. So I look at your ear to try to understand whether it's real or not and I can't make that determination without drawing because drawing focuses your attention. Attentiveness is always the key, whatever that word means. Mindfulness and attentiveness are becoming popular ideas, but that is always the issue. Are you really understanding what you're looking at?

If you can't draw, it's very hard to create form. That's why most of the things we see produced by designers today are basically images found online, replicated, and altered to sufficiently match a desired aesthetic. To some extent you're a victim of what you can find.

Incidentally, that does not seem to be an impediment to professional life. 99 percent of designers work that way. The other day I was doing a poster and I wanted a vase of flowers and a Corinthian column, something that would have formerly taken me six hours to find. In two minutes I had both those pieces of information in front of me and I could use them, but I'm not sure that the speed of that acquisition doesn't become an impediment to observation. This is why people always ask these stupid questions about computer and non-computer. The great thing about the computer is its ability to accelerate your production of an object. Its great limitation is that same acceleration prevents you from understanding what you're doing.

To me drawing is really a manifestation or understanding of what is real, giving you the power to replicate what exists in your mind. Otherwise, like I said, you're just a victim of what you can find.

Time

I always have enough time to do everything that I am assigned. I work very, very fast. I don't have a methodology and I don't have this mysterious process. The idea of process in itself is an impediment to what you do. I know my brain is working all the time, filling itself with every piece of information. It observes everything and knows everything. Most of your time you spend deflecting what you know because things are too complex and incomprehensible. So you just separate off most of what you know and experience in life to limit the complexity and difficulty of making decisions, but I know my mind is totally transparently working on itself inside.

Most of the things I do, I do in a second when somebody calls me on the phone, and they say, "We need a blah, blah, blah." Before the conversation is finished, my brain has supplied an image for me. You learn to trust those images or not. Part of the drawing experience is to help you understand what you're thinking. Drawing itself is a feedback mechanism to adjust your thinking. It's like a way of seeing whether what you're thinking can become manifest, and become real, and become a thing.

Some things you think can't be done at all because you don't have the skill or understanding or because inherently they don't lend themselves to being done. And the key idea here is the distinction between the dimensionality of the world, the atmosphere, light—none of which can really be represented on a flat piece of paper with a pencil.

Coincidence

I'm very conscious lately of the idea of coincidence. I realized my life is consumed by coincidence. Everything everyday seems to me to establish another connected event. There are no unconnected events—that is the miracle of human experience. That everything is linked and at a certain point when you believe that, the link has just become more apparent and the convergence has become more visible.

In the foyer of my house, I have a bunch of Nigerian caps that we bought. Ten little hats all baked by the sun. Exquisite little things, in beautiful colors. I also have a tall seated Buddha. The Buddha's head is exactly the shape and configuration of one of those caps, and when I came home, one of them fit right on top of the Buddha's head to protect the energy that was contained within it. Those are profound mysteries, but you see, there's nothing unrelated. In drawing, very often what you're trying to discover is those connections that are in the world but not visible to you.

Documentation of the Process

My methodology is very random and my assumption is that it's all there all the time. I don't have circumstances under which I prepare myself—but everybody's different. Some people have to have a light meal in the late afternoon and whatever else it is people do. Some people do a lot of studies. I don't have any notion like that because my ideas come from anywhere, anytime, under any circumstance, and it's not logical or progressive.

You know how they tell you that you take an idea, then you refine it, then you illuminate it. There's the whole modernist idea of stripping it down to finally get to the heart of the subject or part of the artistry. I don't work that way. In fact, let me show you a poster and I will show you the documentation of the process.

Here are all the images that I used to get to the final image. They start out with the head of Christ and then I reversed it and I put in a paper print I had done previously. Then I took the two things and I combined them. It didn't work that way. Fluffed them over, it didn't work. They separated. I put this back. Then I had a totally irrelevant piece of material from a series of scarves I did. Then I took the patterning and changed them into a different series of patterns. Then I widened the spaces between them and blackened and thickened it. Then I made it more pointillistic. Then I eliminated everything except the diagonals and I reformed it, integrating a grid into it with white dots. Then I doubled the amount of dots. Then I remembered there was the face of a Velázquez portrait at the Hermitage and I changed it into a series of dots. Then I reconformed the scarves in a Post-it on this portrait, but I didn't like the way it looked because I didn't like the way he looked. Then I remembered there was also a beautiful Rubens portrait at the Hermitage so I substituted the Rubens and I put the layered stuff on top of the Rubens. It was too dense, so I lightened it, and that's how I got to here. It was a completely irrational process, with no logic, just fragments and memory and opportunism.

To me the secret of work is to do the work and the inspiration comes out of the act of working. It's not that you have a preconception of, "Oh, I'm inspired." The actual work itself is what's inspiring. The act of doing the work is everything. I think many people misunderstand or rather misuse the idea of inspiration. It's not that it doesn't exist—everything that motivates you or that causes you to be motivated to work is inspiring—but there is nothing that isn't inspiring. The way this book sits on a table, casts a shadow, and turns—it's astonishing! This is a miraculous occurrence! But everything is a miracle. With that sense of the potential for the miraculous—if you believe it—that's all there is.

Professional Life

I always identified myself with my own work. I didn't know what an artist was and I didn't know what a calling was and I didn't know what a vocation was—I knew none of those things. I knew that my deepest happiness came from the act of drawing when I was a child.

That is the thing that I find most compelling because I thought if I could learn how to draw, I could learn about typography, I could design typefaces, I could do interiors—everything that came under the general heading of "visual activity."

I pursued it and it seemed to me that the most important thing was whether I could learn something by the act of doing it. As you know, professional life consists of being noted for something and specializing. I didn't want to do Push Pin illustrations for all my life. I lost interest and when you lose interest, then you are no longer in the proper place in your life. It means that you're in a factory producing a product and that's not really what you want to discover in life. The thing that has kept me alive professionally is the fact that I'm willing to go anywhere to see what I can learn from it. I've been doing it for a very long time and I still feel I don't know what the hell I'm doing and that's great.

I got an assignment a couple of weeks ago to design socks. What a big, fabulous assignment it's turning out to be. It really got into my head. The first thing to do was to separate the idea that they had to match because if you have two socks and they have to match, think of the man-hours involved in matching after you wash them. If you multiply that in terms of the world, you're talking of about millions of hours a year. Or, you've got a hole in one sock and you have to throw the other one away.

So I got on this idea of never-match socks, which has extended to gloves, tights, and everything else. I was supposed to start with the design of a sock, and I took it to a social level where it changes some economic or psychological perception that people have. That part is so interesting—much more than drawing cute little butterflies. That is another level of activity.

Serendipity

When I don't have work to do, I do something else that relates to it. About twelve years ago, I started doing patterns for no apparent reason except I was interested in Persian miniatures at the time and also some Chinese work. I did a bunch of patterns, maybe a hundred different ones, to see how you could reinvent patterns. There's a case where the computer really helps because it's a genius at replication and you can take advantage of that.

After about a year, some people came and said, "We're rug makers in India, do you have any rug designs?" I said, "Yeah." I took the patterns and they made twelve rugs. That has happened to me all my life—making work in preparation for something that didn't happen yet. It turns out, you attract the world that way.

Time and Money

What I don't do is link speed to money. When you get a deadline, you have to deliver on time. You get a cheap job, you spend a little time. You get a big job, you spend more time. I have no such commitment or idea as that. I will spend months doing a fifty dollar job until it reaches what I think is its appropriate form. I will try not to do the pedestrian work because I have a short time and I will reconceptualize the works that can't be done within the short time. But I've been doing this a very long time and I know my own capacity and also know that time is not the limitation.

Imagination is your only limitation. The answer is always there waiting for you. I love to do jobs fast, but never at the expense of quality. I can do a job fast but I won't do it fast if it's fast and lousy, or fast and ordinary. My demand of myself is always to go beyond the usual. If it's the usual, there's no reason for doing it.

Trifecta

In professional life there are three components. There's you, the client, and the audience. The most important service is to the audience because you're affecting people's lives. You have to take responsibility for that. Then you have a client who has needs that you have signed up for and the needs are usually about selling a product, or an idea, or service—and you have to deliver that. And finally, what's left is your own capacity of yourself—understanding if you're moving forward in your own—not so much professional life—but existentially in your own life, in your own understanding. Those three things have to be dealt with, and if they're not, then the job isn't successful.

Technology

We have a strange way of working here. Sometimes I'll sit down and do some sketches, other times I'll write, and sometimes I just play with language, ideas, words, or narratives—there's always a narrative to what I do, sometimes more obviously than other times, depending on what the project is. The choice of formal elements ultimately has to be intuitive. I'll sit down next to somebody and say, "Okay, let's just set the word in Bodoni and give me this sentence… move those out and put those in…and so on. I depend on accidents that occur in the process of doing something on the computer the same way I used to depend on accidents in a drawing—where you spill a little ink and then extend it to be a torso. By attempting to find the mistakes a computer makes, we use a computer very differently from most people.

I've always said that the computer, which at first seems like a willing slave, turns out to master your brain because of its incredible skill, agility, and power. You don't even know—it changes the way you think about everything—form, color, and time. There's never been an instrument like this in human history, and so the first thing you have to do is establish who's boss.

Newness

The other thing that's more complex is the question of novelty and familiarity. Intrinsically, you're always struggling with a big client who wants the appearance of something new with the suggestion of something old. If designers finally had to speak honestly about this issue, it would be a complicated thing to deal with because obviously you can't get away with something that's totally unfamiliar and expect people to understand what you're talking about. And you can't repeat the same idea over and over a million times and expect to retain people's interest.

There are a handful of things that seem to be the basis for everything and those things seem to be some iteration of what has been in the culture for the last fifty years—with the style modified slightly here and there. But the sources and the ideas are so incredibly ordinary and repetitious. Almost everything you see today looks like something you've seen before. There's so little sense of, "Wow, I never saw anything like it." It's really a kind of endless series of variations of the same thing. I've been thinking lately that it's time for another way to look at this stuff.

April 6 - May 22

R. O. BLECHMAN: BEHIND THE LINES

Here's an exciting collection of R. O. Ble
cartoons, films, commercials and illustrat
can enjoy again his New Yorker and New Yor
cartoons and illustrations and on the ITC
see many of his TV commercials and some of
It's a real Blechman festival.

PIX

June 1 - July 24

TYPOGRAPHY 2: 27th ANNUAL TDC EXHIBIT

This major exhibition sponsored by The Typ
Club, presents examples of typographic exc
wide range of media. The pieces, printed
calligraphic, were selected by a panel of
and include outstanding work by type direc
typographic suppliers, calligraphers, agen
studios, and independent designers from ar
world. The work on exhibition will be pub
annual in the Fall.

PIX

Writing Drawing

Writing and drawing are central to the graphic design process, due in part to the fundamental text/image relationship. Traditional drawing and drafting techniques were of critical importance before the widespread adoption of computers, while today many designers thrive by combining an extensive range of tools—from iPads to notebooks to White-Out correction tape. New technology also allows designers to test multiple ideas, rapidly explore various forms, and put static graphic material into motion in real-time.

 Black tape line study

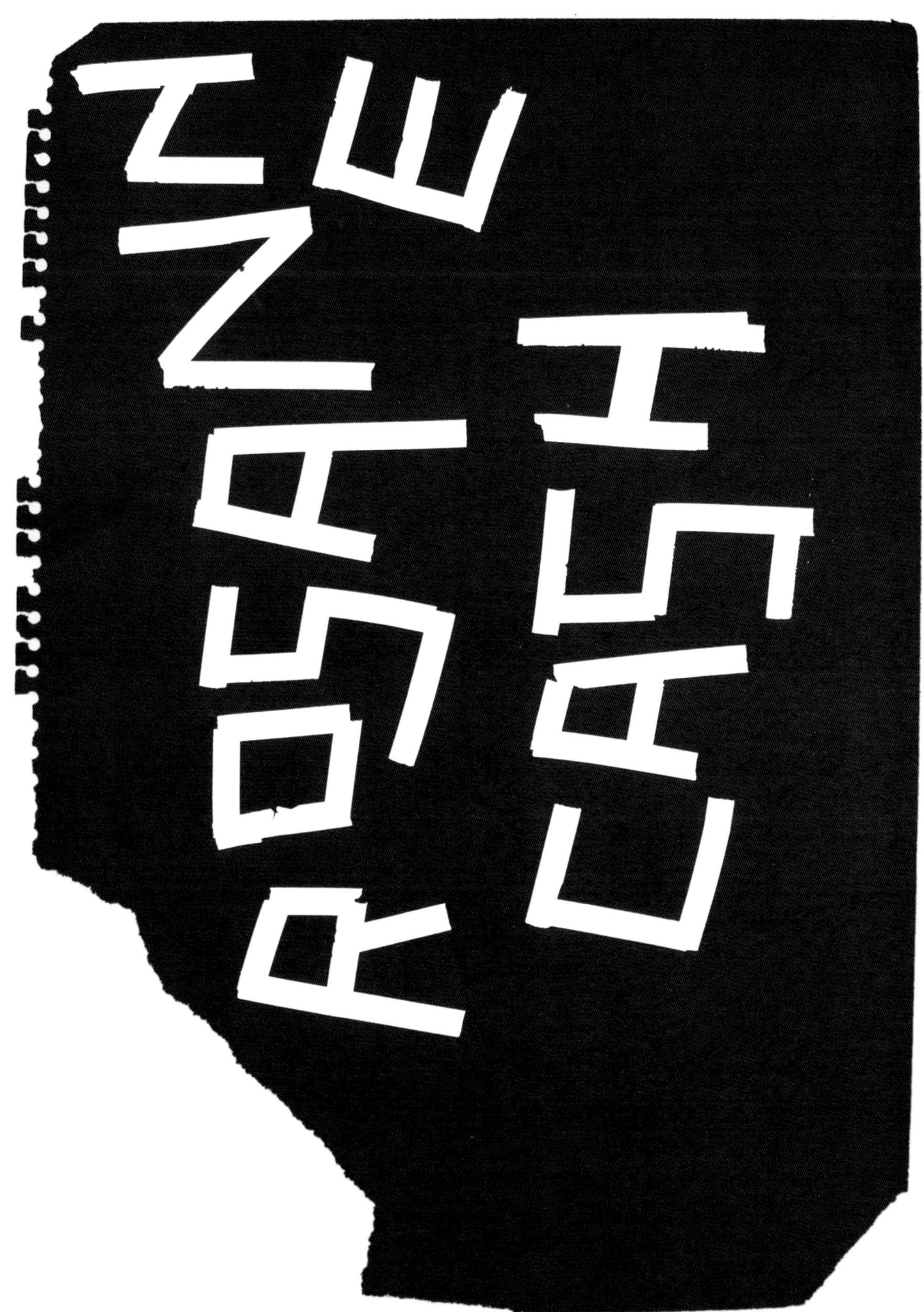

White-Out correction tape letterform and typographic study

REV.
REV
REV
REV
Rev.
REV.
PHOTO

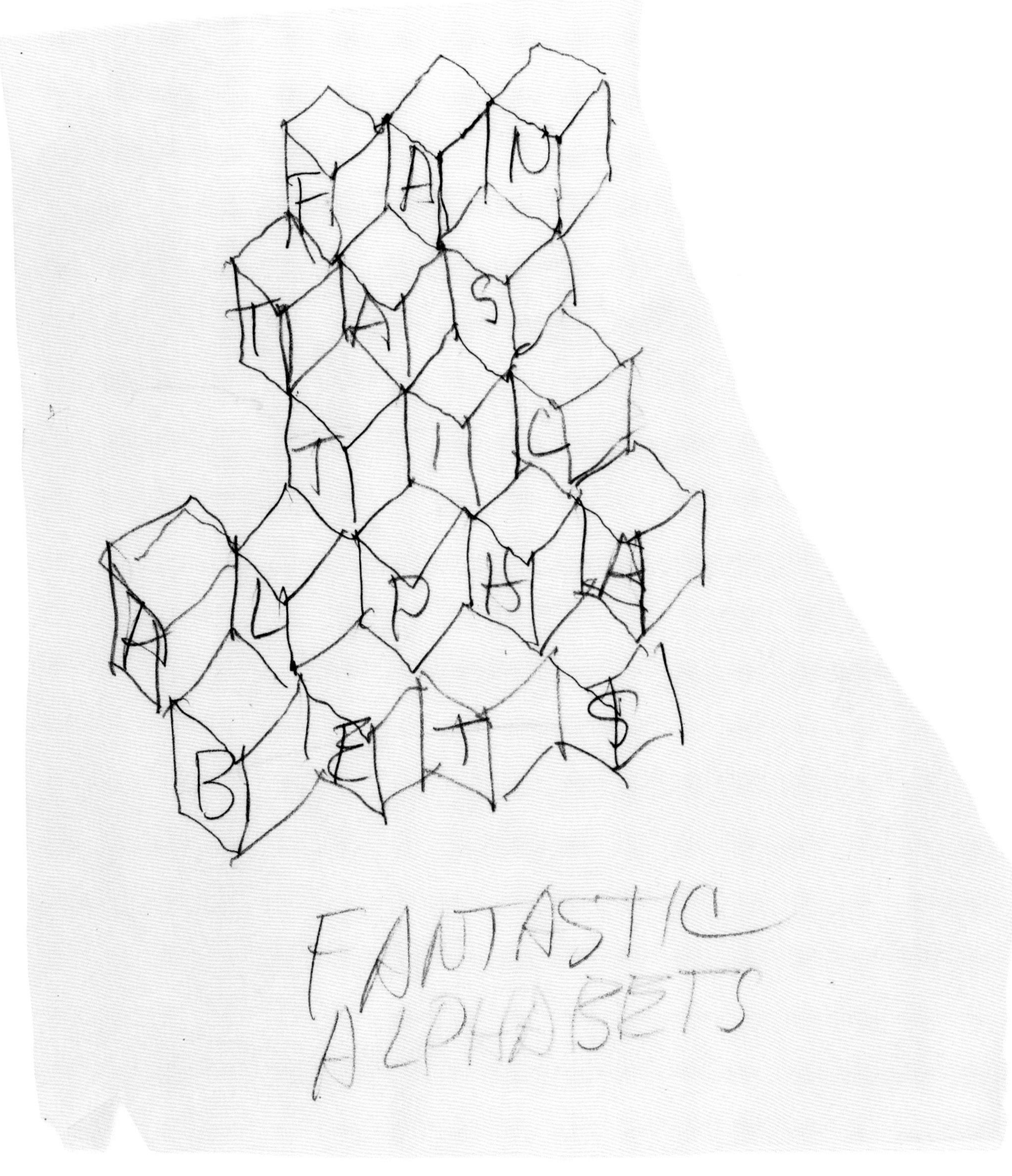
FANTASTIC
ALPHABETS

2

MASCULINE" NO, IT'S FLUID AND SOFT AND OPEN TO POSSIBILITIES.

4 THIS ONE IS DEFINITELY THE RISKIEST.

3 IT'S TOO FIFTIES

4 THE TYPE SEEMS INTRINSICALLY UN-RESOLVED LOOK HOW THE CAP M DOESN'T ALIGN WITH THE LOWER CASE M.

2 YES, I LIKE THESE COLORS. THESE COLORS ARE DEFINITELY NEW.

HOW WOULD THIS TYPEFACE WORK ON THE FENCE?

2 DON'T WE HAVE THIS IN THE FILE ALREADY? YES, I'M SURE THAT SOMEONE ALREADY DID THIS ONE. IT SEEMS SO OLD. SO SEVENTIES.

4 THIS TYPE IS ~~SO~~ TO GRANDROSE ~~[illegible]~~

3 THIS IS THE TYPE IBM LOGO.

3 NOW, COULD WE COLORS?

2 HOW WOULD TH XEROX?

I NEED SOMETHIN AS A LOGO THAT WHO WON'T MESS

I VERY STRONGLY PREFER LIKE THE TYPEF

THIS MAKES IT LO IS A DIVISION OF CO

, WESTERN.

.

EEOKAYAY!

FROM THE

S IN DIFFERENT

ECYCLED PAPER

REALLY ACTS
N GIVE TO DESIGNERS
).

ONE BUT I DON'T

E THE NAT DES MUS.
HEWITT.

/ 4

CONCEPTUALLY, I LIKE HOW DESIGN RISES ABOVE THESE BIOMORPHIC UPPER + LOWER CASE AND IS NATURALISTIC, LIKE IT WAS CARVED FROM WOOD, BUT THE TYPE IS NOT RESOLVED (AND SHOULDN'T BE [YET]) AND NEED MORE RESOLVE IN THEIR INTRINSIC INTERNAL RELATIONSHIP.

I HEAR VERY GOOD REACTIONS TO OUR CURRENT STATIONERY FROM THE VISUALLY IMPAIRED. THEY JUST LOVE IT. THEY SAY IT'S THE ONLY CHANCE THEY GET TO SEE WHAT THE BUILDING REALLY LOOKS LIKE.

Notes from client meeting about Cooper Hewitt, Smithsonian Design Museum identity design

Letterform studies for *58th Type Directors Club Annual*

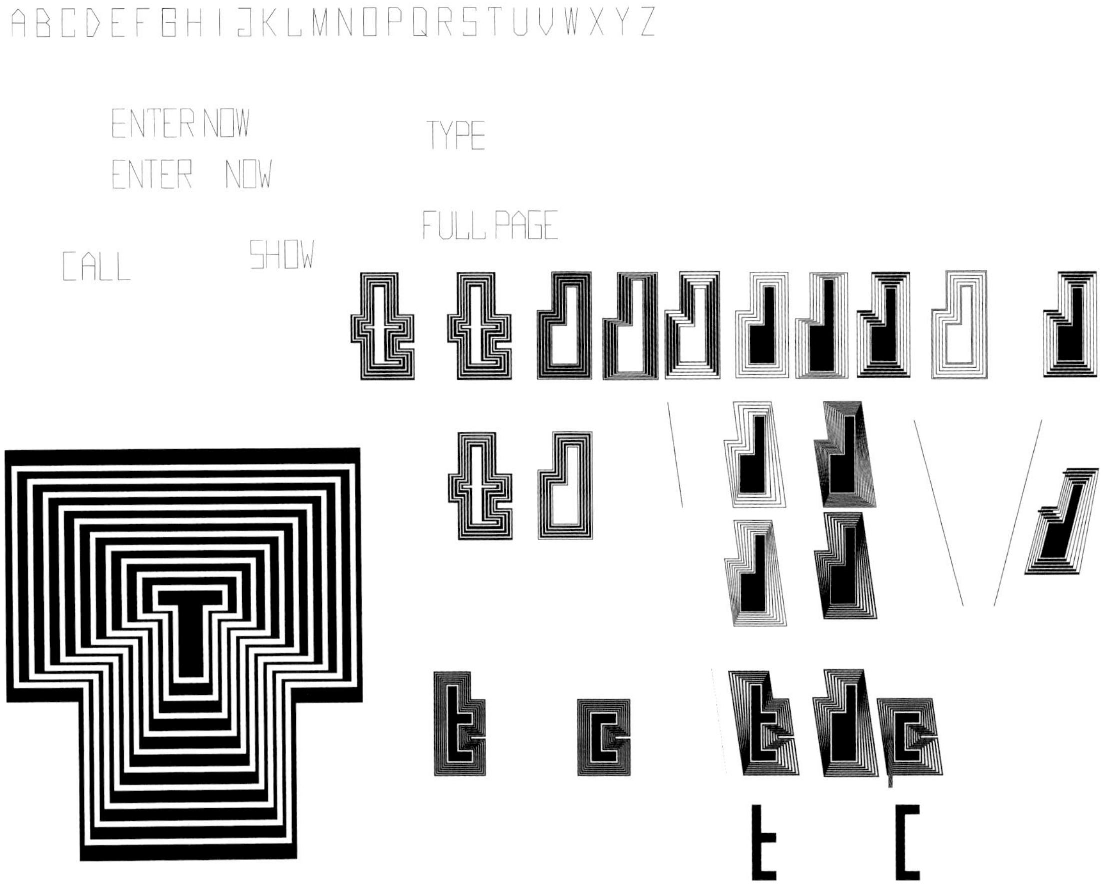

ABCDEFGHIJKLMNOPQRSTUVWXYZ

ENTER NOW

ENTER NOW

TYPE

FULL PAGE

CALL

SHOW

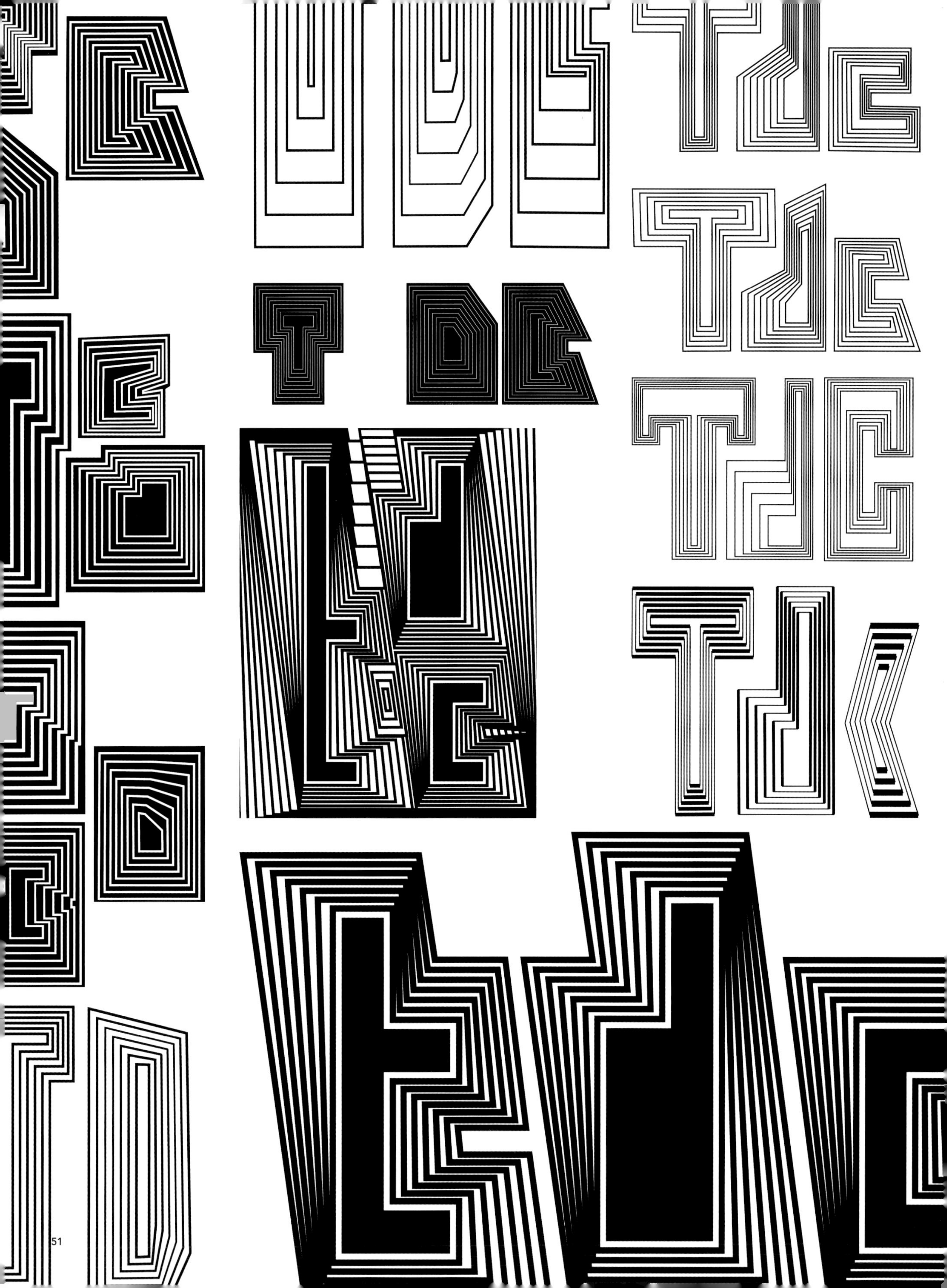

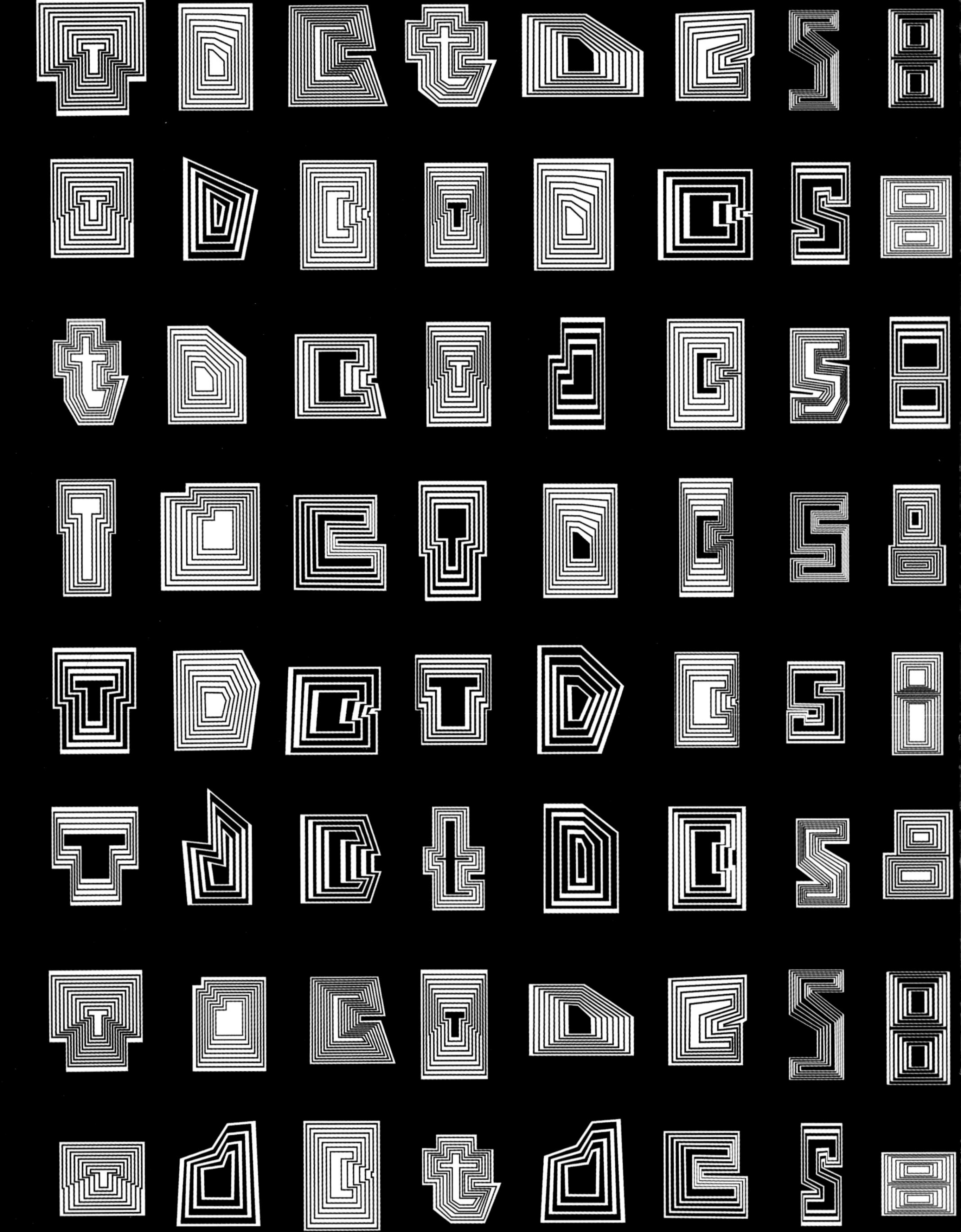

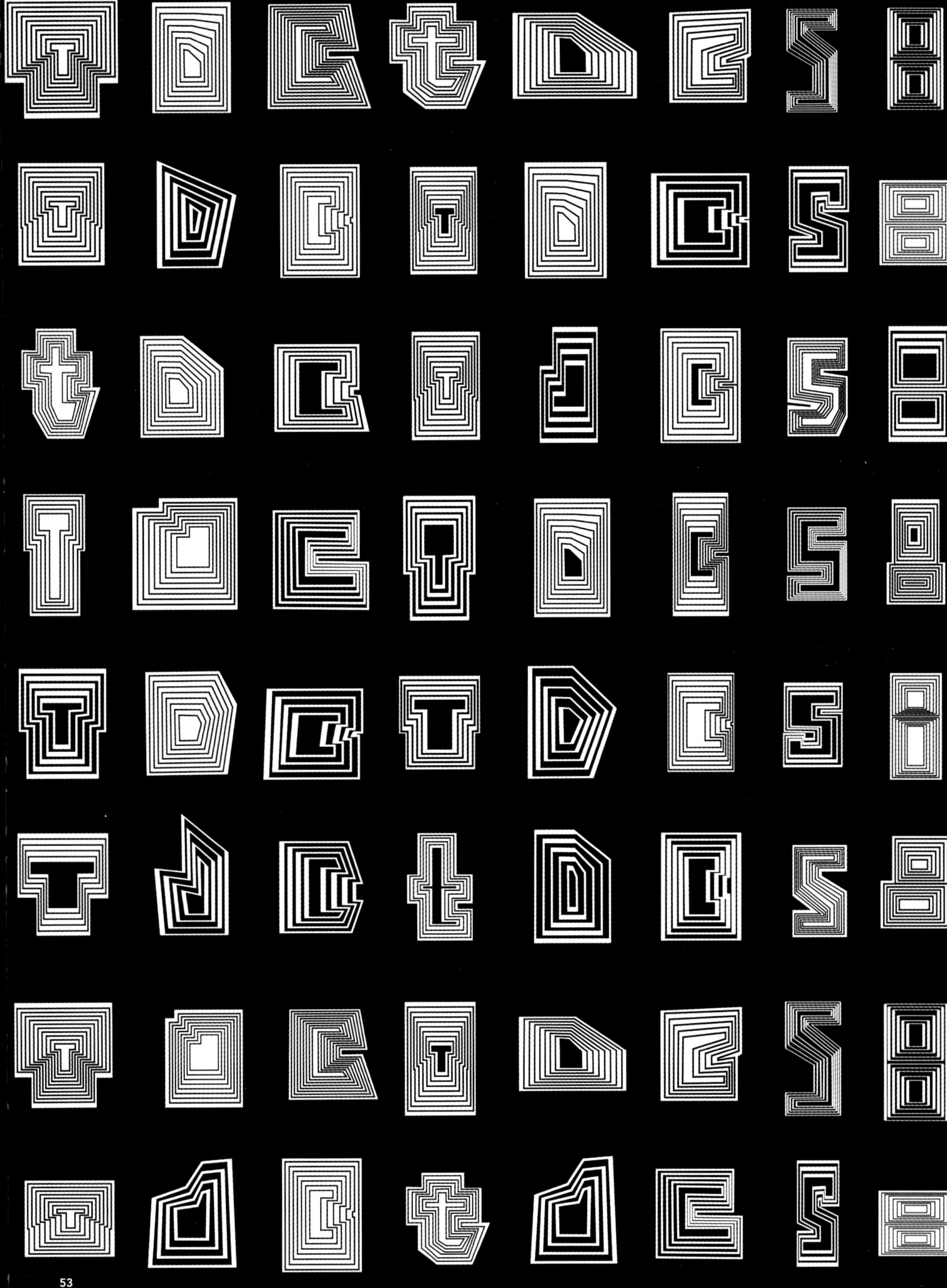

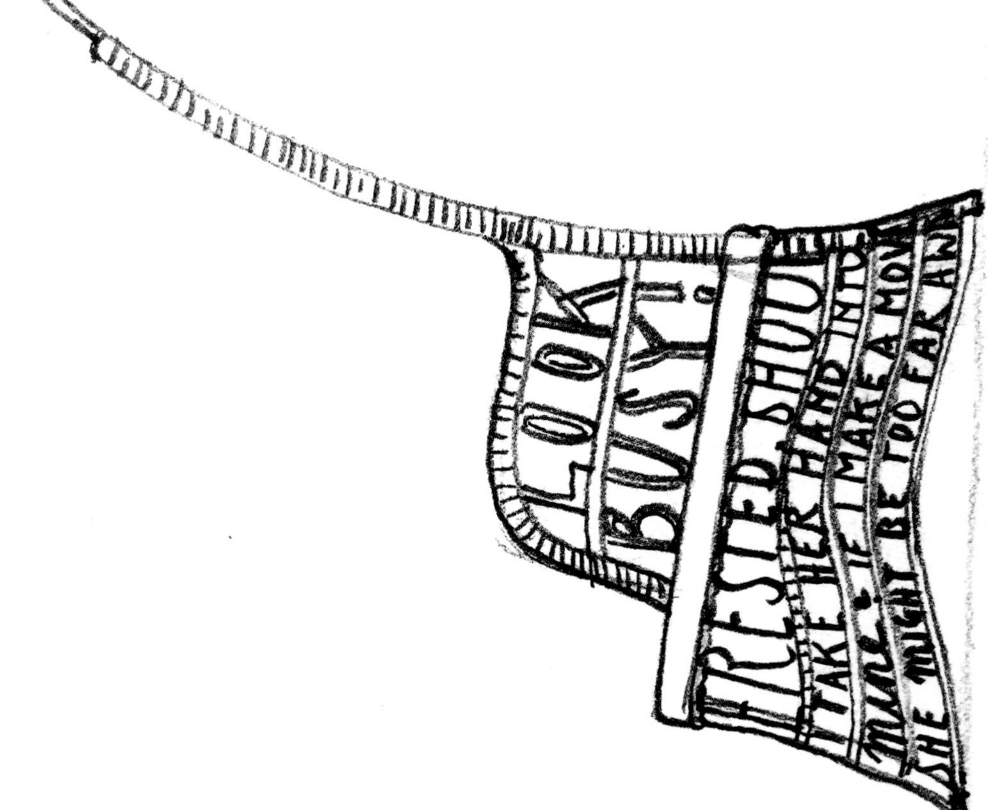
LOOK
BUSY!
TAKE HER HAND INTO

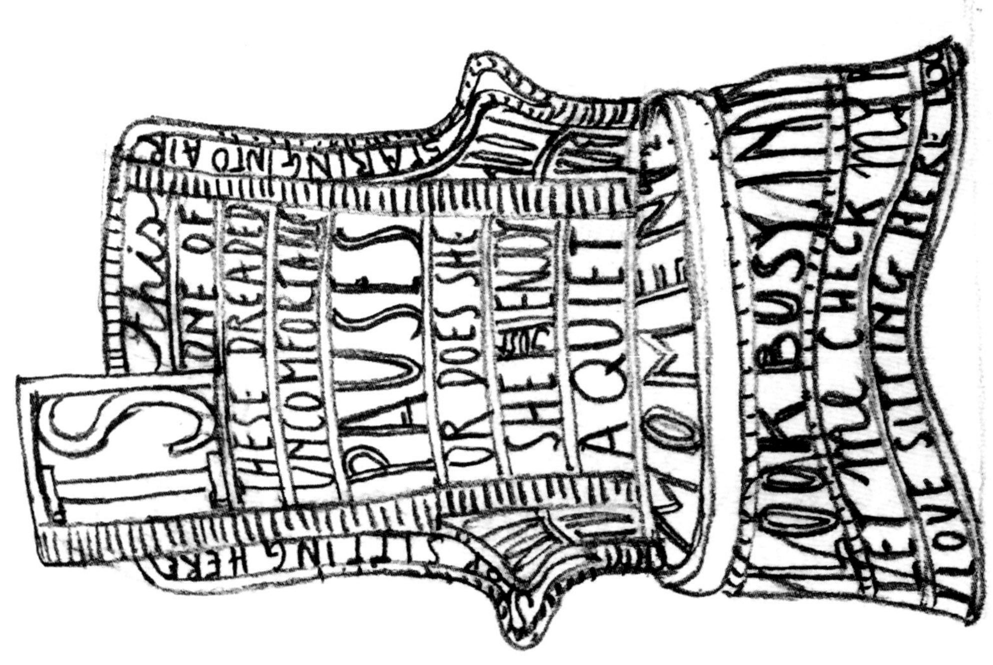
IS
This
ONE OF
THESE DREADED
PAUSES
OR DOES SHE
A QUIET
MOMENT
LOOK BUSY AND
CHECK MY
STARING INTO AIR
SITTING HERE

“Talkative Chair” studies

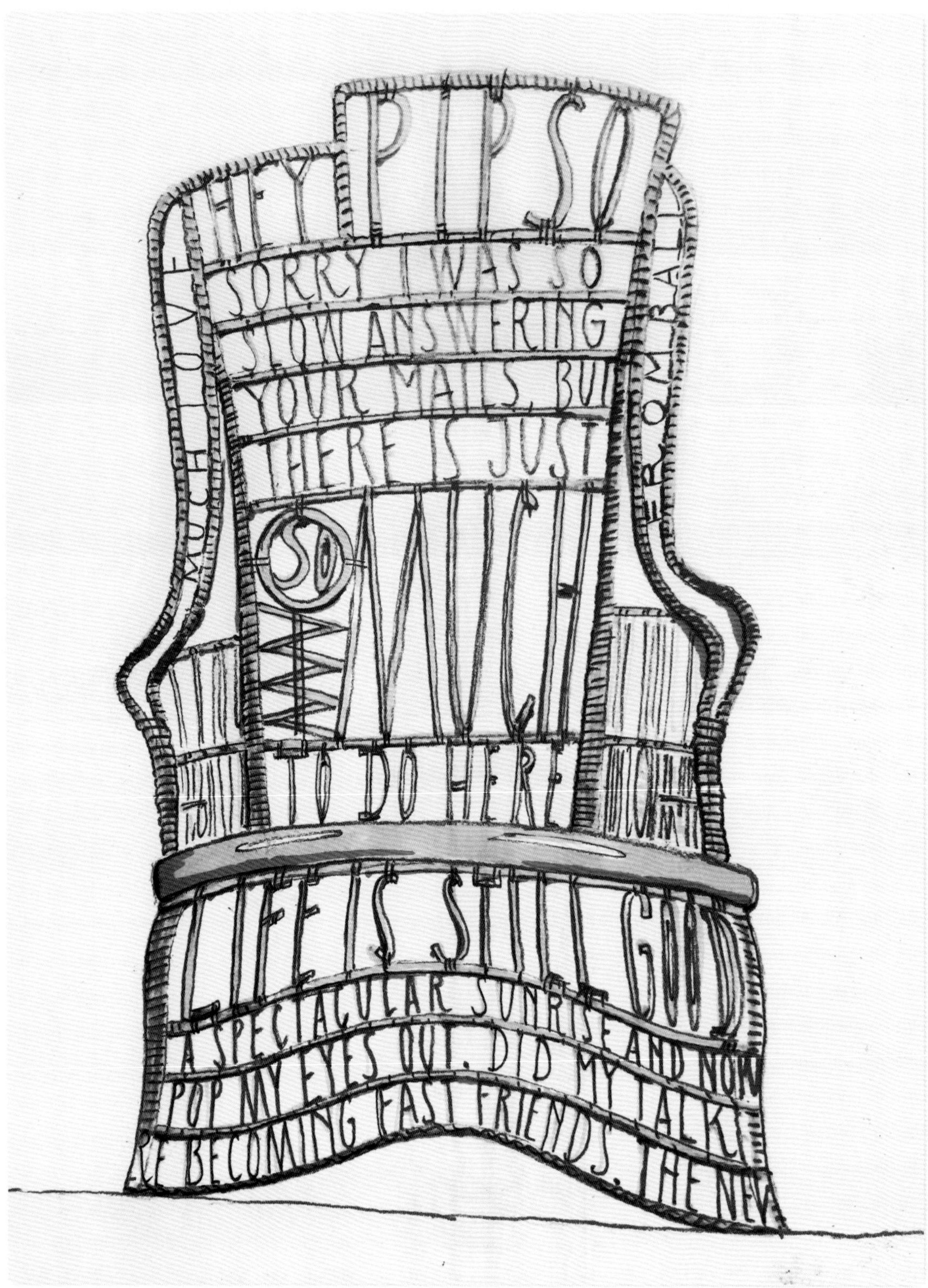
HEY PIPSO
SORRY I WAS SO
SLOW ANSWERING
YOUR MAILS, BUT
THERE IS JUST
SO MUCH
TO DO HERE
MUCH LOVE
LIFE IS STILL GOOD
A SPECTACULAR SUNRISE AND NOW
POP MY EYES OUT. DID MY TALK
RE BECOMING FAST FRIENDS. THE NEW

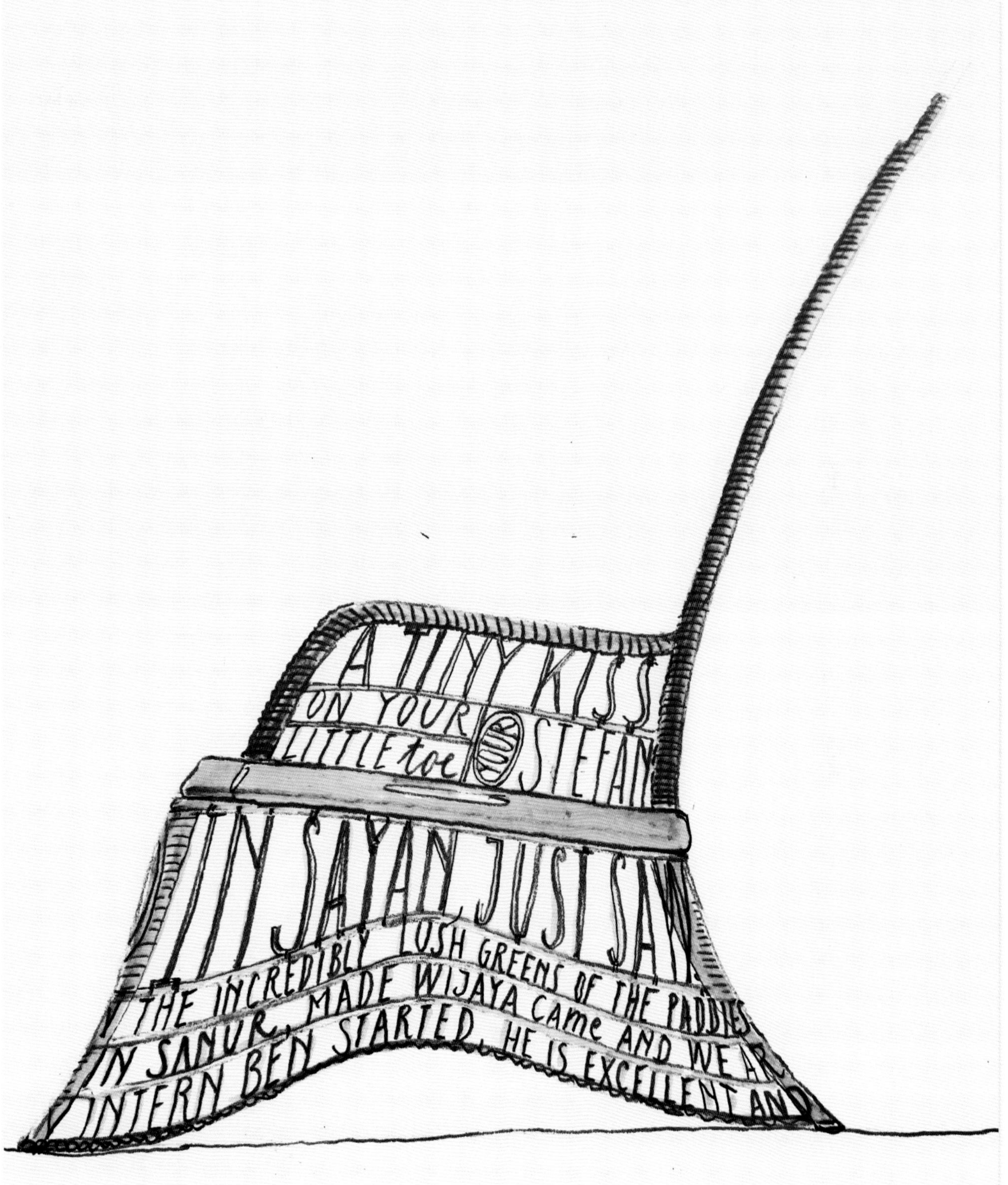
A TINY KISS
ON YOUR
LITTLE toe
YOUR
STEFAN
IN SAYAN JUST SAW
THE INCREDIBLY LUSH GREENS OF THE PADDIES
IN SANUR, MADE WIJAYA came AND WE AR
INTERN BEN STARTED, HE IS EXCELLENT AND

is quite
entirely impossible
Alexander Pope of all
people - snappy writing
it aint -

Silas always picks
the most obscure text
to begin with

No images come
~~Maybe~~ easily to mind maybe
I can do it all with
the words themselves -
Actually there are too many
words for a poster -. Some
of the words might work -
if they're emphasized.

I'll set some type and xerox
~~the words~~ ~~them~~ on scraps of colored
paper and make a collage - sort of funny

maybe it might be
interesting if I photographed the whole thing
~~them~~ with nice cast
shadows to make the poster
~~whole thing~~ more illusionary -

Am I being too trendy with this
word thing? I don't want to
a though I'm trying
to be modern

I'll as
if
ch

Notes and sketches for School of Visual Arts poster

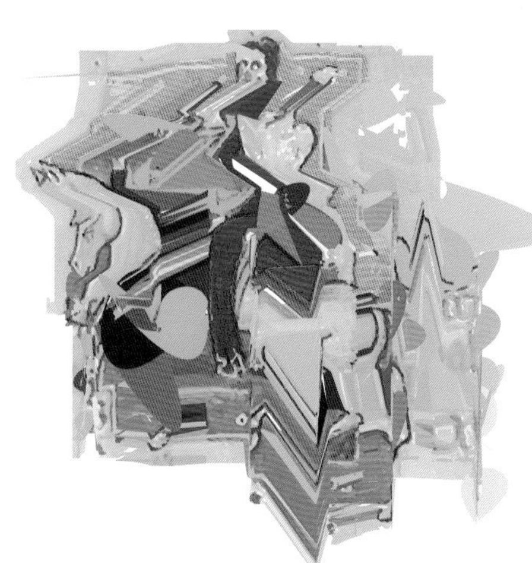

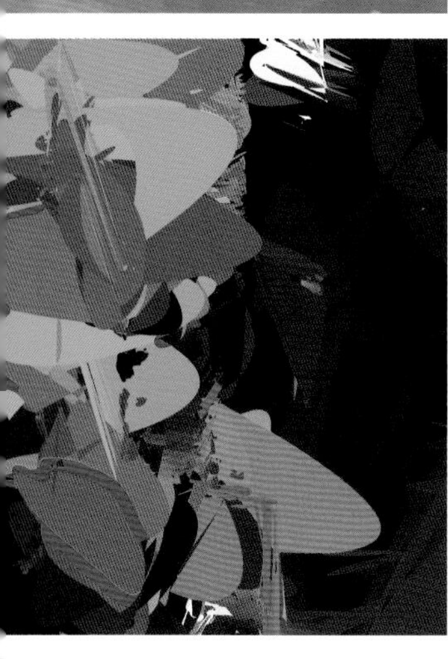

Digital drawings for John Hollenbeck album artwork

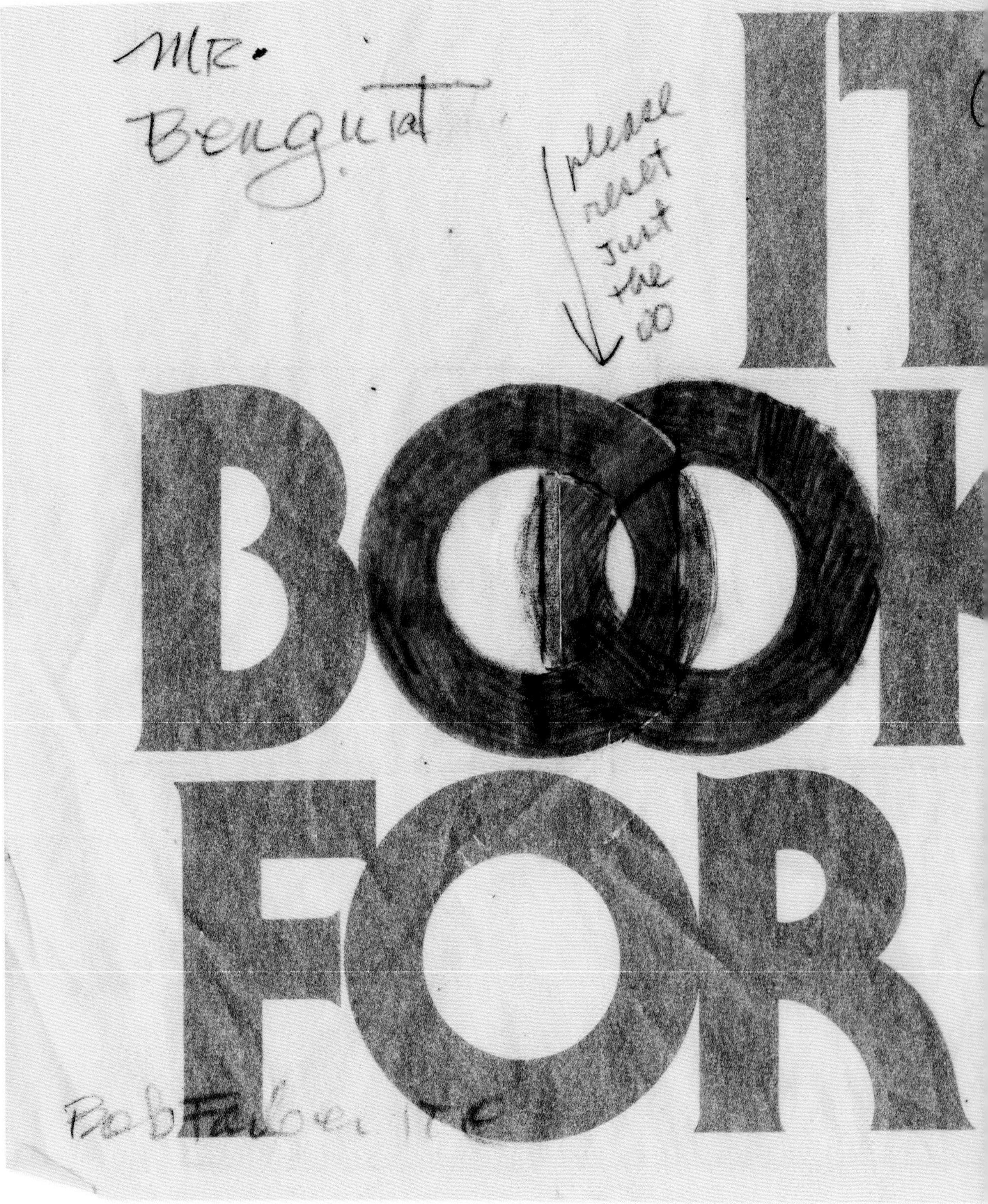

MR. Benguiat

please reset just the oo

BOOK
FOR

Bob Farber ITC

Tracing paper overlay notated by Bob Farber atop Ed Benguiat's artwork for *U&lc* magazine, 1974

P.03

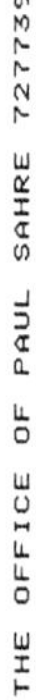
THE OFFICE OF PAUL SAHRE 7277395

AS SHE CLIMBED
ACROSS the TABLE
JONATHAN LETHAM
fig. 1 A
Exceptionally clever...A book of compelling ideas, of intelectual conflict, of human frailty and desire. And its funny. —Dallas Morning Star

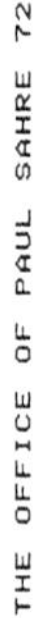
THE OFFICE OF PAUL SAHRE 7277395

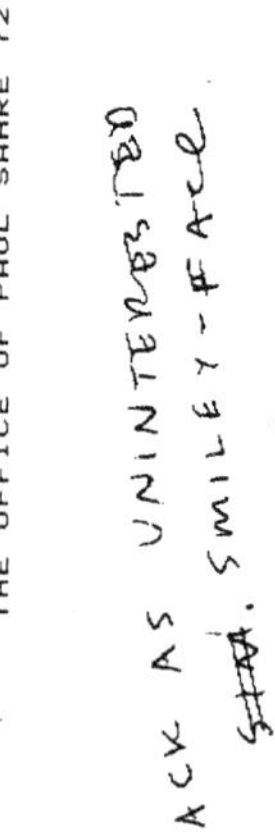

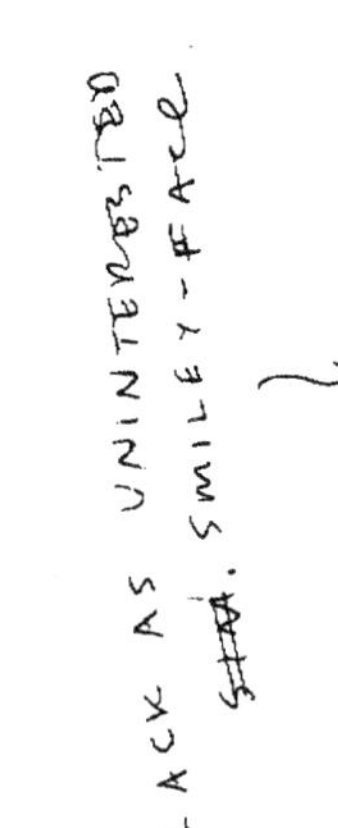

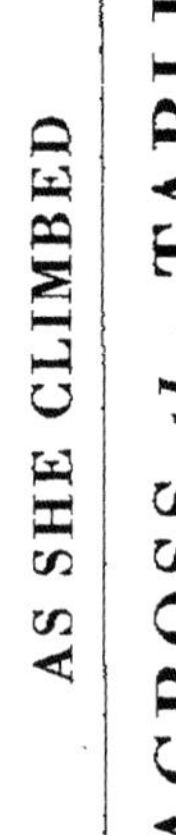

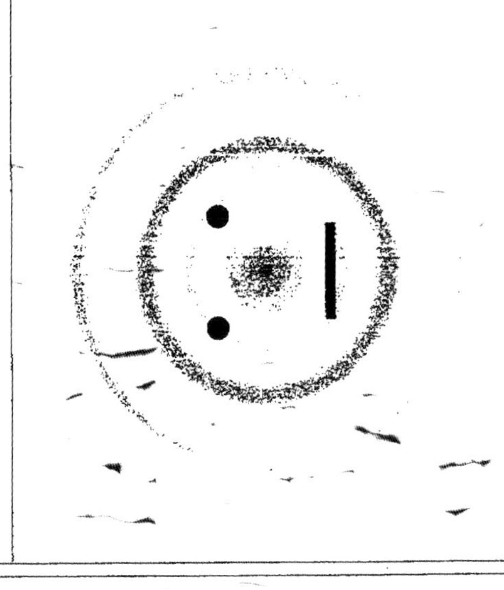
AS SHE CLIMBED
ACROSS the TABLE
JONATHAN LETHAM
fig. 1 A
Exceptionally clever...A book of compelling ideas, of intelectual conflict, of human frailty and desire. And its funny. —Dallas Morning Star

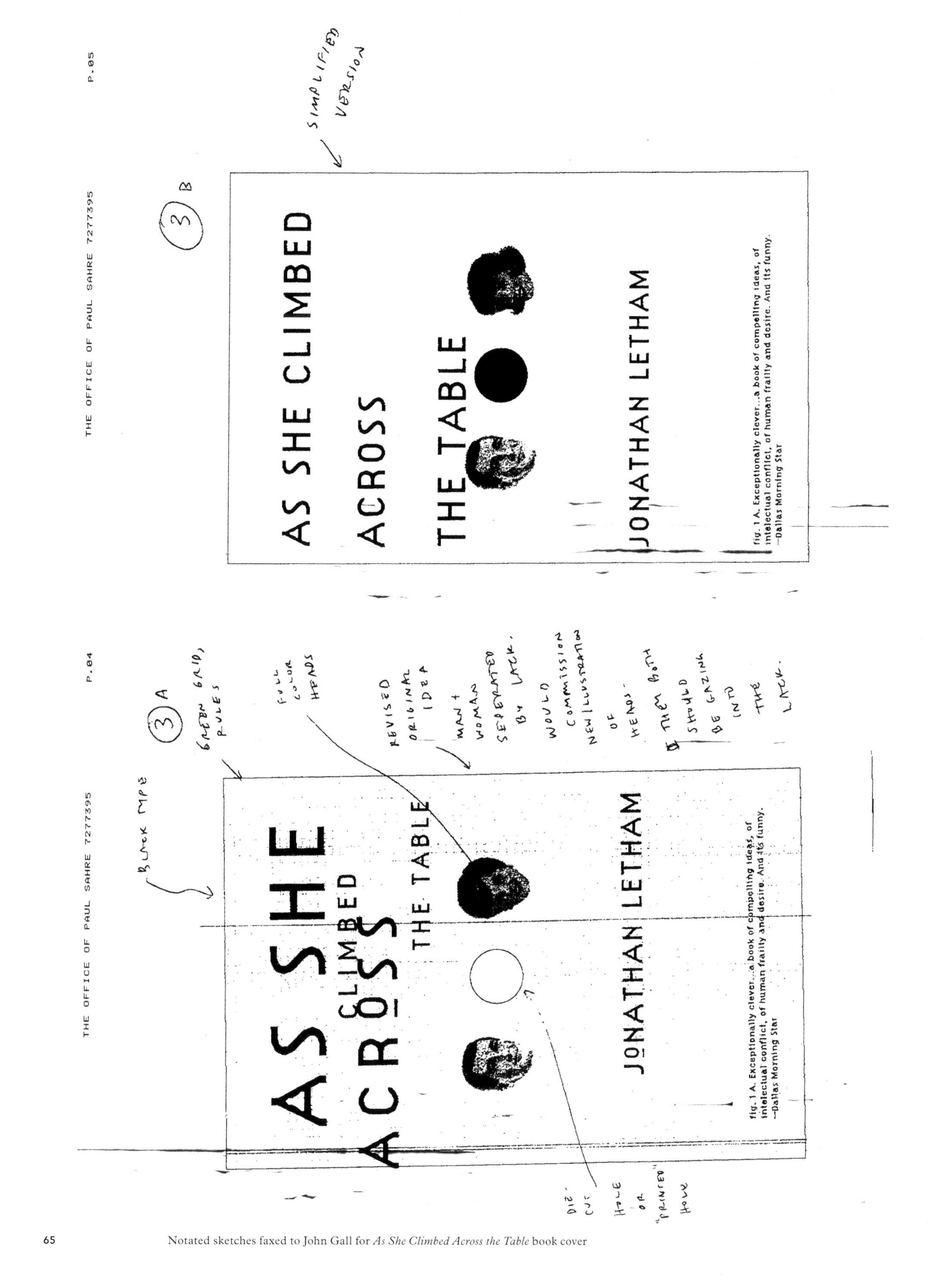

Notated sketches faxed to John Gall for *As She Climbed Across the Table* book cover

VE YOU
crim
i like cigaret
Vape

The thought:
Mean as not nice
is also a meaning of "mean"
(& the letterforms will say it too)
Therefor, Mean means Mean!

"Mean Is Not Nice" notes and letterform studies

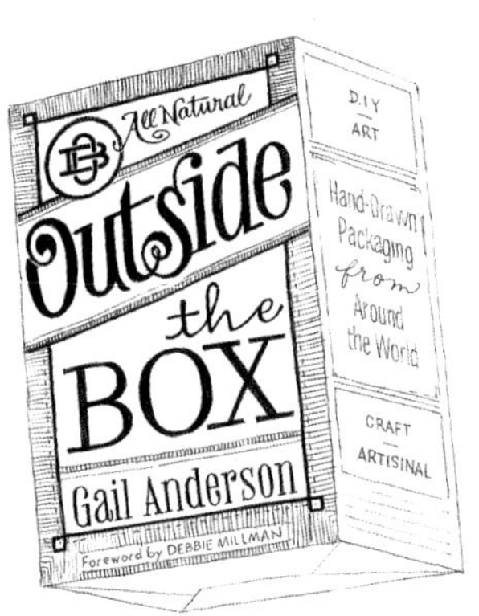

HAND-DRAWN

PACKAGING

FROM AROUND

THE WORLD

Letterform and cover studies for *Outside the Box: Hand-Drawn Packaging from Around the World*

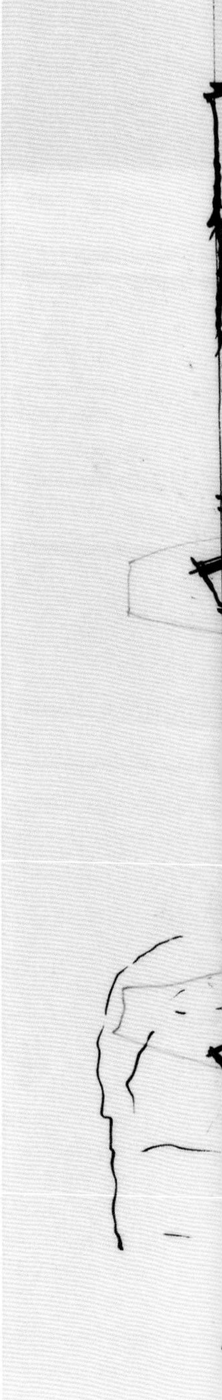

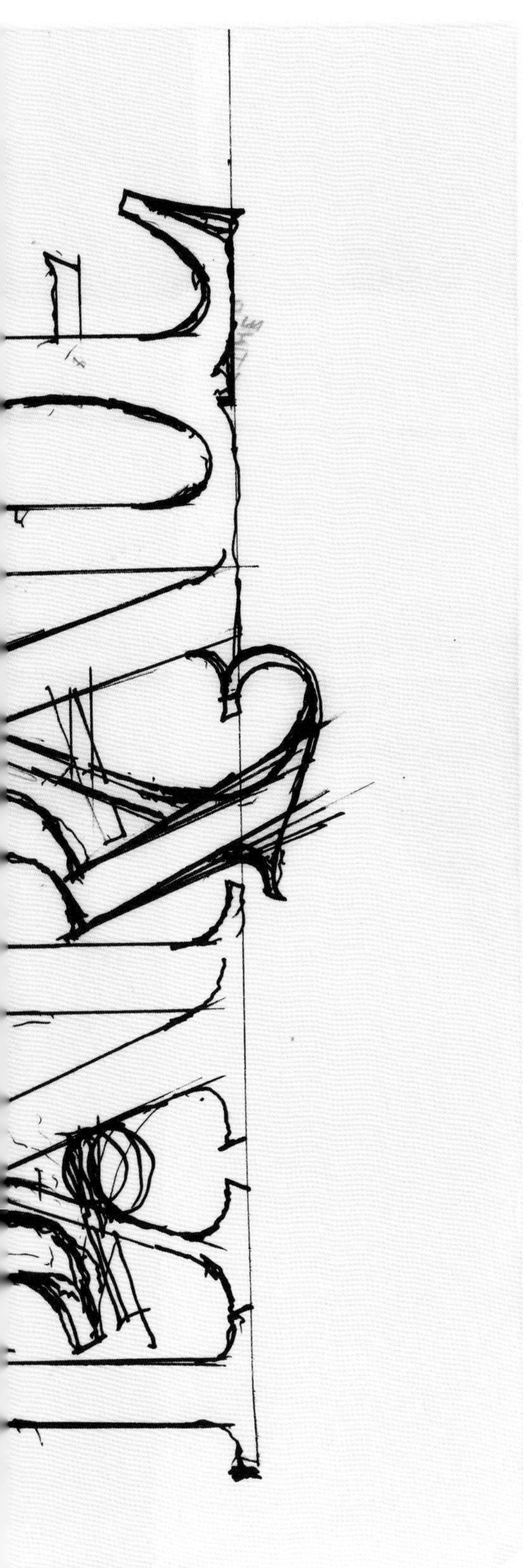

Tracing paper sketches for MTV, *Parade* magazine, and Sony

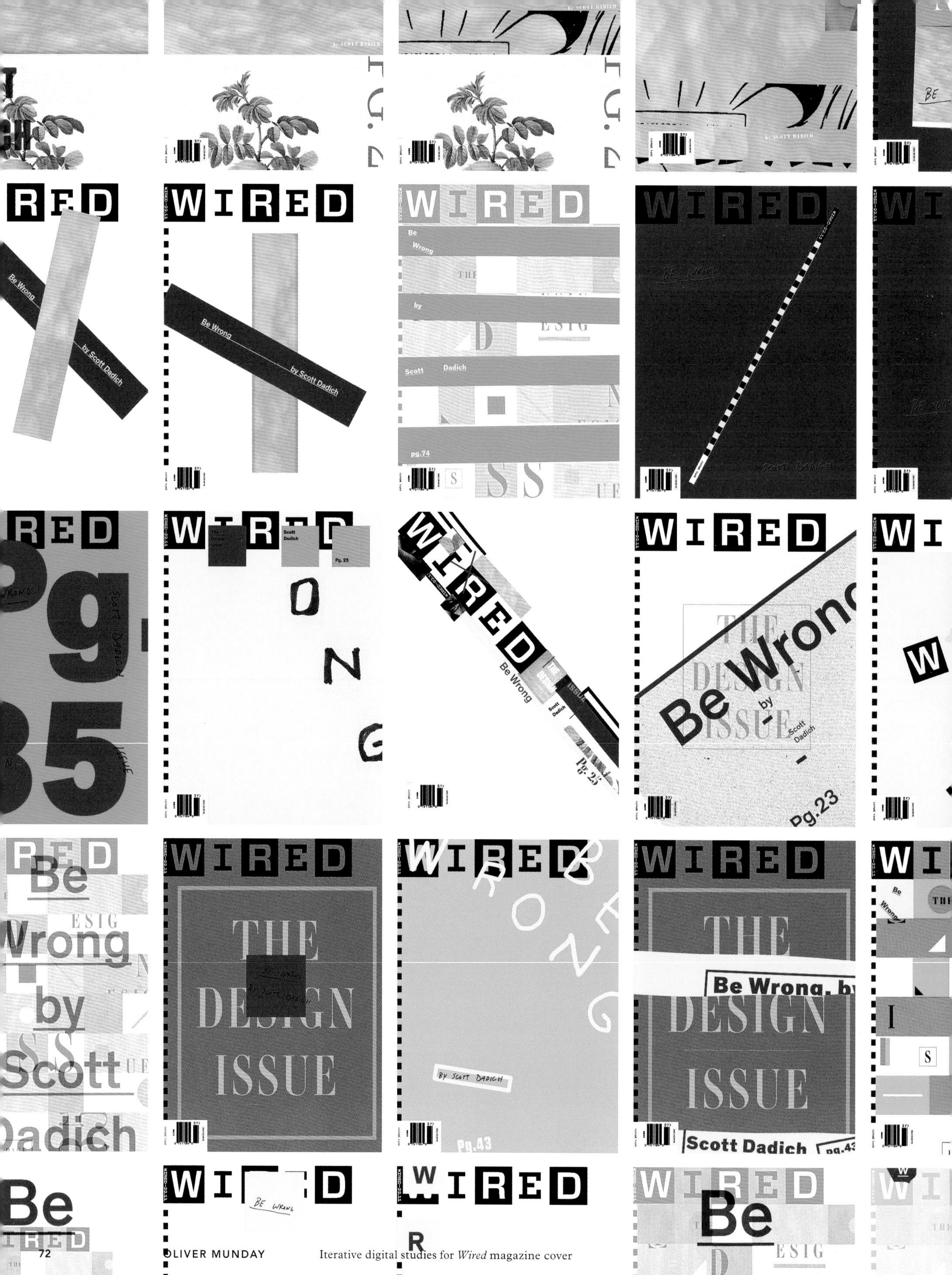

 OLIVER MUNDAY

Iterative digital studies for *Wired* magazine cover

Digital concept sketch for shopping mall campaign

(A) KITTEN IN BEE COSTUME

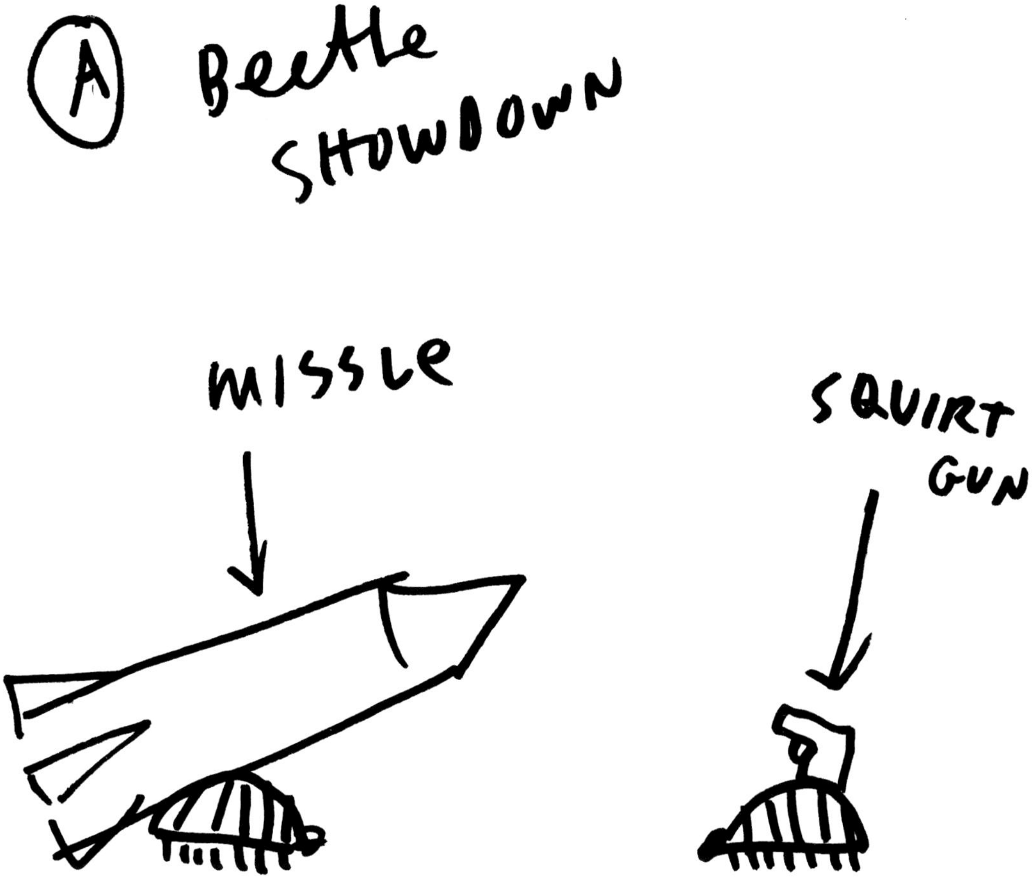

(A) Beetle SHOWDOWN

MISSLE

SQUIRT GUN

Sharpie marker sketches for various clients

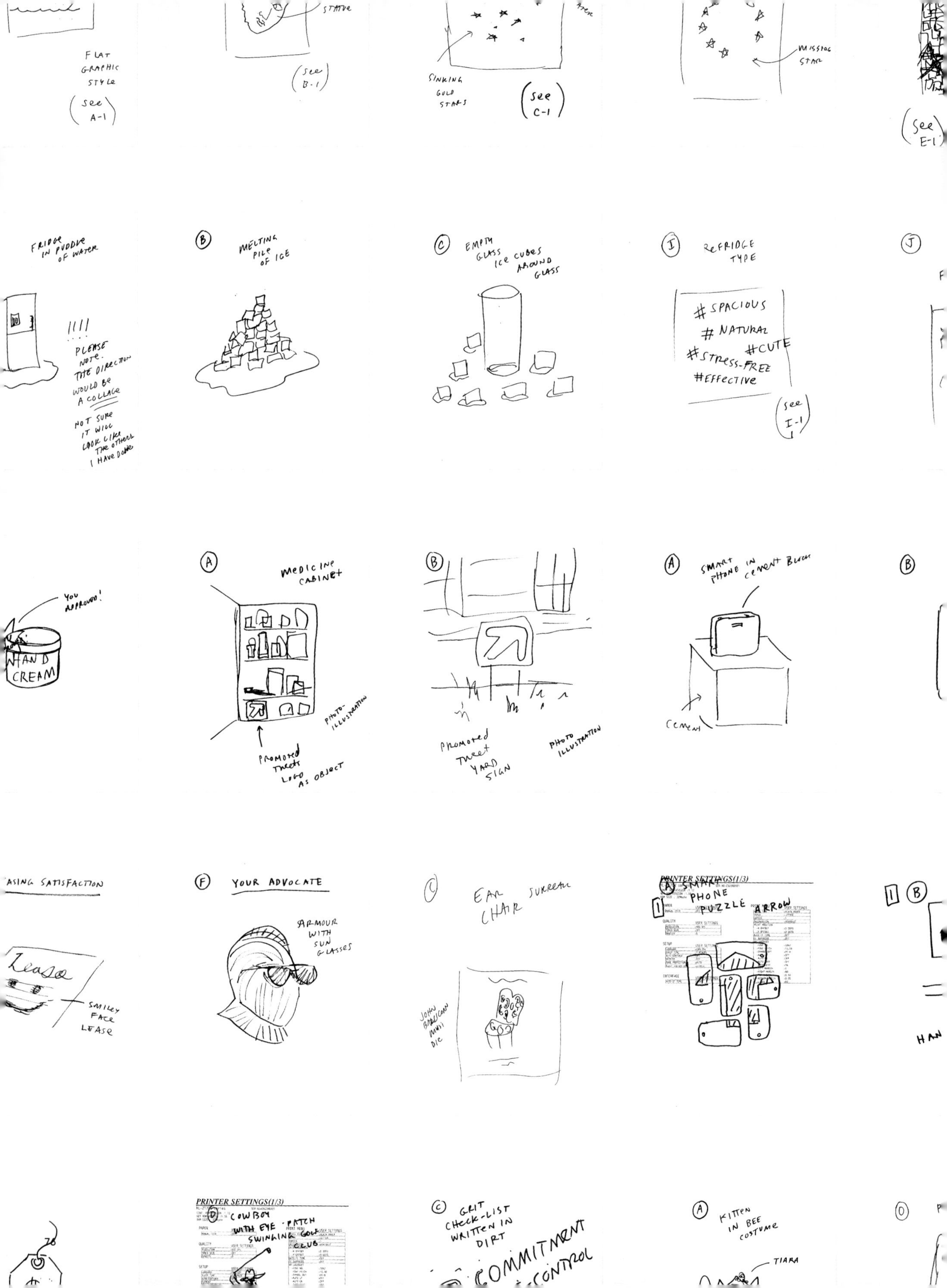
FLAT GRAPHIC STYLE
(see A-1)
STATUE
(see B-1)
SINKING GOLD STARS
(see C-1)
MISSING STAR
(see E-1)
FRIDGE IN PUDDLE OF WATER
!!!!
PLEASE NOTE. THE DIRECTION WOULD BE A COLLAGE
NOT SURE IT WILL LOOK LIKE THE OTHERS I HAVE DONE
B
MELTING PILE OF ICE
C
EMPTY GLASS ICE CUBES AROUND GLASS
I
REFRIDGE TYPE
#SPACIOUS
#NATURAL
#CUTE
#STRESS-FREE
#EFFECTIVE
(see I-1)
J
YOU APPROVED!
HAND CREAM
A
MEDICINE CABINET
PHOTO-ILLUSTRATION
PROMOTED TWEETS LOGO AS OBJECT
B
PROMOTED TWEET YARD SIGN
PHOTO ILLUSTRATION
A
SMART PHONE IN CEMENT BLOCK
CEMENT
B
ASING SATISFACTION
Lease
SMILEY FACE LEASE
F
YOUR ADVOCATE
ARMOUR WITH SUN GLASSES
C
EAR CHAIR
SURREAL
PRINTER SETTINGS(1/3)
A SMART PHONE PUZZLE ARROW
I
B
PRINTER SETTINGS(1/3)
D
COWBOY WITH EYE-PATCH SWINGING GOLF CLUB
C
GRIT CHECK-LIST WRITTEN IN DIRT
COMMITMENT
CONTROL
A
KITTEN IN BEE COSTUME
TIARA
D

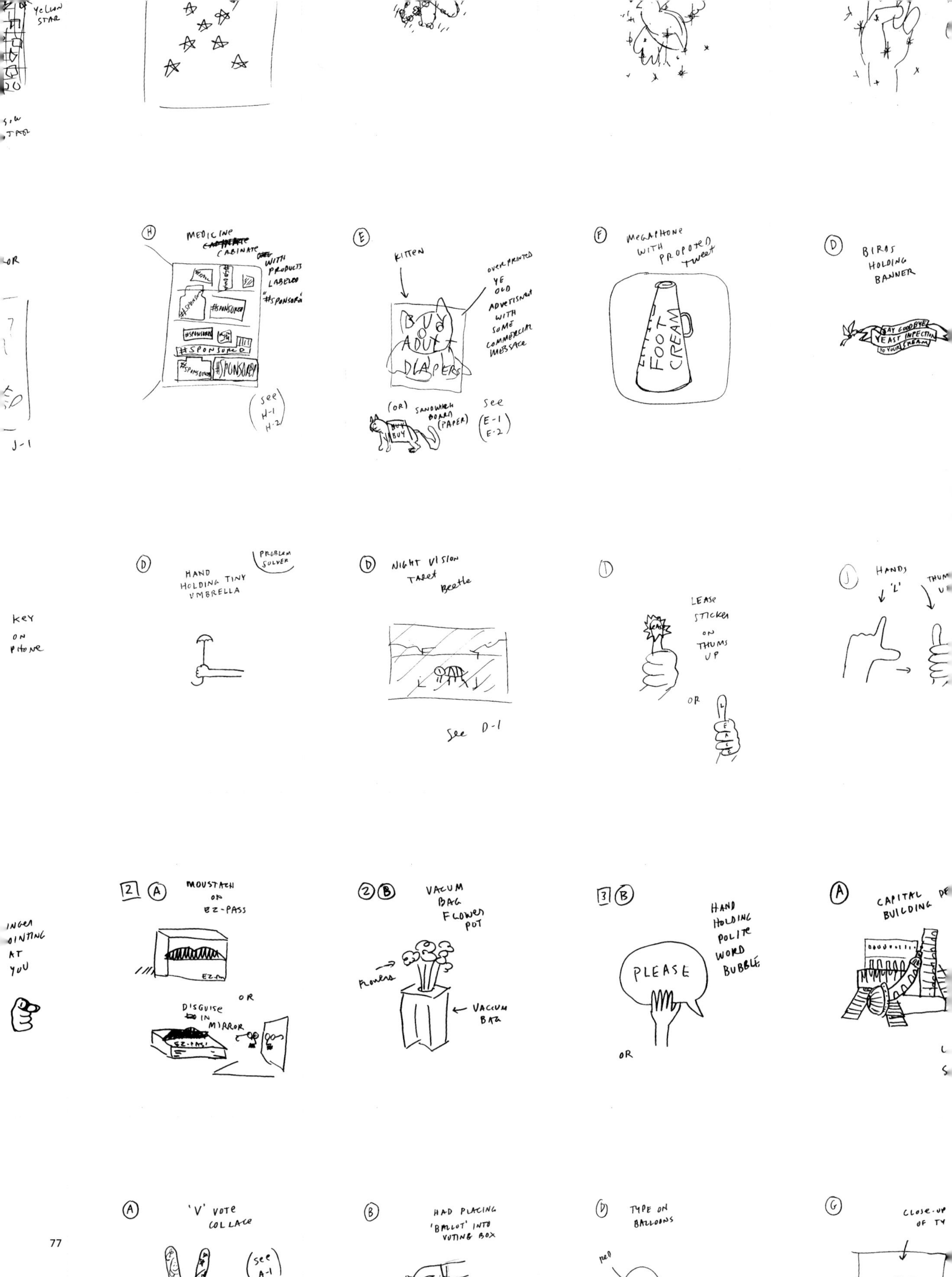
YELLOW STAR
H MEDICINE CABINATE WITH PRODUCTS LABELED "#SPONSORED"
#SPONSORED
SEE H-1 H-2
E KITTEN
OVER PRINTED YE OLD ADVERTISMENT WITH SOME COMMERCIAL MESSAGE
BUY ADULT DIAPERS
(OR) SANDWICH BOARD (PAPER)
BUY BUY
SEE E-1 E-2
F MEGAPHONE WITH PROPOSED TWEET
FOOT CREAM
D BIRDS HOLDING BANNER
SAY GOODBYE YEAST INFECTION TO YOUR CREAM
J-1
D HAND HOLDING TINY UMBRELLA
PROBLEM SOLVER
KEY ON PHONE
D NIGHT VISION TARGET BEETLE
SEE D-1
D LEASE STICKER ON THUMS UP
OR
J HANDS 'L'
2 A MOUSTACH OR EZ-PASS
EZ
DISGUISE IN MIRROR
OR
EZ-PASS
2 B VACUM BAG FLOWER POT
FLOWERS
VACUUM BAG
3 B HAND HOLDING POLITE WORD BUBBLE
PLEASE
OR
A CAPITAL BUILDING
FINGER POINTING AT YOU
A 'V' VOTE COLLAGE
SEE A-1 A-2
B HAD PLACING 'BALLOT' INTO VOTING BOX
D TYPE ON BALLOONS
RED
G CLOSE-UP OF TV
PAST

SIMON
AND
GARFUNKEL

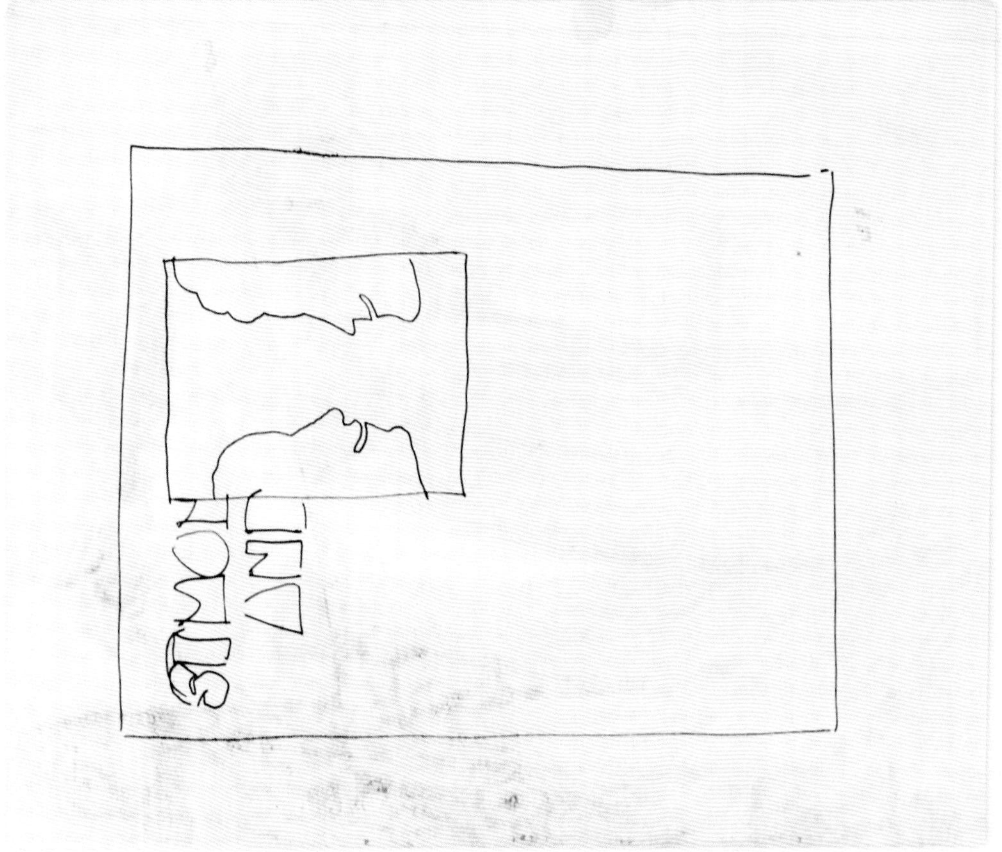
SIMON
AND

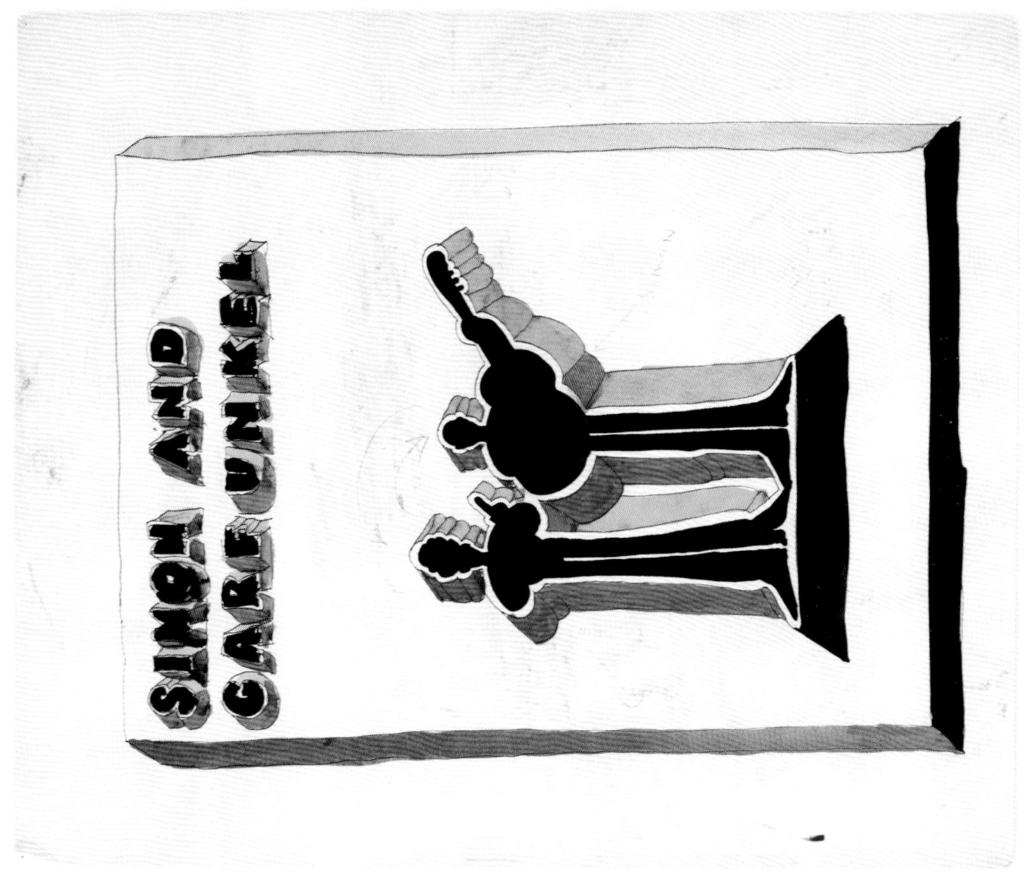

Sketches for Simon & Garfunkel at Lincoln Center poster, 1967

MONTREAUX FESTIVAL JUNE 75

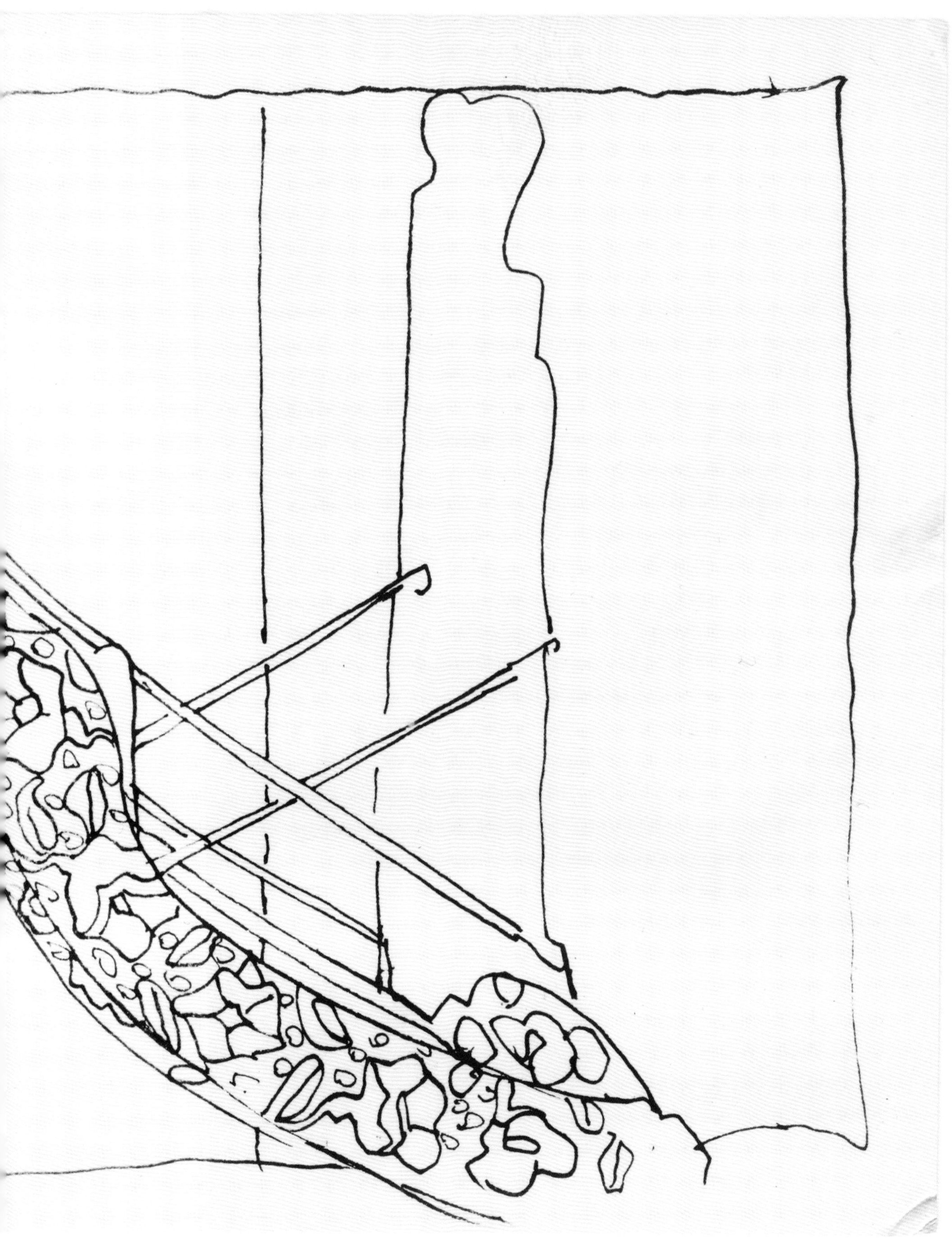

Sketch for Montreux Jazz Festival poster, 1976

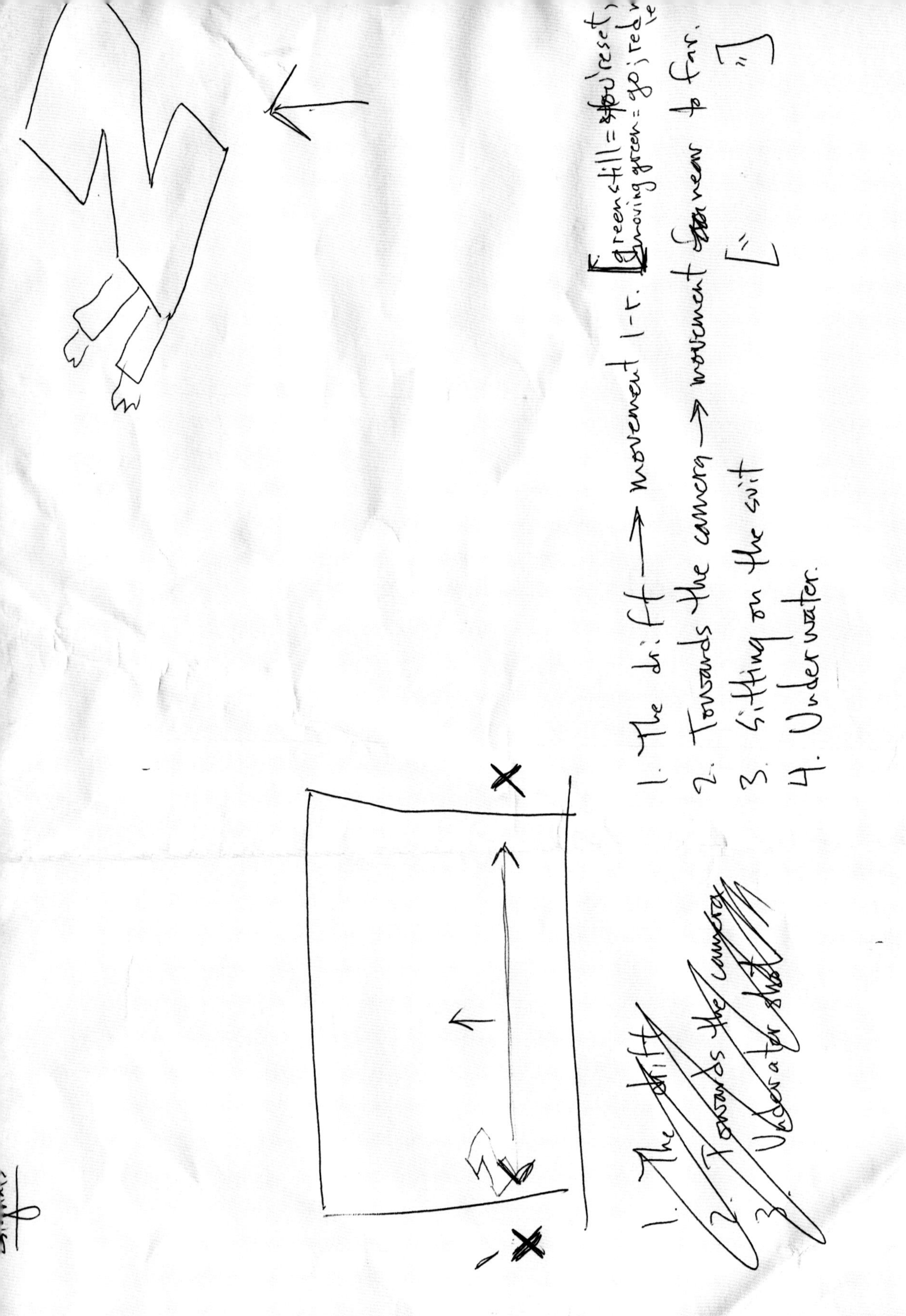
1. The drift → movement l-r.
2. Towards the camera → movement near to far.
3. Sitting on the suit
4. Underwater.

Notes and sketches for self-promotional "Giant Z" project

Frank - I am not so sure that this one is "selly" enough... maybe try saying a little bit more about all the big clients you have worked for... and I think mentioning an award you didn't get is just plain silly!
Frank

Frank - Paul Sahre did this on a book jacket already...

Frank- Where is the wisdom in showing a book which you could not afford to produce? I don't know what you are trying to say here.
Mom

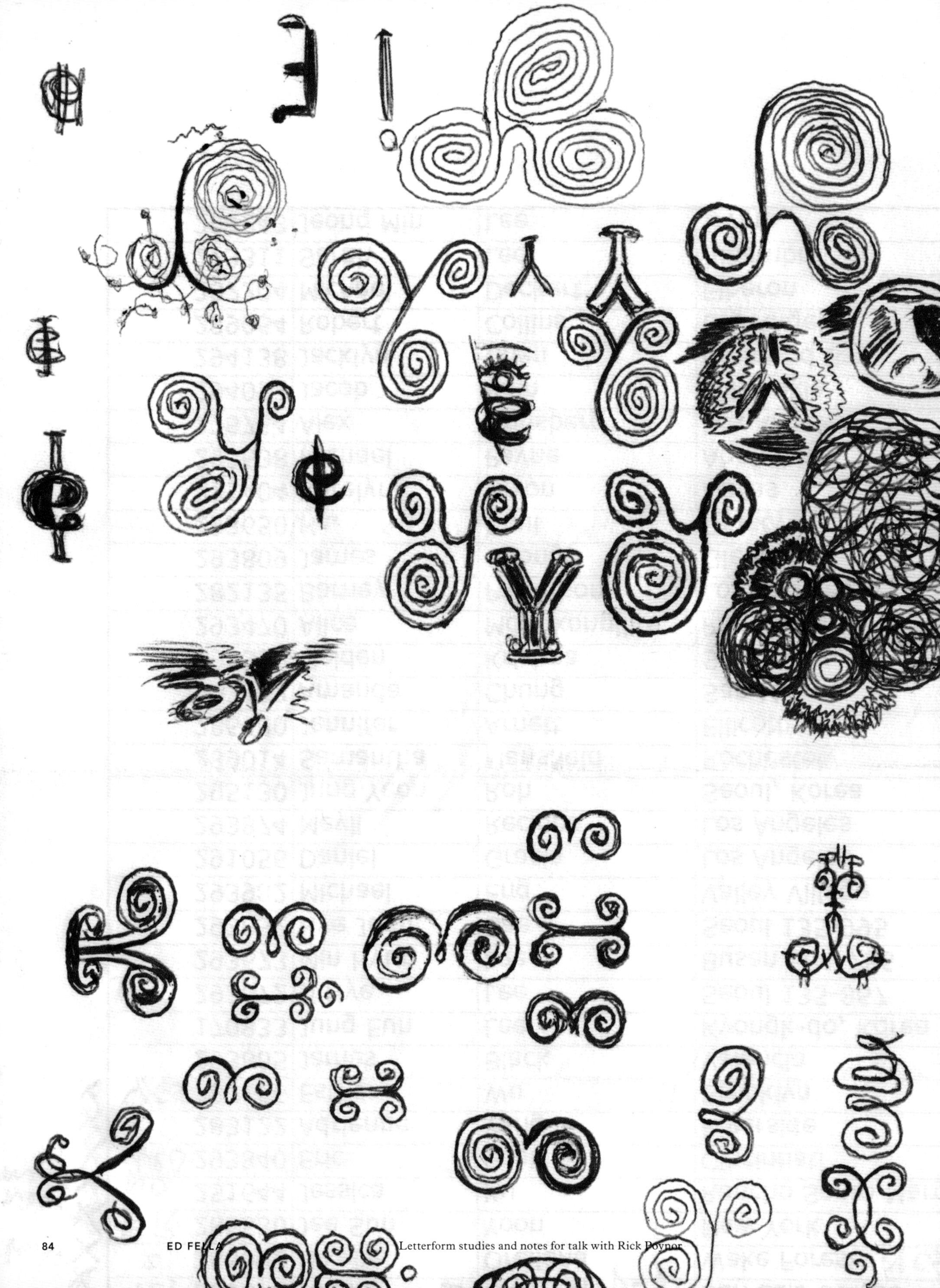

Letterform studies and notes for talk with Rick Poynor

86
IND - IE
- Y
- O
- LAN
~ INDEPENDENT
EEEEEEEE!
I N D
Rick Poynor
Monday
FEB 13th
11:20 AM -
1995 (1990-97 eye mag editor)
interview w/ Jeff & Rich
Emigre
discussion
POMO condition world "culture internet 900 channels
freedom to consume is all! things are as they are
VS
MOD - toward a perfection in culture and society
possible
the desire for a "different" world "progress"
long discussion of 1st things 1st piece
Saunna Hunt
"The extreme Local"
The "mental" environment
VS
The "environment"
* read "NO LOGO" and NINTIES discu

 Preparatory drawing for *Guitar Aficionado* magazine illustration

Ink-jet print with client-notations

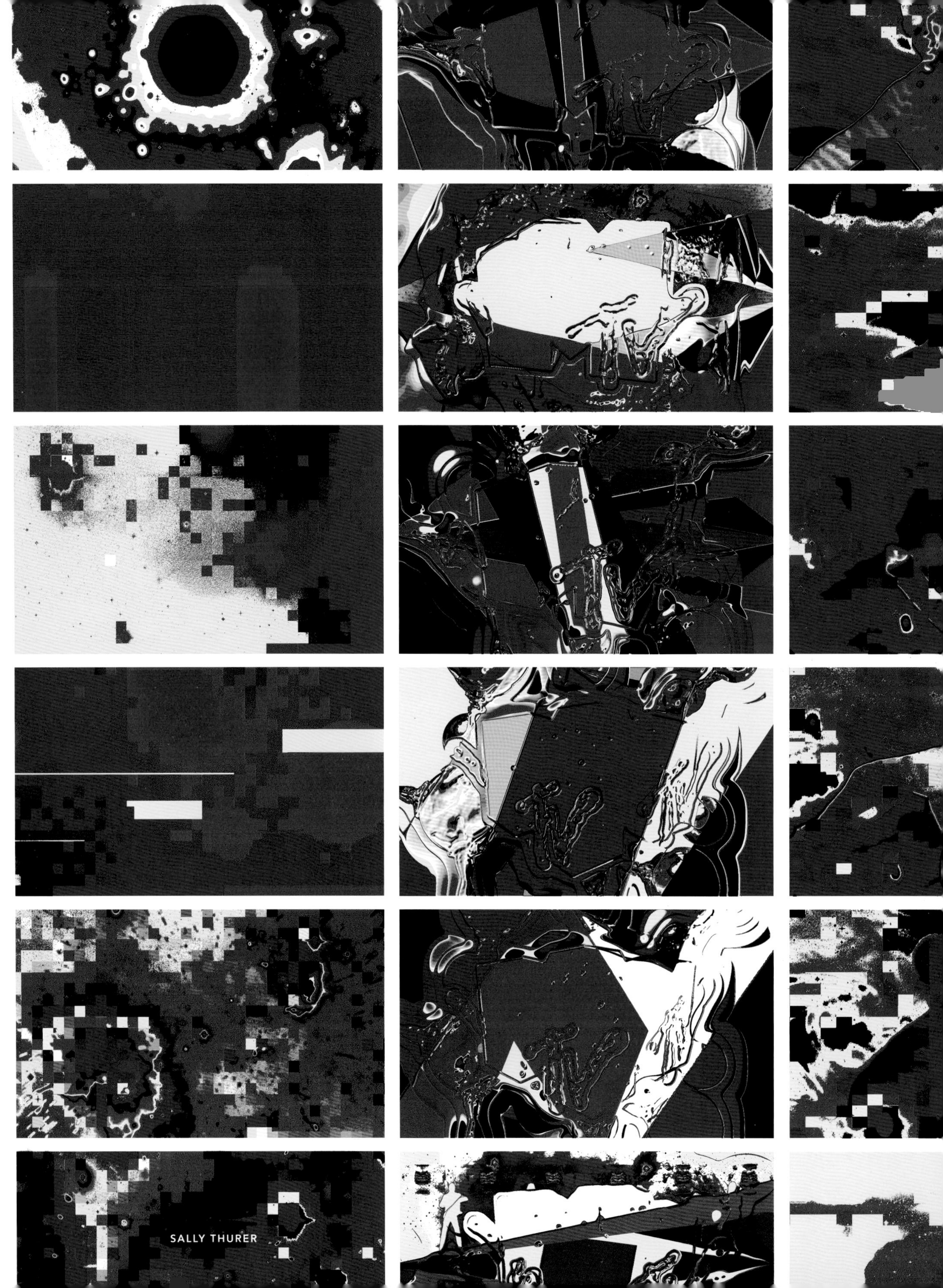
SALLY THURER

Motion stills from MTV's *No Chill*

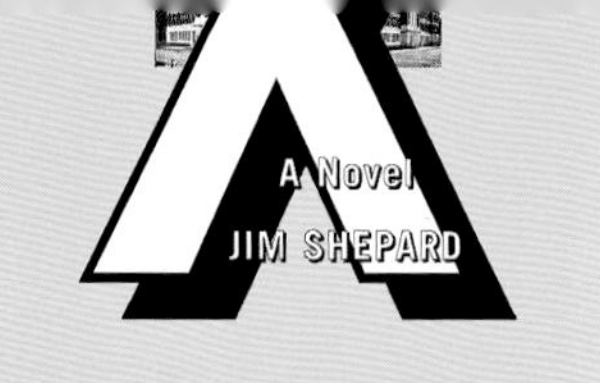

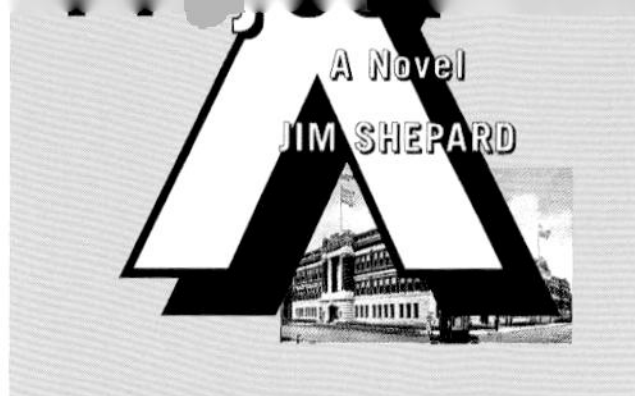

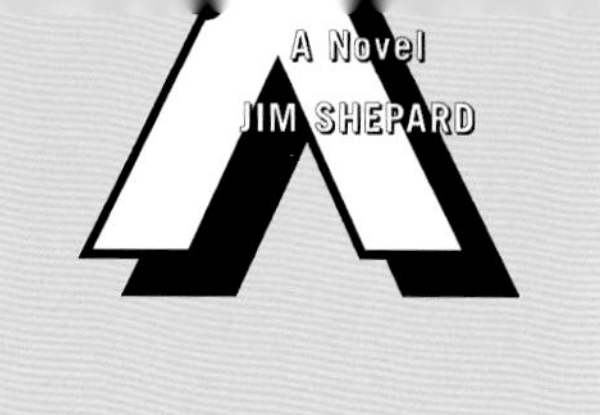

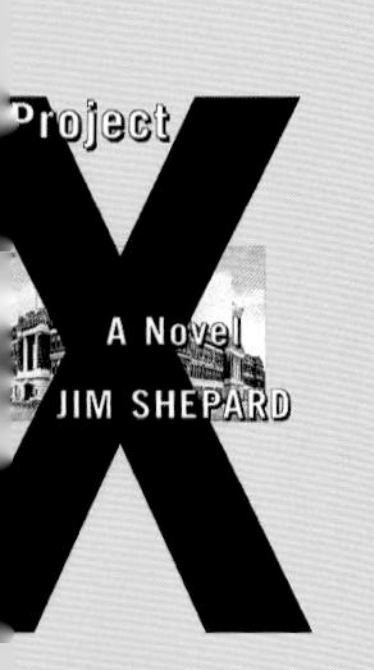

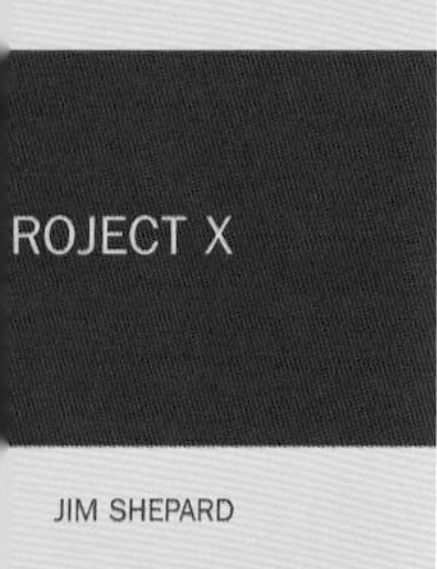

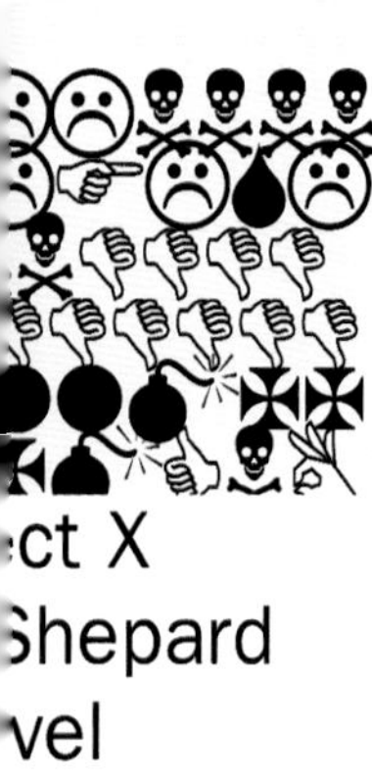

Digital cover studies for *Project X* by Jim Shepard

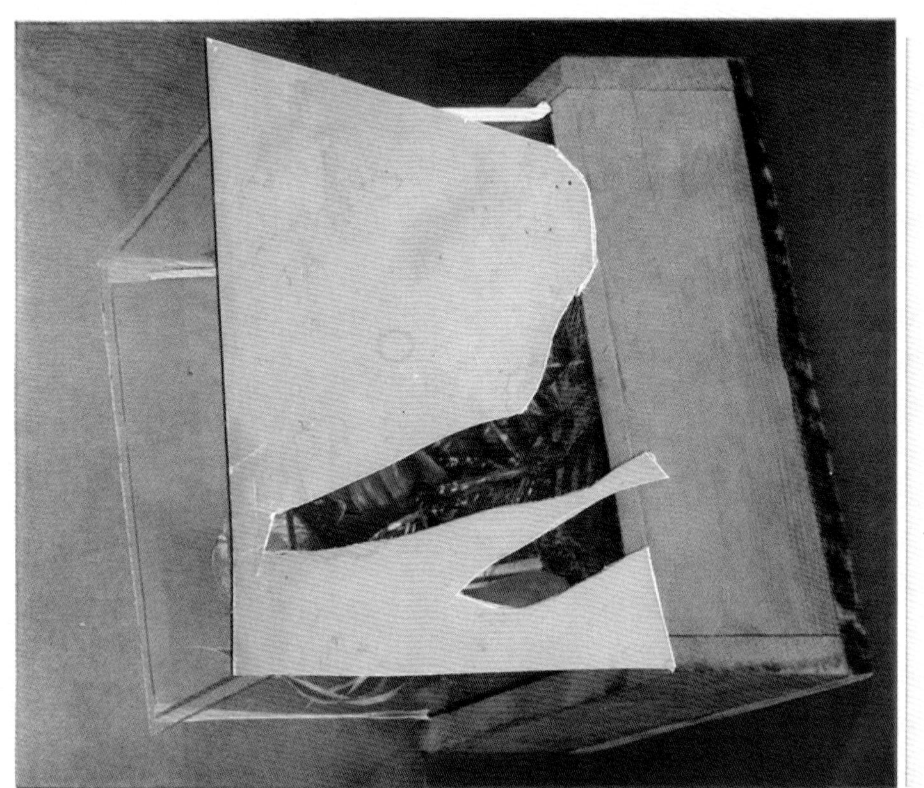

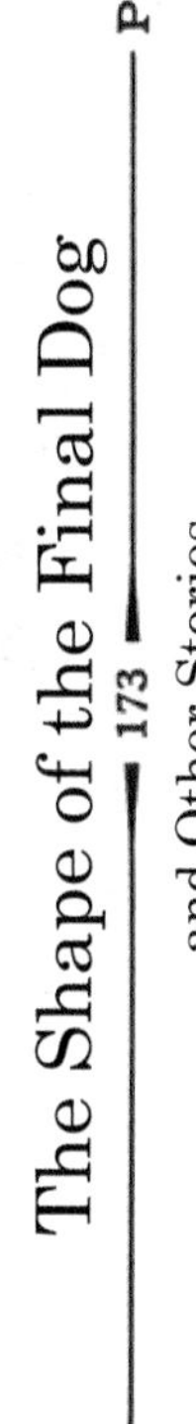

Cover studies for *The Shape of the Final Dog and Other Stories* by Hampton Fancher

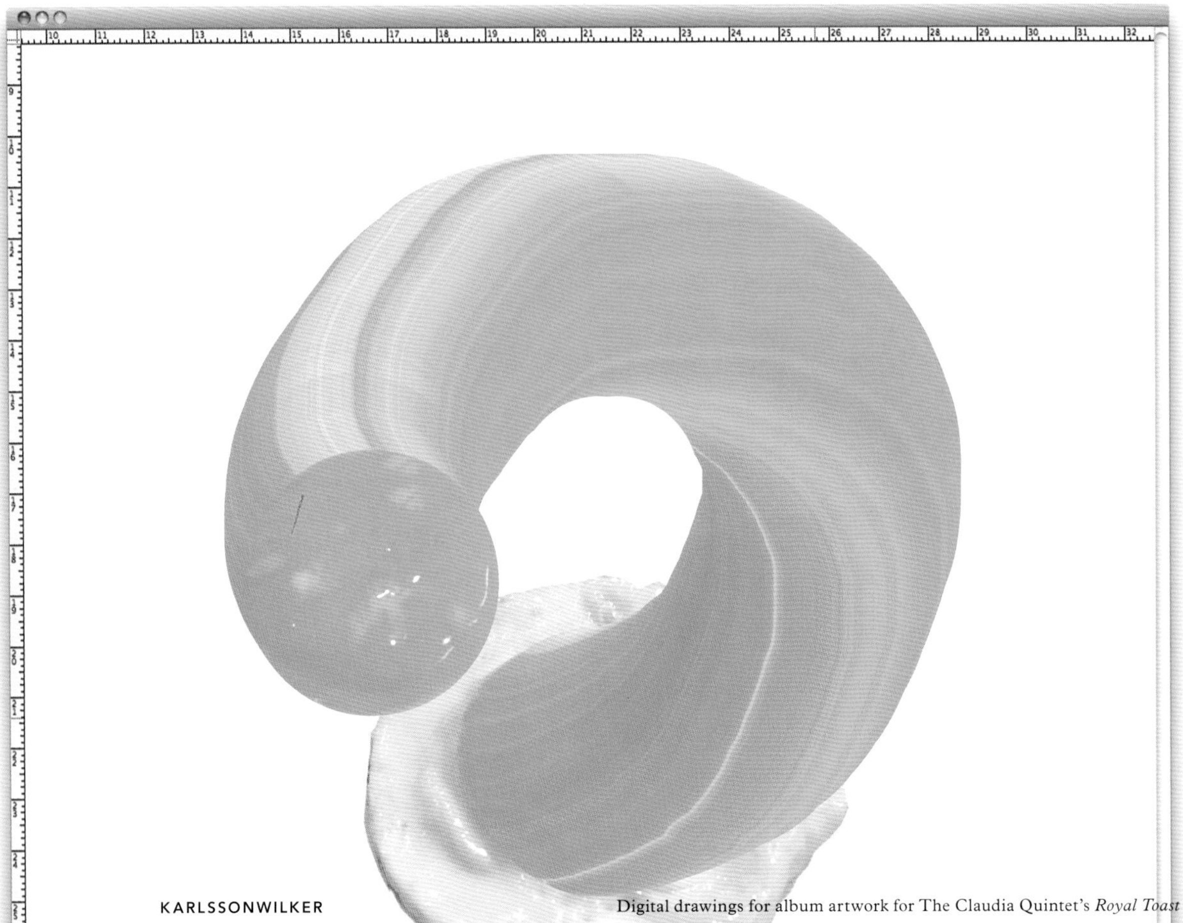

Digital drawings for album artwork for The Claudia Quintet's *Royal Toast*

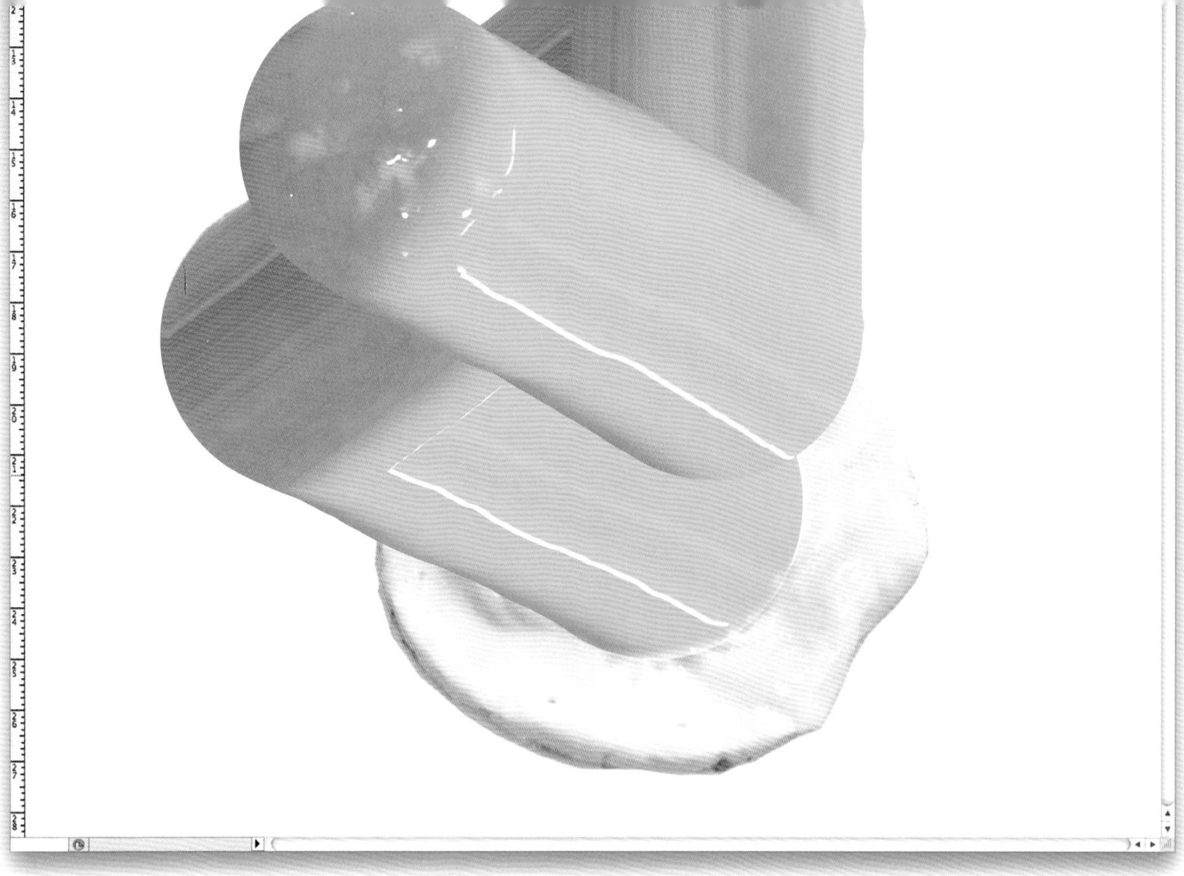

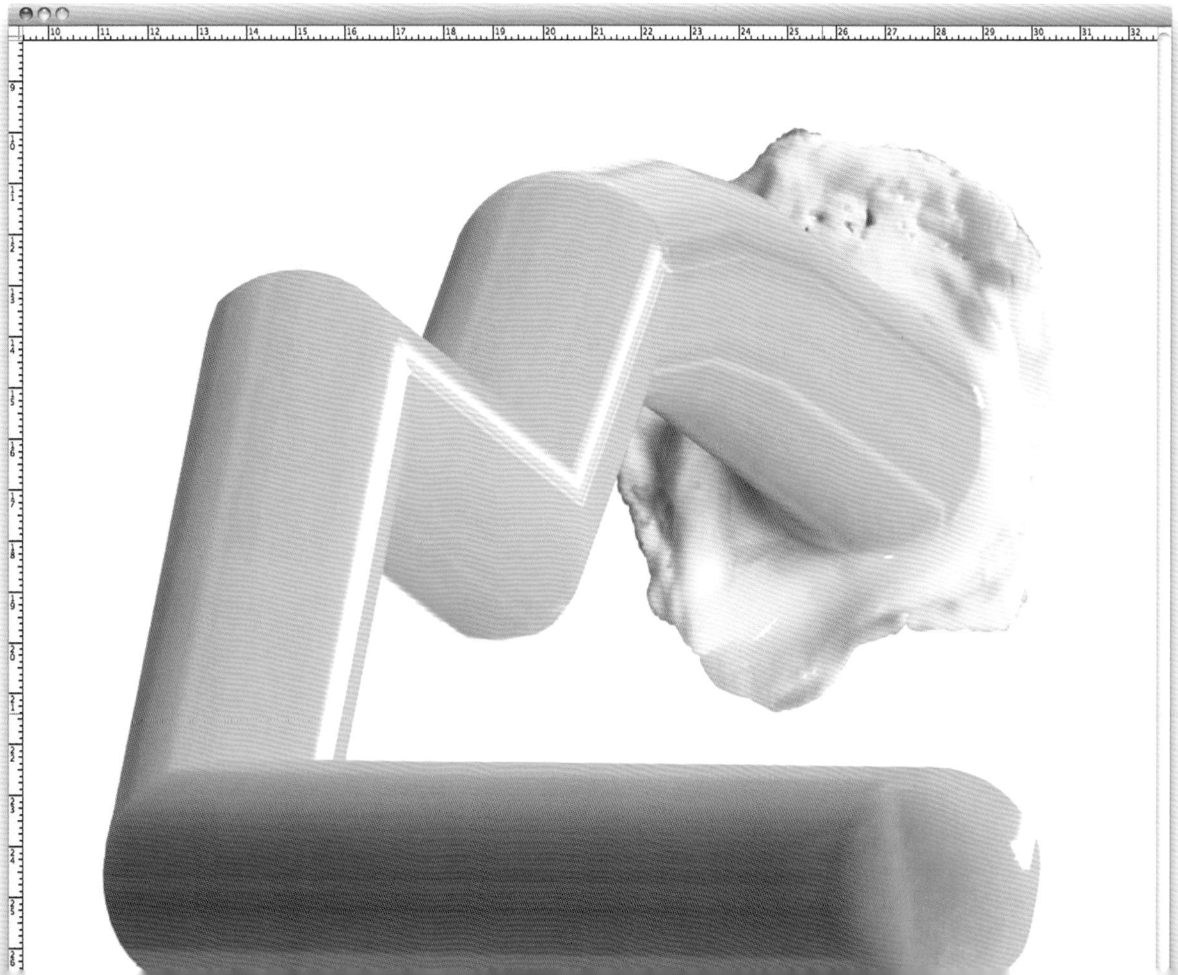
10 11 12 13 14 15 16 17 18 19 20 21 22 23 24 25 26 27 28 29 30 31 32

STUDY #4
ELLIOTT EARLS

PENIS

Digital letterform drawing for Sixteen Tons shop

Digital studies for *Post/Past* poster, The State Hermitage Museum

MY RIGID HEART

is tenderly unmanned

WHAT I
POSSESS
SEEMS
SOMETHING
FAR
AWAY

THE TURGID RIVER
THE WOODS
And
WHAT
HAD
disappeared
PROVES.
REAL.

Needlepoint drawing panels

WARWICK ARTS TRUST
WARWICK ARTS TRUST
nose
eye

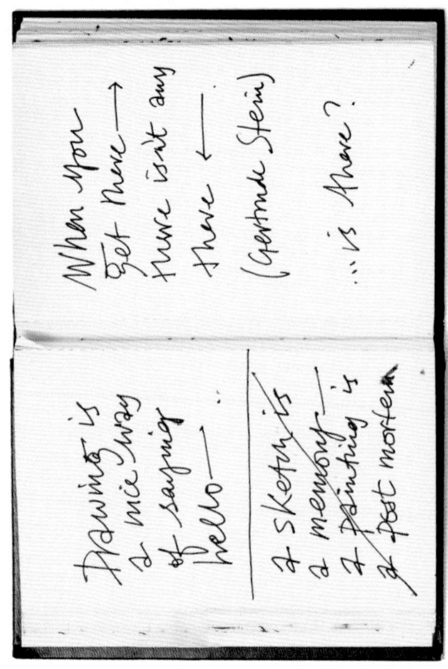
When you get there →
there isn't any
there ←
(Gertrude Stein)
...is there?
Drawing is a nice way of saying hello —
a sketch is a memory
a painting is a post mortem

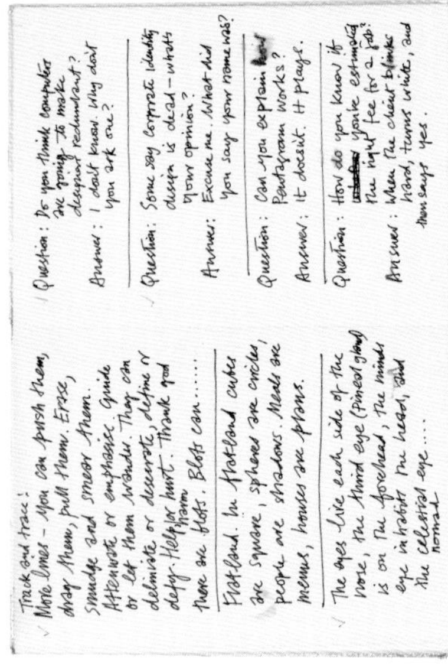
Question: Do you think computers are going to make designers redundant?
Answer: I don't know. Why don't you ask one?
Question: Some say corporate identity design is dead — what's your opinion?
Answer: Excuse me. What did you say your name was?
Question: Can you explain how Pentagram works?
Answer: It doesn't. It plays.
Flatland. In Flatland cubes are squares, spheres are circles, people are shadows. Meals are menus, houses are plans.

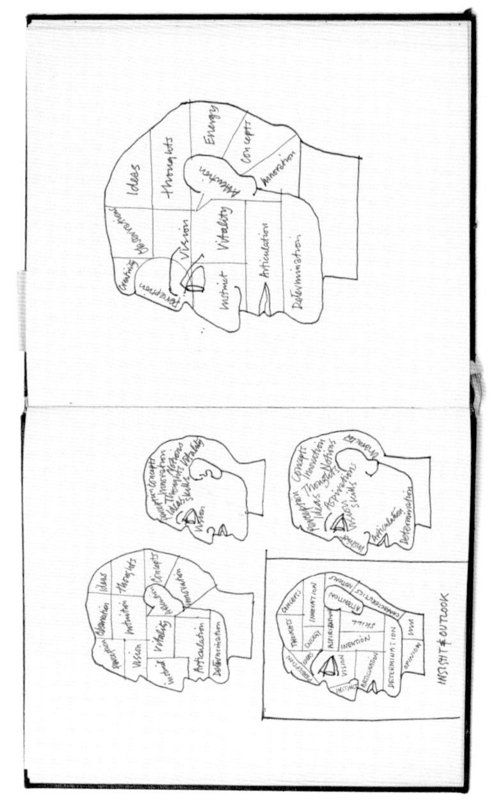
Ideas
Thoughts
Energy
Concepts
Immersion
Vision
Vitality
Instinct
Articulation
Determination
INSIGHT & OUTLOOK

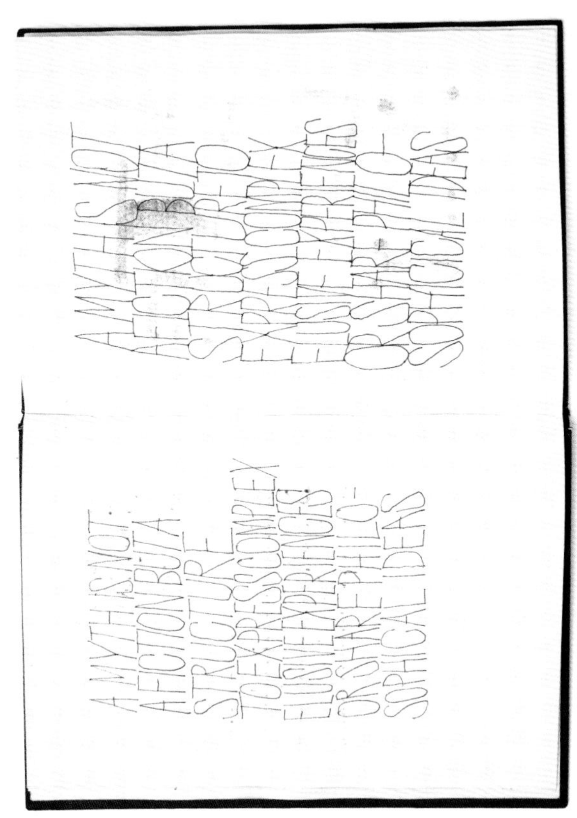

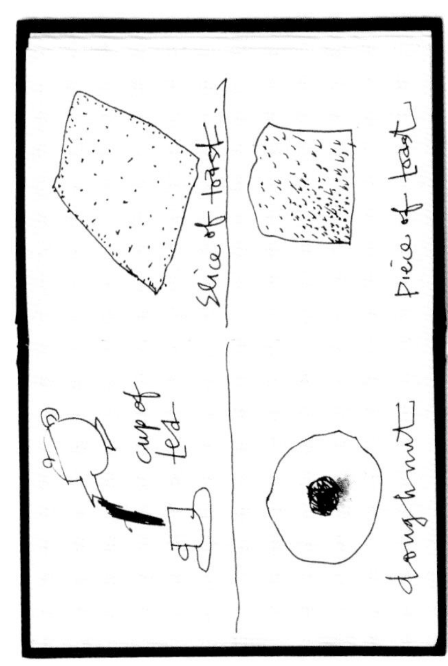
cup of tea
doughnut
slice of toast
piece of toast

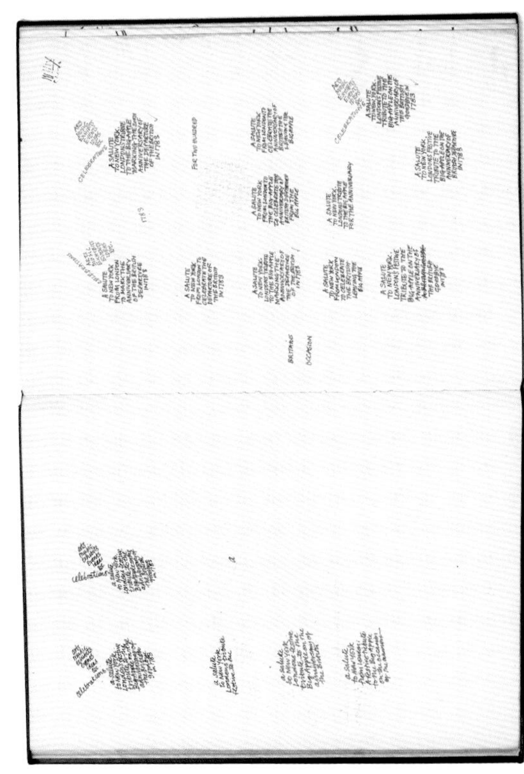

Holders Balance
Sunset/Sunrise
Chattel House

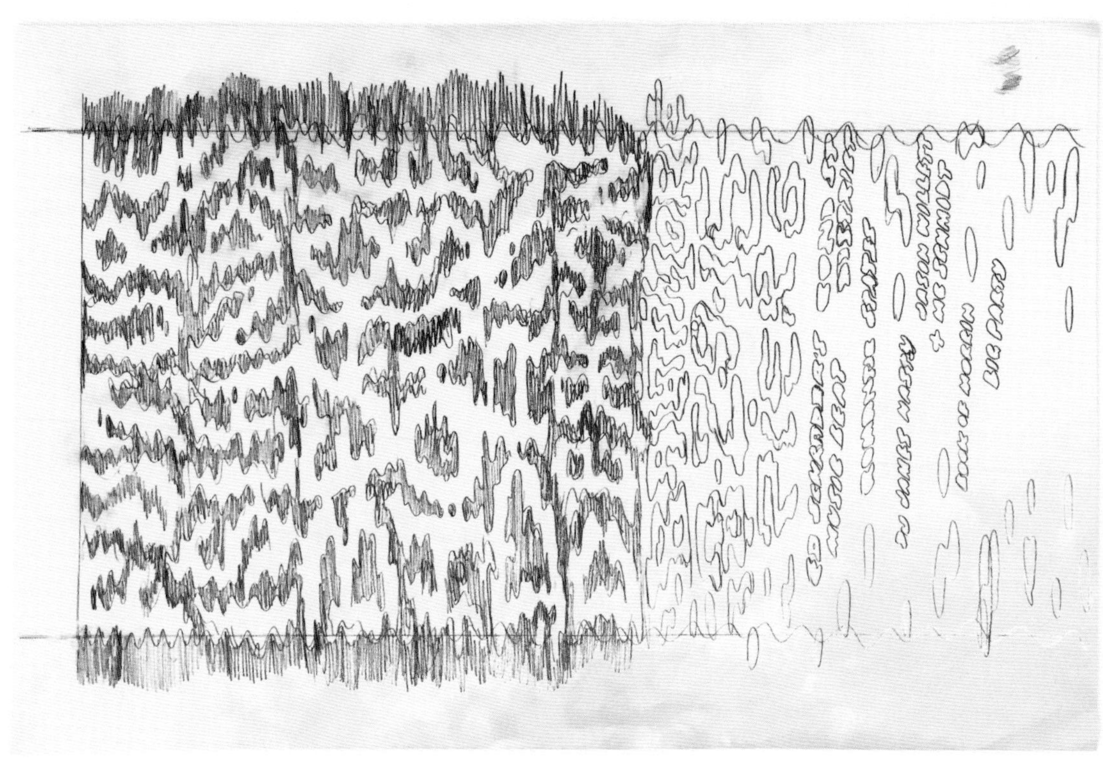

 Sketches for Windjammer poster

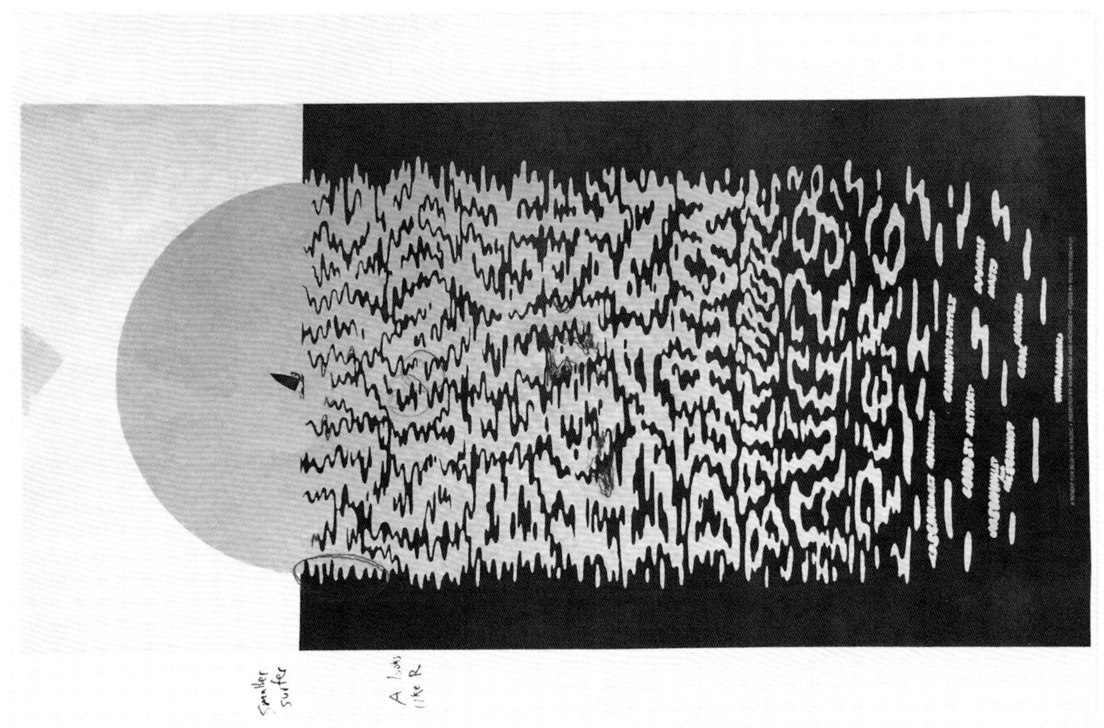

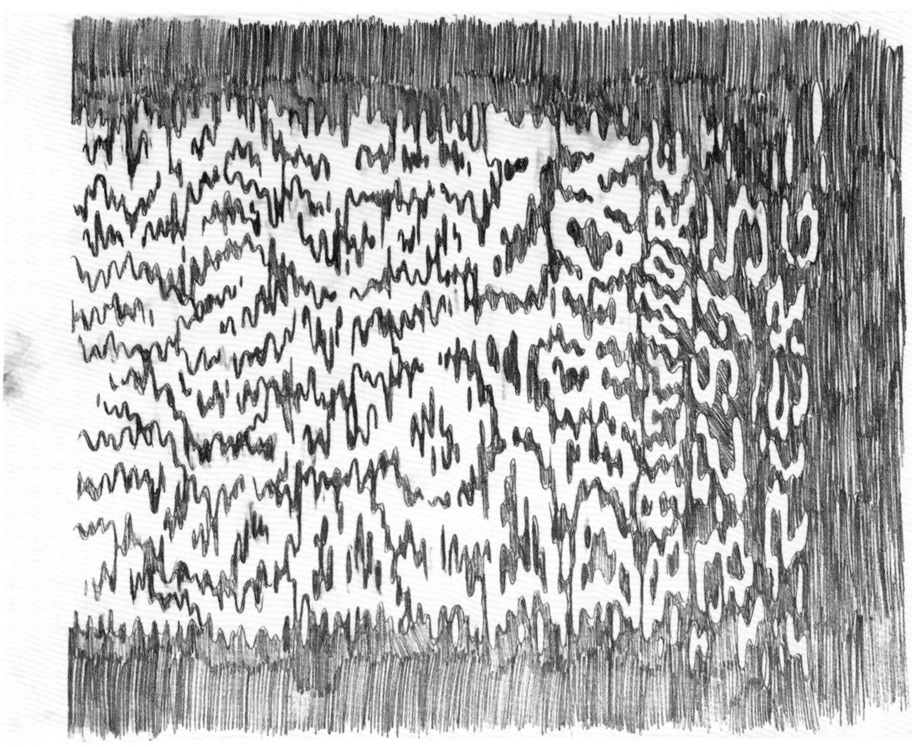

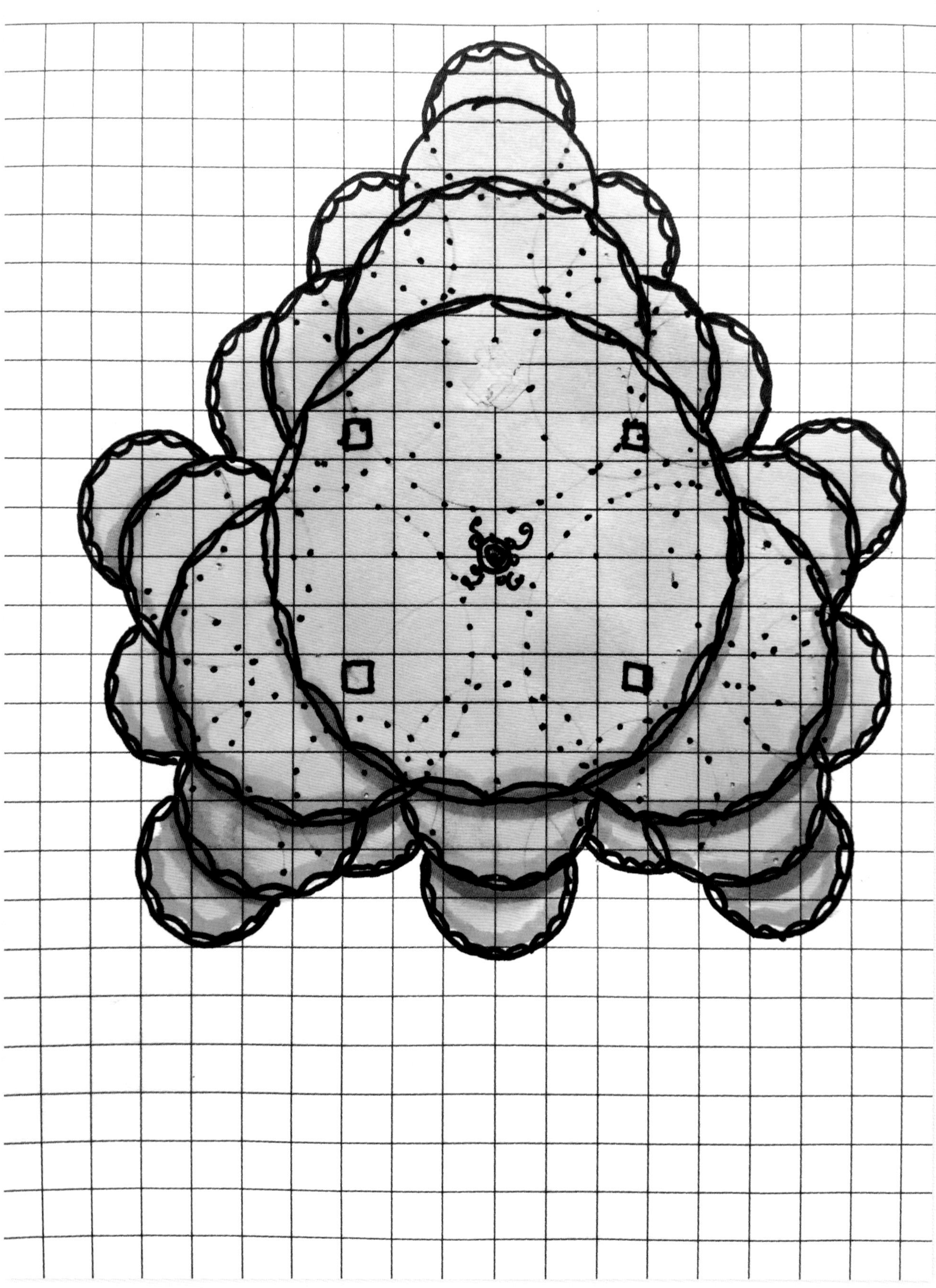

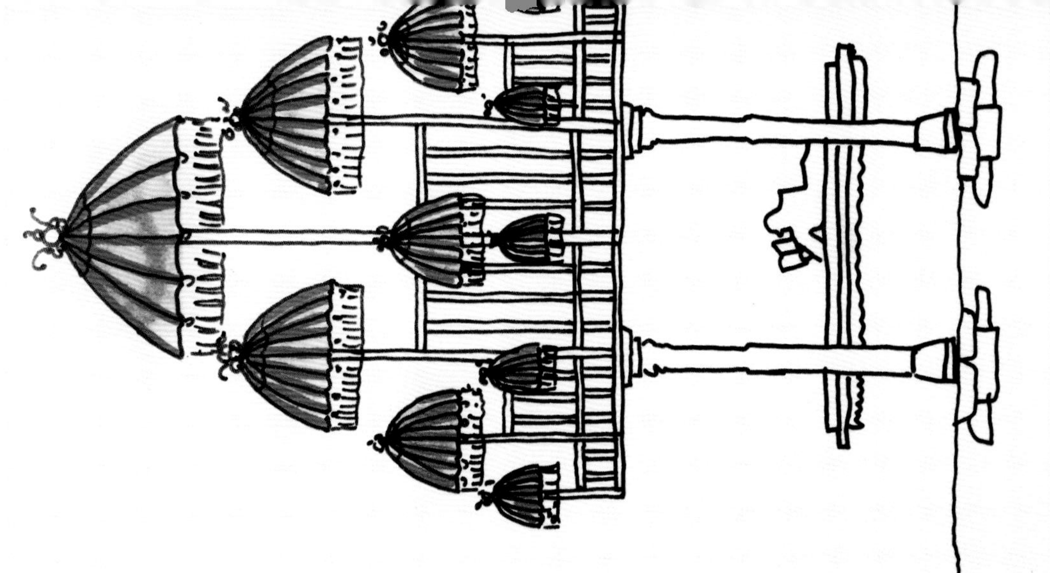

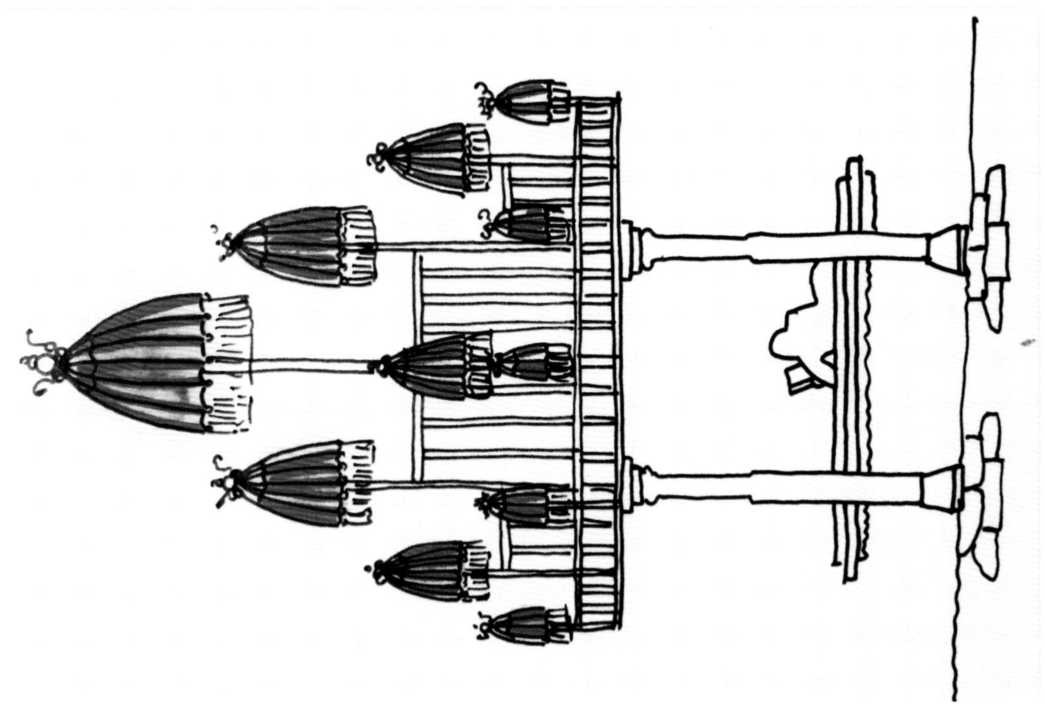

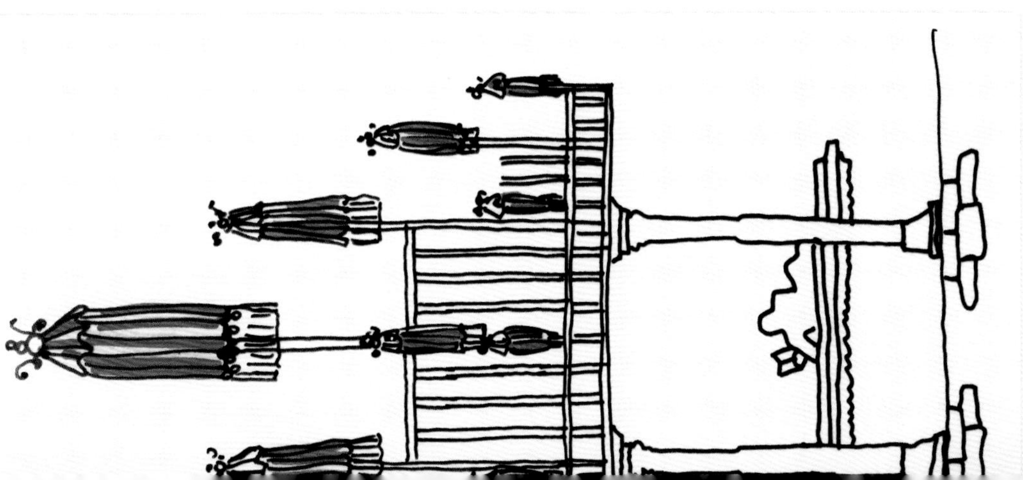

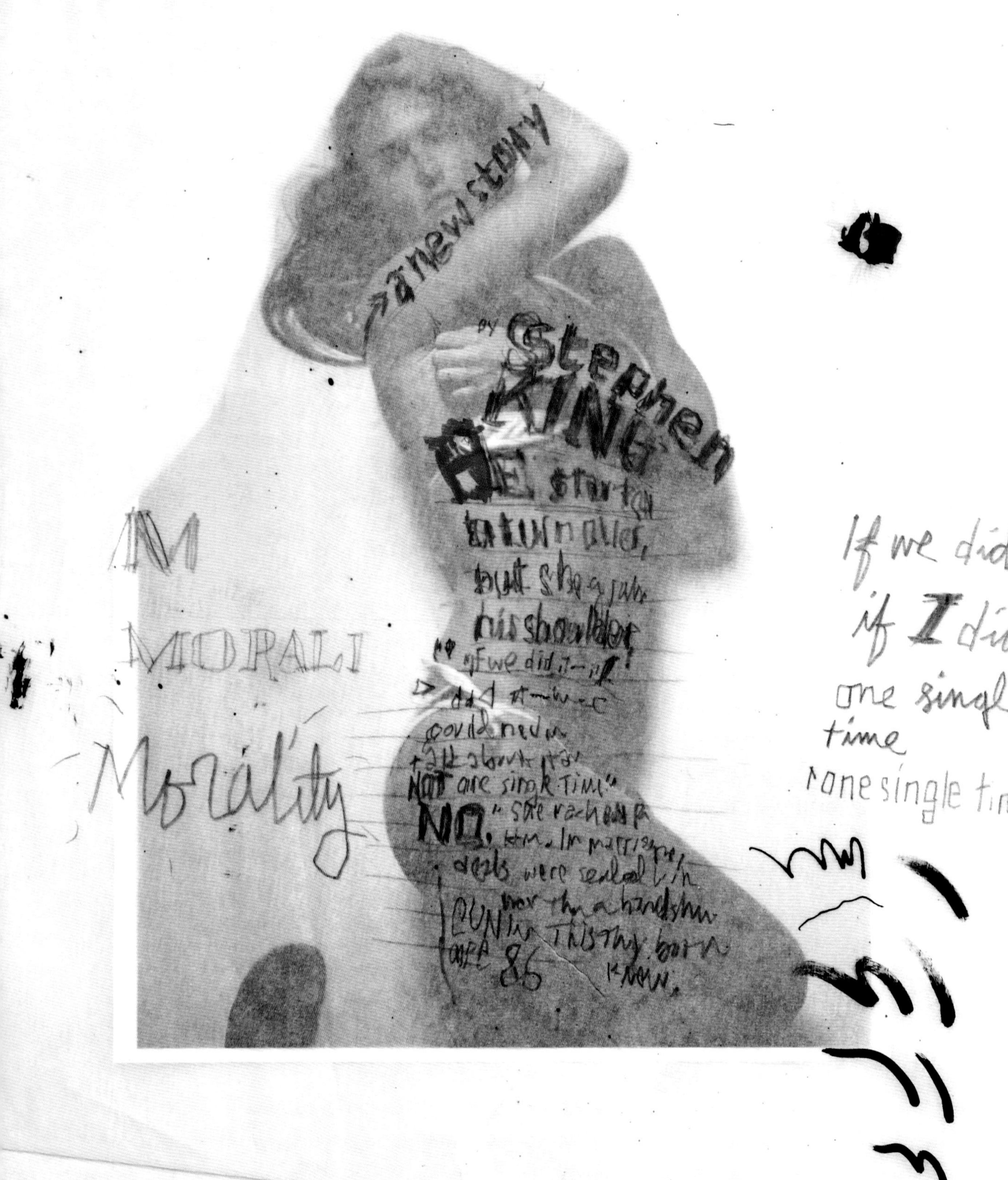

Preliminary drawings for July 2009 *Esquire* magazine cover

He started to turn over but she grabbed his shoulder. «If we did it,—if I did it—we could never talk about it afterward. Not a single time» No.» She reached him. In marriages, deals were sealed with more than a handshake. This they both knew... STORY BEGINS ON PAGE TK

Karls sonw ilker

December 15, 2014, July 16, 2015

Partners

J/ The studio has always been fairly playful and experimental so the difference between just me or just Hjalti and the two of us together is that there's one more head and two more hands experimenting and playing since my work has always been outside of "me." It's a part of me but the thing I'm working on is not. I think it's more like a scientific relationship to the thing, or project. In that sense I can do with it whatever I want and he can do with it whatever he wants and I would not take it personally if he breaks it. It's just the more that's being done in front of me, the better. So I'm doing my best by myself and there's another guy with a different sensibility.

H/ Better…

J/ Yes, sometimes better, but not often [laughing].

Play

J/ First, I wouldn't call a design project problem-solving, but rather just a thing. I think of any project as a thing I spend time on.

The process has always been very analytical but not cold. Maybe using the words playful and analytical don't go together for some, but I think they go together extremely well. For us there's almost a systematic way of playing. Since a lot of play isn't logical you're constantly shifting, bouncing back and forth between the making of things and letting things happen, and then reflecting on what happened.

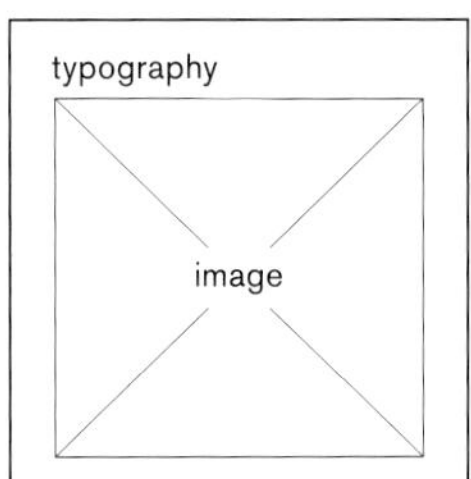

This sort of approach has always made sense to me and I can't really say why. Growing up in Ulm, Germany, everything looked one way, which was flush left, lowercase—which is very unusual in Germany—Akzidenz Grotesk, strict separation between type and image, square format. Ulm School of Design. That's the way they did it. When I left Ulm, I was happy that everything didn't look like this anymore.

Working with People

H/ When I was at school and for a few years after, I was not a very good collaborator. After I graduated I freelanced at a couple of places and always felt very protective of what I did. If I did something, I thought it should be left just like that.

That changed for me when I started working with Stefan [Sagmeister]. It was clear that he was the boss. He would sketch something, give it to me, and I would do it—and then we would go back and forth until he said it was ok. That was a big deal for me. I had to get better at working together. I realized that his comments were really good. Learning to trust that feedback was also a really big deal.

When we decided to start the studio I didn't know Jan very well and still thought my work would be "mine." But from day one it has never mattered if I did it or if it was him or even someone else in the office.

J/ I think that only works if the joy of the process is the ultimate goal. If you need your name to be bigger than everyone else's then it's going to be complicated. To work together, a small ego is very helpful.

Back when we started the studio, we would sit in front of one computer and Hjalti would work for ten minutes and then I'd say, "Ok, let me try." It was like a game where we had no idea what we were doing, but we were having fun. There are no rules, but a common interest in reaching something that's unusual, has some kick to it, makes us laugh—or not—and is strange enough to tickle something in us.

That's really how we worked for the first several years even though we actually had two computers, but one was very, very slow. We had only one project at a time anyway and it was much more fun that way—as opposed to me in one corner working on my thing and him in another corner working on his. In working together, on one machine, we were able to surprise each other faster.

H/ There was always this thing where the Illustrator file started out here with some stuff and then Jan would take what I did and add some stuff there, and then maybe within a couple of days or a week there was a lot of stuff. We'd also have all this leftover stuff, which we'd drag out and add back into whatever we were doing.

J/ You cannot be precious with the time you put into a project. "Oh, I already spent a day on this and now you've come and changed it!" I could work for five days if Hjalti was away and then he would come back and delete everything but one piece and do a little stupid thing to it, and I would still say, "Well, it really *is* better."

H/ We did this for eight or nine years. Now it's a little less—or maybe more—structured, but we still sort of work like this.

J/ We're much faster now.

H/ That's true. We don't need to sit there for a week.

J/ I wouldn't say we work less now, it's just that we can get "there"—to that point—faster, which allows us to push a project even further.

H/ Sometimes a job comes in and we don't do anything on the machine, but we just talk about it.

J/ But the talking is usually very vague. There's not a distinction like you have between an art director and designer where one person creates this goal or mission statement or idea that says, "That's where I want to go." For us it's much more in the making and spending time with it—that's where the project happens. We don't try to come up with a conceptual construct that is so brilliant and then you execute it and it's lifeless and boring and not sexy—totally not rocking at all.

Play vs Concept

J/ In a conversation about making, you can come up with a starting point and then the trajectory is open. You're just trying to find an interesting starting point from which you can get to a place that is unknown to you. When you talk about a concept, it's not really a starting point but an end point that demands, "This is it and we're not going to go outside of this." So when you talk about concepts you already have a hunch of how it's going to be at the end, even if it's very faint.

Professionalism

J/ We have a terribly kept archive so we almost never look back at the work we've done. We don't give a shit when things come back finished. Sometimes once a project leaves the studio for the printer our interest fades and we move on to the next project.

H/ If you asked me to name my five favorite projects, I could tell you, but it's not like Jan and I sit here and look at what we've done to see if it was successful or wonder about what we should have done. Although lately we've done a little bit more of it.

J/ But that's part of the recent "professionalization" of Karlssonwilker. Which I don't think is great but we've been at this for so long—fifteen years or so—that I do think it's great that we try something different.

H/ I wouldn't say we were unprofessional before but now we track time and have four people on the payroll. We had always set up the company to make money. We never saw ourselves as artists. We've always paid the rent and the work we do always generates some income.

J/ Even if our office is more professionalized than it used to be, we still expect anyone here to work the same way we always have. They have to break a project down and explore and play.

I would actually like to do it myself but sadly these days I have other people to play for me. I do still play but it's different. The playfulness—it's in everything. It's not just the beginning of the process. Even with typography there has to be some playfulness, otherwise you just reproduce what you've done before. I think that in everything—even with the most mundane thing—playfulness will get you further.

Handwork

H/ I took a few classes in that old way of hands-on design work and in my first job out of school we did rub-downs and stuff like that. In general I don't see much of a correlation between that kind of handwork and what we do now. I did see it when we did lots of dummies and presentation boards. But when was the last time I took out an X-Acto knife or printed something out? I don't know.

At Stefan's we did a lot of it. When we'd do a CD, we'd print it out and look at it and then both of us would look at the spine and there would be fifty versions of one CD. I'd take the stuff out and put it back in and glue it. It was really, really a lot of work. It was great while it lasted but I don't miss it.

J/ I think that printing stuff out—CD dummies or evaluating typography for text in a book—it's not raw enough. When you try to control everything I think it's a sign of—not weakness—but that you feel vulnerable.

H/ A lot of times we have these projects that only live on the computer. There isn't a single print-out until the thing comes back finished.

J/ It's awesome if you just rock 'n' roll the shit out a thing and it comes back finished and you're like, "Whoa! Nine point type can be *very* big!"

H/ If I did print something out—and I wouldn't—but if I did and showed it to Jan he'd say, "Don't show me this shit. Why would I look at that?" Even with the colors, we just pick a blue or a red—maybe a little light or dark—but matching colors, I don't really care.

J/ I don't care about obsessing on these details because they won't make or break a project. It will not matter with our way of working.

I think that if you work conceptually then you had better make sure everything is "perfect" because in that case the yellow you've picked has to be just that yellow to match whatever it is you're referring to.

So those days of building dummy after dummy and staying late at the office to build another one—those days are gone. It's really boring. It also means you have no idea what you're doing—that your sense of design isn't there.

H/ It's not that we don't care—but it all takes place in this vortex—the screen or the playing or all of it.

Although—if I could say one cheesy thing—just last week I was thinking that I miss this X-Acto thing a little bit. Like, maybe I should take a wood-carving class. My mom is 78 and she took this class and she's making these little birds out of wood and I love them. She paints them and they're so cool and I think I really want to do it.

Outside the Studio

J/ Ella [Smolarz] and I do have a band—maybe not a band, maybe a performance group—called Hedonic Treadmill. We make what we call existential techno, which is the greatest philosophical questions put to music—humanity in a techno song. All we do is 154-beats-per-minute songs. They're all the same and they're around a minute each. But the lyrics aren't about "She doesn't love me anymore," but much more existential than petty relationship stuff. We've played four gigs I think—mostly at art galleries. I do the beats and music stuff and Ella sings.

H/ Shouts...

J/ Screams...and the beats are more calculated. I just press play because it's all prerecorded.

Second Interview / Jan Wilker

Logic Struction

A lot of these projects for Skirl Records—and we've done dozens now—can take a full three, four, five weeks. We don't listen to the music at all—that's not part of the deal. We try to stay away from what they do because it helps us to not fall into the cover-design traps created by an album called, for instance, "Black Crow." That sort of shit that is so dumb.

Shelley Burgon and Trevor Dunn's *Baltimore* was especially great because we spent two weeks playing with that stupid Photoshop tool Liquify that I had always made fun of. For this project we embraced it and became masters of the tool. We played with making these squiggly forms with just two fish we had bought and then scanned. We made hundreds of studies and even turned them into type.

The funny thing, and the thing that this project taught us, is that the musicians are all extremely ecstatic when they see the album artwork because in a strange way what we do is completely parallel to their work as experimental, free jazz musicians. They do, to the extreme, what they do best, and so do we. More often than not, they think that we listen to the music, that we know everything about them, and that that's why they see themselves in the work we do.

Once a musician said, "I really hate that color." And we said, "Ok, no problem!" Because there is no right or wrong—your guess is as good as ours. By not working conceptually, we didn't build a big structure out of logic. Nothing falls because nothing has been built. So if you want to have it yellow instead of blue—consider it done! That is so revealing and refreshing.

Start to Finish

There are a few ways of illustrating how we work at the studio. The first one isn't concerned with the end point, so you scribble that out. You just end wherever you end. The end point doesn't play a role here so it doesn't exist. This path is only so windy because that's how it went when you were doing it, but in retrospect it could be a straight line because in that universe it made sense—it was all linear—not in a grand A to B way but in that one thing happened, then another, and so on. Instead of knowing your target you aim your arrow, shoot it into the woods, and see where it lands—then you just go looking for it.

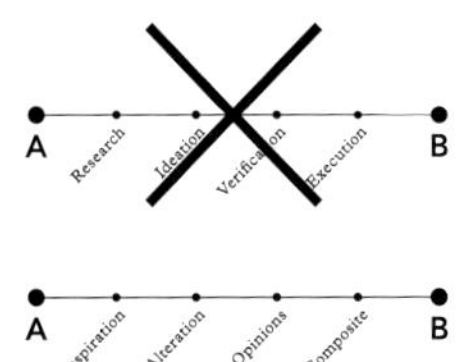

The next one is the boring linear thing which is billable—research, ideation, verification, and execution. This is how the bad graphic design projects get done and you see it all the time. The problem with this approach is that "Research" is actually "Inspiration," which immediately puts you on a wrong path because embedded in "Inspiration" is "Ideation," since "Inspiration" includes visual examples. What that means is, your chance of arriving at something original is out the window and "Ideation" becomes "Alteration." Since there's neither real "Research" nor "Ideation," then "Verification" cannot happen. If anything, you'll merely talk to your fellow designers or the uninformed client—neither of whom are objective—so "Verification" becomes "Opinions." And "Execution" becomes—I don't know—you're just putting it together without thinking, right? Like something rather mechanical. Maybe "Composite"? So instead of research-ideation-verification-execution, what you have is inspiration-alteration-opinions-composite.

The last one, and this is really important for me, is where A to B defines the project, but you can redefine the start and end points and break it open. You as the designer can make it bigger and look for different approaches. It's about repositioning. So in a way, this A to B two-dot diagram really needs to have a step or two taken back to understand how you might approach a project—and not just jump right into the "Research" phase without questioning that starting point—which is what A implies.

By doing so, you could say that for one project you're going to start by ignoring it for a while and go for a retreat. What a refreshing thing that would be. Then for your next project you say, "For this project, I will have sex with the client—no matter what the client looks like." What a cool approach!

Maira Kalman

January 22, 2015

Early Days

There was the Saul Steinberg show thirty years ago, which was a stupendous influence. When I saw that body of work, I said, "Oh, ok." I looked around at all the things that were interesting in art and poetry and film and realized, "There's a place for this kind of thinking." For me at first, it was going to be illustration. Then it became illustration and writing. Then, because I was working in a design studio with Tibor [Kalman], there was design too—so it was all open. There was no limit, no boundary.

The writing continued in various ways, in different assignments, in working at M&Co. Sometimes there were captions and some were more like cartoons, so I was always writing somewhere. When we were working with the Talking Heads, after I did the first book with David [Byrne], it was clear that I could incorporate actual writing and actual paging into a book. When I did the drawings for the book, I had complete freedom to do whatever I wanted. Nobody was sitting over my shoulder saying, "Let me see the sketches, then I'll decide if I like it." Once you decide that somebody is going to be your collaborator you say, "Do what you do," for the most part.

I understood the spirit of what was going on and hoped that I would bring something to it.

While I had occasional doubts, for the most part, I think I had the attitude of, "I'm going to do whatever I want to do. I'm going to continue doing it. It's going to evolve and change. But I'm going to do absolutely what I want to do. Otherwise, what's the point." At the time I had inexplicable self-confidence, along with great self-doubt.

M&Co.

Officially Tibor started M&Co. with two other people—Carol Bokuniewicz and Liz Trovato—but I was there in a lot of capacities and was clearly an important part of the equation in different ways throughout the years. From the beginning our expectation was to do really smart work, with a new voice, with a sense of humor. I don't know if it was unique, but for us, we had a very similar attitude toward things. You see something and you do it, do it intelligently, and have people around you who help you make it good.

We found that the observation of the world around you includes many things that are digressions and many things that are unexpected and are not part of the point. Very often, those things are more interesting than the point, and that's what we both observed when looking at the nature of work—how you go off point. The challenge of course is how you go off point in a way that isn't self-indulgent, but that's communicative. There was always a sense that you wanted to communicate, "We're in this together. We all have a sense of humor and a sense of yearning for some kind of beauty." That allows you to include things that may be seemingly random, but aren't necessarily so.

An Outsider's Perspective

Tibor and I both came from Europe. Neither of us studied what we ended up doing. We were both voracious readers. When you come from another culture and you absorb a new language, your sensors are very open and very aware, and it's an advantage to be an outsider on many levels.

That advantage though depends on how much you assimilate. Of course, we came here when we were children and we had perfectly lovely lives here. It wasn't as if we were suffering by any means, so we both had this keen observation of the culture and the things around us that delighted us in the culture. For the most part it came as a positive rather than a critique. Tibor ended up being very political, being in SDS [Students for a Democratic Society], and wanting to overthrow governments and all that. But the sentiment was very positive. He wasn't a negative person and I think we both brought that with us—that we came to a place where we actually said, "Wow," as apposed to, "Oh no."

Today I'm a reporter. I am talking to and dealing with the culture, but I don't have an agenda. I don't need to reveal anything about the culture, or propel the culture along, or make things better. I just want to tell you a point of view.

Writing

My own process has to start on paper—with either pencil and paper or pen and paper. I do still carry journals that I've had since I was 18. I have the entire history of my sketchbooks and writing notebooks, and basically what I need is a sense of order and a sense of freedom at the same time. For example, when I'm working on a book I start creating these note cards with thoughts and ideas and sketches that I've taken from my notebooks, and I start elaborating from a specific idea and I start to write. I type. I have my favorite pens that I use in my notebook. I have to feel that there's some kind of warmth and air going through me when I'm doing it, and the last thing I would do, is do it on a computer because that would be death. That would be the end of the sense of making mistakes or falling onto something that is inspiring or has some emotional resonance. I finally end up writing a complete manuscript that has to go to an editor, and then revisions and revisions. Then I paint with gouache on paper, which is how I paint, but the initial part of it is much simpler, in a way. It's just trying to find the track through paper and pencil.

What's great about the note cards is that you can shuffle things around. You can throw things out. You can look at things later. They're not that big. You can spread them out on the table. You can add and subtract. So you're really assembling. [Vladimir] Nabokov worked this way and I'm sure many other people and artists do too. The note cards work especially well because my stories are non-sequential in many ways and interstitial—so I can move them around until I'm happy.

Make No Mistake

I used to use the word "mistakes" a lot and say that mistakes bring good, and of course, these are things you don't expect to happen—something that goes wrong in a drawing or whatever. Today I don't know if I want to use the word mistakes anymore. I just want to say that something happens and then something else happens and then something else happens. There is no right way, so all of the zigzags that you make getting toward something—painting something the wrong color—all of those things that take you hopefully to a place that you like in the end, it's all a part of the process. I'm not even sure what I meant by mistake because it's all a mistake, it's all one big mistake.

Sometimes you're too uptight in the beginning and you need to kind of look at it and go "Ugh-gh-gh" and loosen up and say, "Wait, there's too much here." It's just like when you overwrite. I often write three or four times too much and I look and say, "Ugh, that's horrible." So how do you clarify and edit and reduce it? Sometimes I think I don't need to touch it and sometimes I think it needs to be torn up and thrown away.

Sometimes I wish I were really lazy and I wish I could just do it once and get it over with and go to the movies or something, but for the most part, what I like to do is love the process. You don't always love the process, but when I'm loving the process of editing, I'm finding the better voice.

Time

I think time and deadlines are both essential, especially for illustrations as they have a lot to do with speed. You don't have time to mull over something for many months. You have an assignment and it has to be done quickly. You have to hand it in on time and it has to be appropriate for the assignment.

I actually talk a lot about this in my installation at the Cooper Hewitt, which is basically about slowing down time. In the exhibition there are a pair of shoes that I call "The Shoes That Slow Down Time" because they are too big for me. I bought them in a thrift shop in England and when I wear them I have to be very careful and conscious of every step I take.

We could talk about how important it is to slow down and restore your soul and your brain and all that, but really I think the deadline is the greatest thing that was invented. If, in and around that, you find ways to not think and just be there and to replenish what it is that needs replenishing—you find it. One of the ways that I found I was able to do that was to do drawings with a needle and thread. One particular set of four panels was created when my mother died. It was a painstaking process and the needle makes you work very, very slowly.

Walking

In terms of practices outside the studio—I walk. I also travel and love music and film and architecture, and in many ways everything I do is part of my process, but if I had to say what is the thing I do—I walk.

I walk with the purpose of walking and looking—not with the purpose of solving this problem or getting somewhere. I mean, sometimes I need to get somewhere, but I don't have to figure it out by the time I get to point B, all I need to do is be a human being. All of these things feed me in extraordinary ways and make me feel exhilarated. Even just the action of walking a few miles, the cleansing of the mind that happens when I'm moving, restores me—it restores my faith in living.

I do it everywhere I go—even when I travel I don't like to be places I can't walk. I couldn't ever live in a city where I can't walk. I could never live anywhere in the United States but here [New York], because this is the essence of a walking city.

Influence

It's difficult not to be influenced when you think something is really fantastic. So when I'm reading W. G. Sebald or Robert Walser or any writer that I love, there's something that seeps in—a certain slant. It's the same thing with music. There are certain rhythms in the music that I listen to, a certain aspect that is entering into how I'm painting. When I paint I listen to music all the time—but when I write I don't listen to anything.

Ludwig Bemelmans was also a huge influence. Not as obvious is Hilary Knight. Charlotte Salomon was a beautiful painter and writer. Of course visually Émile Bénard and Henri Matisse and conceptually Eva Hesse, Lucian Freud, and Fred Sandback, among others. I look at a lot of people who enter either literally or obliquely. I might not be aware of that influence, but I'm thinking about a thought process or I'm inspired by a certain kind of clarity of vision that somebody else has and I'm wondering, "How did they get there?"

Do What You Do

I don't really do that much personal work—by which I mean 99 percent of what I do is on assignment. Having said that, many of the assignments are "do what you do," but it's a little bit different because I don't wake up thinking, "I wonder what it is that I'm going to do." It's me waking up and saying, "Ok, I'm doing a book about dogs. What is that?" Or I'm doing this column for the *New York Times*, so, "What does that mean—The Principles of Uncertainty"? I have to craft a story, but I know there is a framework, a deadline, and that there's an editor waiting. I know it's a real thing for real people and on that level, everything I do is commissioned. I love that. I prefer that. My preference was always to be very connected to the real world of commerce and the media. That always was something that I related to. I never thought about a gallery. I always thought about newspapers, magazines, and books. That is my calling—communication.

It's a real desire. I don't want to not communicate and hopefully I can do so by being myself. Exploring what that means and bringing in my own voice and trying not to second guess what somebody else might like, but finding out what I think is the essence of who I am, in the changing ways through the years, and to communicate that.

Working

If you aren't living the labor, I don't know what you're doing. It doesn't always have to be deadly serious—of course it can be fun and mad and wonderful. But the actual making of things—the essence of working—brings you to the next work, and it never ends. So whatever thing you finish today brings you to the next thing tomorrow.

Ed Fella

January 16, 2015

The Nature of Design

Graphic design has to communicate something. The way medicine has to cure something and warfare has to kill something. It's the very nature of something, and the nature of graphic design is that it has to communicate some kind of message. It can be very ambiguous, but it still has to do it. When it doesn't do that, it becomes art. Art doesn't have to communicate—the criteria are different.

I'm an artist and a graphic designer because I had a Bauhaus-styled education in the 1950s—when art and design were one and the same. As a student you were a typographer, a photographer, a painter, a printmaker, and so on. Sometimes you did "social" work, and sometimes you did "pure" work. We didn't even use the more loaded terms "commercial" and "fine" art.

Part of that communication, or functionality of design, is dressing something so it's visually appropriate. Is it going to go to a funeral or a beach party? A designer needs to know which outfit is more appropriate for the occasion. I think that a big part of what we're doing is dressing things visually, in a manner appropriate to the receiver, the demographic, the audience. It's the presentation of something but also how it's received. This is the whole thing between connotation and denotation—the literal meaning of something versus the feeling or what it invokes.

Early Days

My parents were immigrants who came from Europe to America in the 1920s and '30s. It was a typical working-class Detroit home—my father was an autoworker and my mother was a maid.

I had one foot in art and another in literature—especially the avant-garde. In a lot of ways that's because I was a kid in the first half of the twentieth century, which was all about these revolutionary movements—Cubism, Surrealism, Dadaism. When I went to high school, that's all we learned about—these avant-garde art movements.

After high school I won a scholarship to go to art school, but in those days art schools weren't college, they were more like trade school. We didn't have to take physics or math classes—all we had to do was take studio and art history classes. It was an amazing kind of education.

For years after I also attended "adult education" classes—as they were called—in downtown Detroit. This was in the 1950s and you have to remember, adults were expected to be well versed in literature and culture. So I went to these classes where you didn't have to write any papers or anything—you just had to read books and talk about them. I was always interested in writing and poetry and of course art. I subscribed to *Art in America*, *Artforum*, *October*, *The New York Review of Books*, among others. I was interested in what was called "high-culture art."

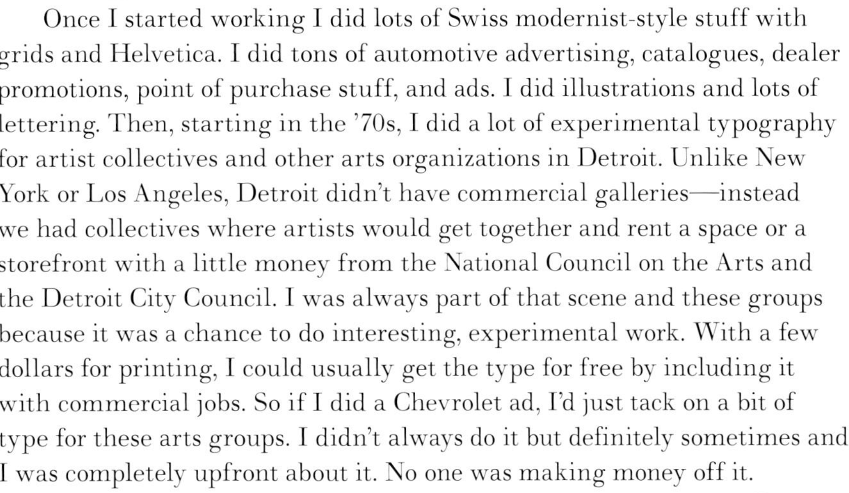

Once I started working I did lots of Swiss modernist-style stuff with grids and Helvetica. I did tons of automotive advertising, catalogues, dealer promotions, point of purchase stuff, and ads. I did illustrations and lots of lettering. Then, starting in the '70s, I did a lot of experimental typography for artist collectives and other arts organizations in Detroit. Unlike New York or Los Angeles, Detroit didn't have commercial galleries—instead we had collectives where artists would get together and rent a space or a storefront with a little money from the National Council on the Arts and the Detroit City Council. I was always part of that scene and these groups because it was a chance to do interesting, experimental work. With a few dollars for printing, I could usually get the type for free by including it with commercial jobs. So if I did a Chevrolet ad, I'd just tack on a bit of type for these arts groups. I didn't always do it but definitely sometimes and I was completely upfront about it. No one was making money off it.

I had the chance to create a whole body of work—posters and all sorts of other things—which was all experimental and outside the realm of commercial work.

The Era

I really consider myself a part of that 1960's Push Pin [Studios] generation. Although because we were in Detroit, we weren't as lucky as Push Pin in New York. Commercial work in Detroit was so tied to the auto industry and there wasn't any editorial or publishing work. People did interesting, avant-garde work when they could and just for the hell of it. It was a lot of that psychedelic stuff that was really big in the 1960s. All that psychedelic work was meant to be completely indecipherable to the "squares," but if you were in the psychedelic culture you could read those posters and figure it out. They were deliberately created to obfuscate the messages, but their style implied a meaning and an audience.

I was really interested in connotation and context. There's popular culture, avant-garde culture, academic culture, museum culture, and so on. Not only are there different cultures but also a perceived hierarchy—from high to low. That was my whole thesis as a graduate student at Cranbrook [Academy of Art]. I wanted to bring the vernacular and commercial arts into the high culture—which is exactly what post-modernism was, in graphic design, in architecture, and so on.

Historicism was seen as "authentic" and post-modernism was "inauthentic"—it intentionally tried to skew styles. It straddled a period of pre- and post-computer. It was also part of the de-skilling of art and design where you could make things looser and more casual—where more things were allowed than before. Before post-modernism things were more prescribed and crafted, and you had to have a certain capability. This isn't really necessary anymore—twenty-first-century design is way more nonchalant. I love it and

I truly think it's interesting—and the sensibility is global. And of course, now you see this nonchalance in the high-culture world. Go to a museum or book fair or look at a high-end magazine—everything has this style.

Personal Work

Today my work changes based on my own interests and my own agendas. I have a dialogue between me and myself—instead of a dialogue between a client and myself. In a way I become the client since I'm interested in doing things or having things go a certain way or exploring certain things—but I'm the one doing it. The bigger change is from a public forum to a more private or at least personal one. But that's the idea with personal work—right?

Ownership

You make your work but once your work is made, it belongs to the society, culture, or world that you live in. You don't have a right to it anymore. In fact I think a lot of designers destroy their work because they feel insecure about it—which is foolish. You made it at a certain time and place, under certain conditions, and that's it, that's all it is.

In literature there's this idea of the fallacy of intentionality—that once you write something and it goes out into the world, you no longer have a right to its meaning. Its meaning then belongs to the audience. For example, I draw a swastika and say, "This is a symbol of love." And you say, "Bullshit! You can say what you want, but this is not the symbol of love, this is a symbol of hate." I say, "Oh no, no—I'm telling you it's a symbol of love!" That's ridiculous, right? That's an extreme example but I'm saying that the culture, the reader, the audience has the final word on what something means.

Moment in Time

A big part of the process is that it resonates within the culture—that it has a context—that it has a particular meaning at that point at that time. This is another thing I would always argue with the modernists—this inane idea of "timelessness" because nothing is timeless. Everything is within its time and that's precisely what is so interesting about it—that it is part of a moment, a place, continuity. Everything belongs in its particular place in history.

Wisdom

That's the one thing I have left at my age—wisdom. When you're young you have energy, creativity, flexibility—all these wonderful attributes that you're going to lose when you're old. But after you live your life you will have the wisdom of experience—you've lived through history and hopefully you've gained something from it. Our entire lives become a narrative, which we then look back on and see a lesson, a story.

You don't realize until you're toward the end of the book and you say, "Oh my god! This is a great story!," that you've come to some conclusions. In fact, I think it's this awareness of who we are and the world that we have to be in that makes designers more than just craftspeople—it makes us professionals.

Seymour Chwast

March 11, 2015

Early Days

After graduating I had to get a job to make a living—I was a commercial artist and I knew how to make funny drawings. Herb Lubalin fired me from *Esquire*, but they were cutting back so I don't know if I was really "fired." Ed [Sorel] and I got fired from a bunch of jobs so along with Milton [Glaser], we decided that we should try to get freelance work. We had tried that while we were in school and it seemed to be the only way out, so we wouldn't get fired anymore. We made portfolios and showed them around and created a promotional piece called the Push Pin Almanac—all of which really helped us to get to do that work.

In high school I learned about design and wanted to be a designer. I learned about poster art and wanted to make work like that but I tended to do funny drawings—especially at my first job at the *New York Times*, where they were doing these simple promotional pieces that called for funny drawings.

My teacher had come from Germany and done a book called *Graphic Design*. From him I learned about A. M. Cassandre, Toulouse-Lautrec, and those guys, but I was also attracted to the work of Ben Shahn and others like him where there were messages—oftentimes political—in the work itself.

Brainstorming

When Milton and I were running the studio and a job came that wasn't for either one of us in particular, he and I would sit down together and think of ideas, make sketches, and then go away and come back again. We'd follow the best idea we'd had, whether it was his or mine.

Today I think my first ideas are usually the best. I'm not sure there's a reason for it—maybe just a prejudice that I want my first idea to work. Sometimes I don't have more than one idea. Sometimes I put it off and come back to it. Sometimes I get an idea when I'm getting up in the morning and am still half asleep but my mind is clear and the solution appears to me. Most of the time I have a sense of which way I'm going and what I want to do. When I put it down on paper sometimes it works, sometimes I find out it doesn't work.

I like to think that I use design principles in my work no matter what I'm doing—whether in illustration, a children's book, or something that's purely symbolic—using type or not. The three most basic principles that are important to my work are contrast, scale, and color. Scale in particular is very important and that's why I love posters. There's nothing mysterious or magical about it.

Technology

When I was teaching I would tell students, "You have to do your thumbnail drawings and your sketches on paper and then go to the computer because the computer only knows answers." If you work directly on a computer, it's too finished, too concrete, while if you make sketches there is a funny, fuzzy kind of thing that you can manipulate into something that's good. On the computer, it's either good or bad—I think you have less room to play.

I have to work on paper. Then, of course, it's brought into the computer. For most projects I work on a translucent paper pad. Over the years I've gone through a few different ones because most have gone out of business. Right now I'm using a Bienfang Graphics 360 pad. I like it because if I find something that I want to keep from one sketch or move it around, I can trace it, redraw, and continue to develop it in another sketch.

Doubt

My biggest fears are that I've done this before or that I'm imitating someone else or that I'm doing something that everybody is going to think is stupid. Five minutes into every drawing I think I'm never going to be able to draw again. At the sixth minute something happens, but in the first five minutes I find I'm struggling and nothing is going on. I say to myself, "Ok, that's the end. This is the end of my career."

Outside the Studio

For me, immediacy is the reason why I started doing woodcuts rather than etchings and engravings. With woodcuts, you see the results right away—you cut into the wood, you make a print, and it's there. It's also physical, which is good.

I think the painting Paula [Scher] does is a way of relieving the tension on the weekends—a way of getting away from the work she does during the week, which is on such a different level and always takes so much out of her. Her painting, especially the maps—while she considers everything very carefully—is easy. She doesn't mind repeating the same thing over and over.

On the weekends I also paint—which I try not to make look like illustrations. They've been mostly about war and battles, airplanes fighting each other. Those paintings started as drawings I made when I was a kid during World War II. Now I'm doing other aspects of war but a similar kind of topic. The paintings today are smaller—usually about four by six feet or less—but they're my obsession.

Abbott Miller

May 19, 2015

Working by Hand

I'm a little romantic and nostalgic about that previous, primitive relationship to drawing and cutting and moving things around on a page. I still do that when I have the opportunity to lay things out on a table, push them around, and really think. I want to use a different word than "analog." I have to spatialize things in order to understand them and I do it in a three-dimensional environment, in an interior environment, and I do it with page materials too.

The digital technology is burying a little bit of those hallmarks of the paper basis of design. I do feel like that has shifted. It's just not efficient, so most of that ideation is at the very beginning or it's in some more organizational mode of literally getting a big surface and laying everything out. We still pin up stuff on a wall to look at the organization of a book. I cannot just rely on the embedded, buried nature of digital files. I know that's a big difference between me and younger designers who do not need to print it out and see the whole landscape.

Early Days

I think that Cooper Union poster is very representative of a way of working at that time, which was total cut and paste. For me, it was a very direct way of appropriating the tools at the library to make graphic design. There was this fascination with the dryness of using the pages from the book to promote the

event by the author and then making it into an information graphic. So literally pasting together pages that were photocopied out of the book. This particular poster was called *The Age of Plunder*, which was a title that Peter Wollen had given to us, and we weren't really clear what he meant by it but that was the topic of his lecture. So I plundered all of the images, which created another layer of abstraction in the poster because there were all these blank spots within it. So, for me, the craft of graphic design at that time was tied directly into any other kind of making that I was doing at Cooper Union.

I was conversant with how to make things in the shop and the parallels between the two were very—I don't want to call that poster a piece of sculpture, but there was no real difference to me. I was doing the same kind of things—editing and manipulation of stuff—with three-dimensional objects at that time, so for me the cut and paste world connected graphic design. I did a lot of stuff with architectural elements and found objects so that kind of common ground between text and three-dimensional stuff was specific to that period. There wasn't an alternative way of making things.

So many aspects of graphic design at that time had a manual component, something that is much more buried now. That component connected it back to drawing and art-making. I remember creating a typeface and we had all these analog pieces of equipment. This thing called the Luci [Lucigraph] looked like a photo booth but you could put a book or an image on the bottom and dial it up and down to enlarge the image and then trace it. It was a camera obscura-like thing, where you saw this dim apparition of whatever was on the plate down below.

I did this typeface called Helvetica Antique which was based on Caslon Antique, which was the only font in our type book that had little bits and chisels eaten out of it to represent that it was old. I remember using the Luci to draw those edges and redraw them onto the skeleton of Helvetica. So that was an amazing crossover between drawing and graphics at that time, without me ever being that drawing-oriented person. It was just how you made stuff.

Content and Design

We—me and Ellen [Lupton]—had a sense that graphic design was actually sitting in the middle of all of these interesting currents and that it historically had been linked more to art-making or fine art or picture-making, but that it could just as plausibly be reconnected to its longer history of being related to printing and publishing. We thought that design could be this common denominator where research and writing could be practiced right alongside design, and design could actually be formative, not just gathering up of content. That's where exhibitions and publications really came together—they both require this narrative environment that could be words and images and objects all brought together, but they were ultimately connected with a kind of didactic or pedagogical mission or message. It was putting design back on the plane where it always should have been. Instead of working with editors and publishers and writers, and always being the vessel through which those ideas get shared, why can't you position yourself in a way where you are the generator of that content? I think the big question is what does that mean about the final product?

That is something I'm still answering because I'm still doing projects where I'm more in the—I don't want to use the word "passive"—but I'm more in the hired-service mode. Then there are those where we are generating the content. Ideally, you don't make a value judgment. You want to think about using all aspects of your intelligence and not putting up borders even if you're not directly the author. Any good designer does that.

When working on a project where you control the content, you find yourself able to indulge the schematic thinking. Oftentimes design creates a harness around the material, whereas if you're working on content, you can be more focused on drawing out, which I would argue is more of an organic approach to creating a story—whatever that content is, that's the storyline. If I know that I'm able to shape it from a design perspective and that I can steer the content, then I look for bigger, faster moves.

That's a thrill because there are a lot of lost opportunities if you're not able to think about design and presentation at the outset. It unleashes a different freedom in the early framing of a project, where you can say, "What if we did it all backwards? What would that allow? What if we split this show right down the middle and there's a collision of two elements?" I think those kinds of spatial, conceptual moves are what you can do when you're in both the design and content seat.

When you're not, it doesn't mean that you can't implement those, or propose them later, but it may be that you're working against a kind of script that has had its own evolution. It's a little abstract sounding, but I think that's the big difference. You're going to have this totally different take on the structure of the project.

Drama

I don't think that we ever really sit down and think differently. It's just a question of, "What's the stuff and what are the moves that we can make?" I think that design thinking is that kind of filtering—how can the design actually dramatize and foreground these things? We just did a show at The Jewish Museum called *Revolution of the Eye*. This incredible curator, Maurice Berger, had the show in his head from day one. We were working with someone who is such an obsessive thinker that his themes and the interplay of everything was in his brain already as he did the checklist. Our role was a bit more passive, essentially to dramatize it. We had to visualize it for him. He was a curator who was very interested in design, a great partner, but in a funny way it was less of a revelation. It was more like everything finding its place, doing it really well and beautifully. That's great because the dialogue is so clear, but it wasn't a project where we ended up somewhere surprising. There are two different paths, and it's nice to have both ways.

I think of it in terms of the word "dramatize" because it unfolds within that, beauty and meaning. To dramatize something is to make it look really strong, but also deliver it with force to a viewer or a reader. In book design it can be just a simple move—shifting from one page to another, slightly bigger, slightly stronger crop. Cropping to me is so related to writing, because it's about zeroing in on the right moment, the right scale. It's like finding the right word. If you crop something really beautifully, it sings in a way. Dramatization is about the persuasive factor.

Time

I don't ever really connect the depth of insight and duration of working on something. It's part of this legacy of design thinking, which can move in these lightning jumps of associative logic or pure association or backflips that if you tried to articulate them or verbalize them, they just wouldn't make any sense, but it's the classic brainstorming scenario.

I find that when I work on projects I have to work with someone. I don't do well in isolation. That ideation part where you're kind of just shooting the shit about a project is really my favorite part. I should say my favorite part is when you get on something really good or interesting as a strategy or an approach. For me that conceptual framing, which is more about the approach, is the richest part of design. I tend to get impatient at the backend, getting it done and executing it. I go nuts with how long the process is from those great insights to the finished installation. It's not a good thing, my impatience. But for me, the pleasure of the projects slowly diminishes. There's a pleasure point when it's done and photographed and you can look back and see that it turned out well. But those periods of the back and forth and the editing—the tedious stuff—is why I will always need to work with a team. I don't want to go back to doing all that myself. I'm not good with that.

Gratification

I value the ideation part the most because there's a conceptual purity. That's the gift part of design to me, the one where it doesn't matter what happens later. That was a really powerful realization. My very first boss out of college was Richard Saul Wurman, who had this phrase that was something like, "Having an idea and not doing anything about it is like never having had the idea at all." I always thought, "No it's not! You still have the idea." There is, to me, a beauty in conceptual art. It's the Yoko Ono *Grapefruit* moment.

Doubt

I'm rarely wracked by doubt because there's always a job to be done and the question is more, "Is this going to be a really good one?" You know you're going to come through. You don't know if the stars will align and it will be profound or beautiful, but you're going to get it done. If I were more manic about things and tried to insist that absolutely everything that we did was a revelation, there would be more doubt and the big existential crisis.

Writing

One thing that surprises students is to learn how much writing occurs in the course of any design career. You're constantly articulating what the project is and sharing that with your client in some form, even if it's just in the letter of agreement. That verbalization and writing are always tied into the definition of a project and until you have that, it's really difficult to move forward. There is the functional aspect, but then there's also this aesthetic or stylistic aspect of a desire for clarity. Ellen's writing is so pared down—the more minimal the sentence, the better. I'm less focused on that. There's residue of speech in a lot of what I write, but for me that's another kind of clarity. I have similar goals in writing and design.

Outside the Studio

I have this side obsession with environment—home, furniture, and landscape. I'm a little nutty about it. I could so easily go off into those areas of work. I'm not qualified, but I could. I think that landscape design is incredibly interesting. It's not like I'm a good gardener. It doesn't come from a horticultural standpoint—it comes from a spatial standpoint. The same with my obsessiveness about interior space. Part of exhibition design is this very responsible, message-oriented element, and then part of it is interior design. I've always known that I get a fifty/fifty mix, and I love that.

As a kid I thought I was going to be an architect and I drew buildings. I also did all those construction toys. Then I became very intimidated by the formality of architectural training. I was just not gifted in terms of the math part and I retreated to the safety of graphic design—keeping it flat. I love that. I have cherished what it means to come out of print. That, to me, is a totally valid perspective and it's not like I've suddenly become so spatially adventurous. It's really cool to become dimensional out of the flatness of graphics.

Prototypes Tools Photography

The ability to visualize, create, and document is critical throughout several phases of the process. Before computers, this was often labor intensive and expensive, but today's technology offers designers the ability to render, iterate, and plan with incredible precision and speed. However, some "techniques" such as thinking, walking, and modeling by hand persist despite technological innovation.

Wax letterform manipulation with heat-gun

NSPB1X38 282x218x108 mm (Inside)
You become
who you
pretend to be.

FOR BEST RESULTS
SAFE FOR USE BY CHILDREN
PC-5M
Sharpie
black/noir
Sharpie
black/noir
D'HUILE
MARKS ON MOST SURFACES!
Broad Line
MARKER
300-S BLACK
Sharpie
Opaque Paint Marker
Sharpie
Opaque Paint Marker
MARKS-A-LOT
Color
OPAQUE PAINT MARKER
USAGE
Posters, point of purchase signs, charts, graphs. Designed for use on paper. Can also be used on metals, stone, plastics, vinyl and glass.
DIRECTIONS
Shake well with the cap on to agitate ball. To prime, depress tip until it is saturated. Test on paper before use. Replace cap after use to prevent tip from drying.
WATERPROOF PERMANENT
DRIES INSTANTLY HEAVY DUTY
USE IN A VENTILATED AREA
DO NOT BURN EVEN WHEN EMPTY
KEEP AWAY FROM CHILDREN
SC-6600 MADE IN JAPAN
uni PAINT
OPAQUE, OIL-BASE PAINT
FOR BEST RESULTS:
PX-30

 Laser-print reference photograph for July 2009 *Esquire* magazine cover

 NATASHA JEN Scanographic concept sketch for apparel graphic

Photographic documentation of self-promotional “Giant Z” project

STRAIGHT VIEW

DIMENSIONAL VIEW

PERSPECTIVE VIEW

FACING DOWN PRINCE STREET

FACING UP PRINCE STREET

STRAIGHT VIEW

Digital renderings for Pennsylvania College of Art and Design environmental graphics

Digital rendering for Parkway Film Center environmental graphics

Set photography for Google Classroom commercial

Miniature book mock-ups for *SVA 2009 Senior Library* and *Victore or, Who Died and Made You Boss?*

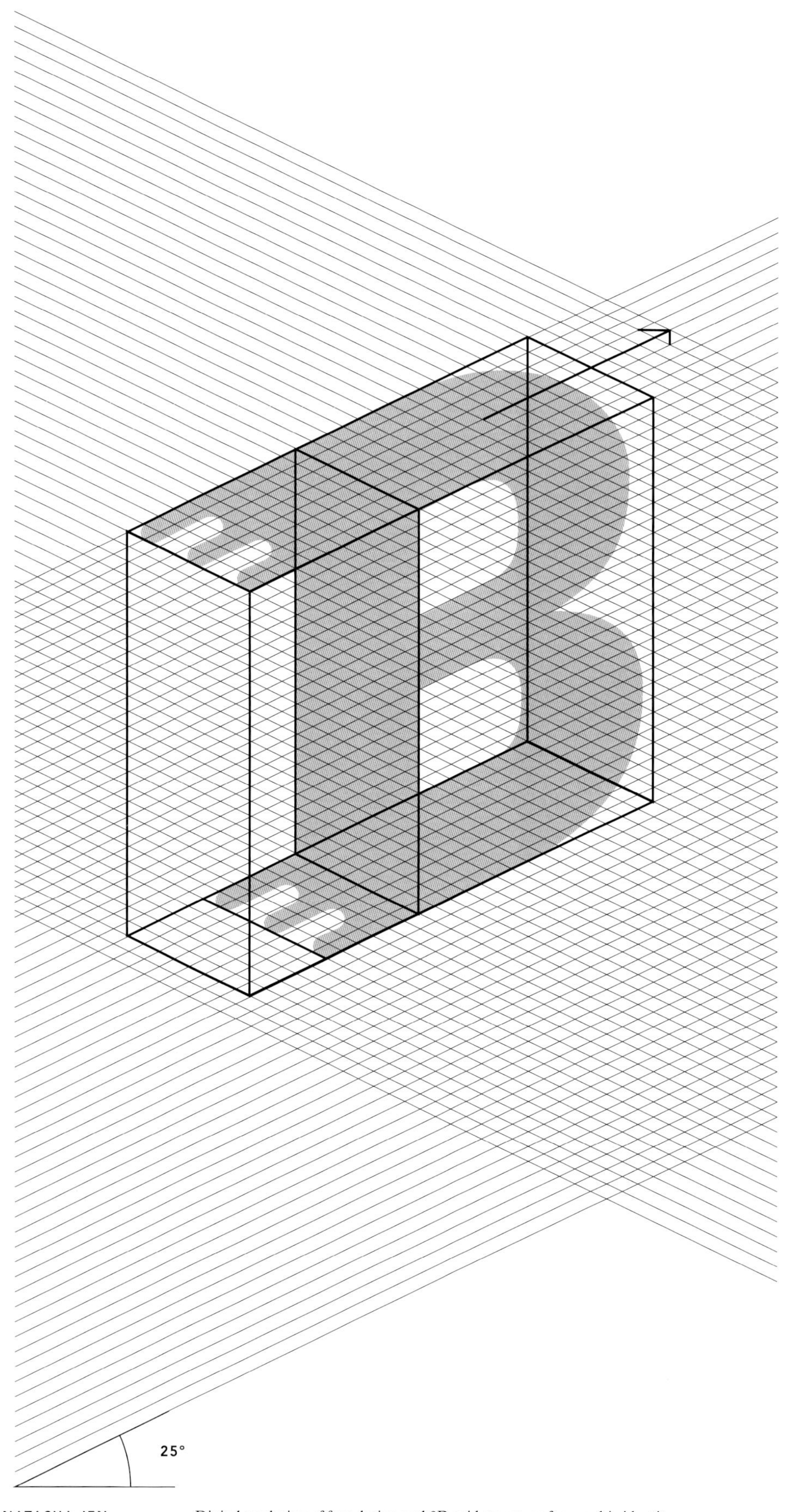

NATASHA JEN

Digital rendering of font design and 3D grid structure for graphic identity

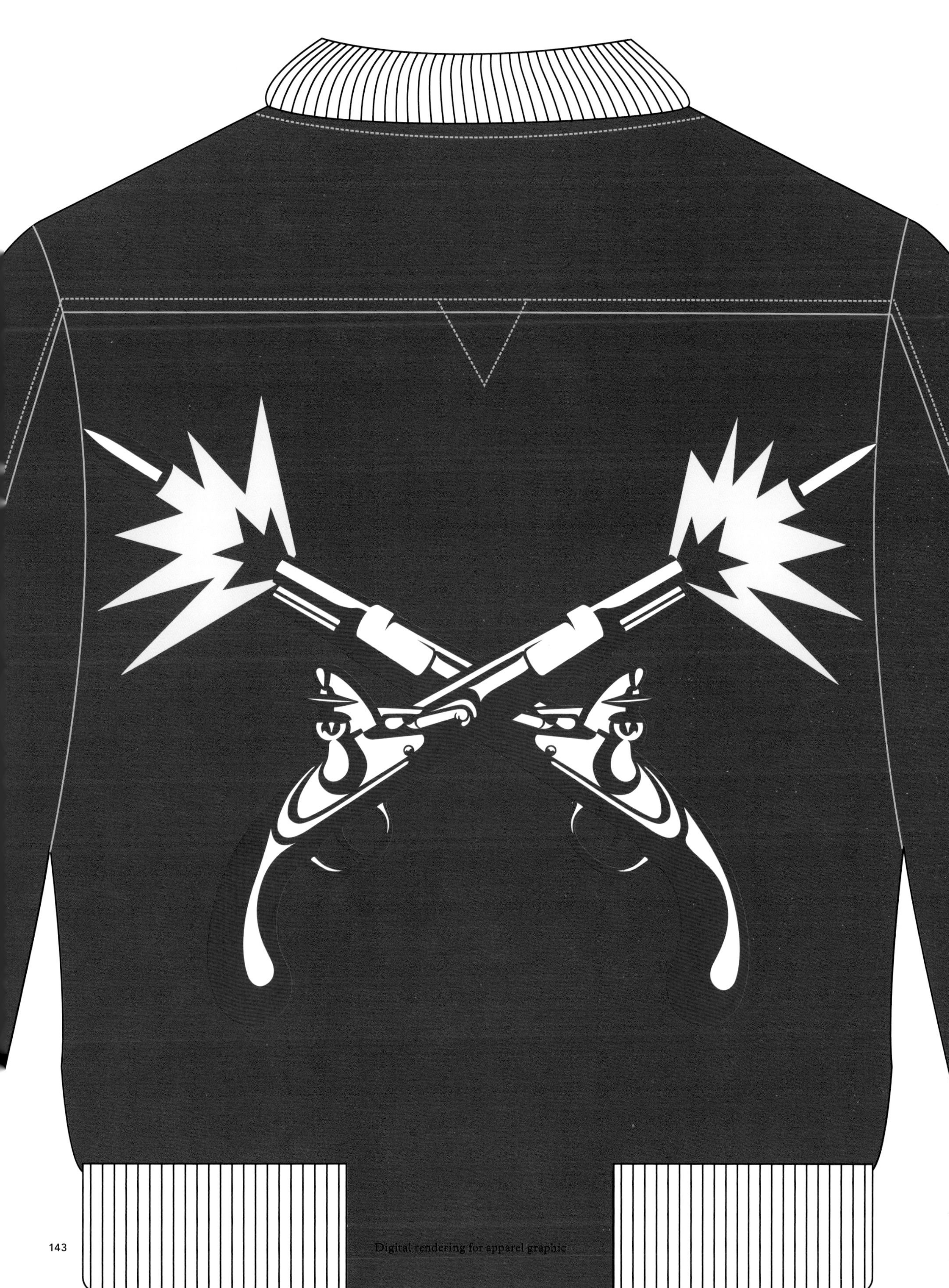

Digital rendering for apparel graphic

CARIN GOLDBERG Ink-jet print of photograph

 STEPHEN DOYLE Photographic documentation of photo shoot

Photo shoot set-up for illustration

 Set photography for IBM "Phones and Food" commercial

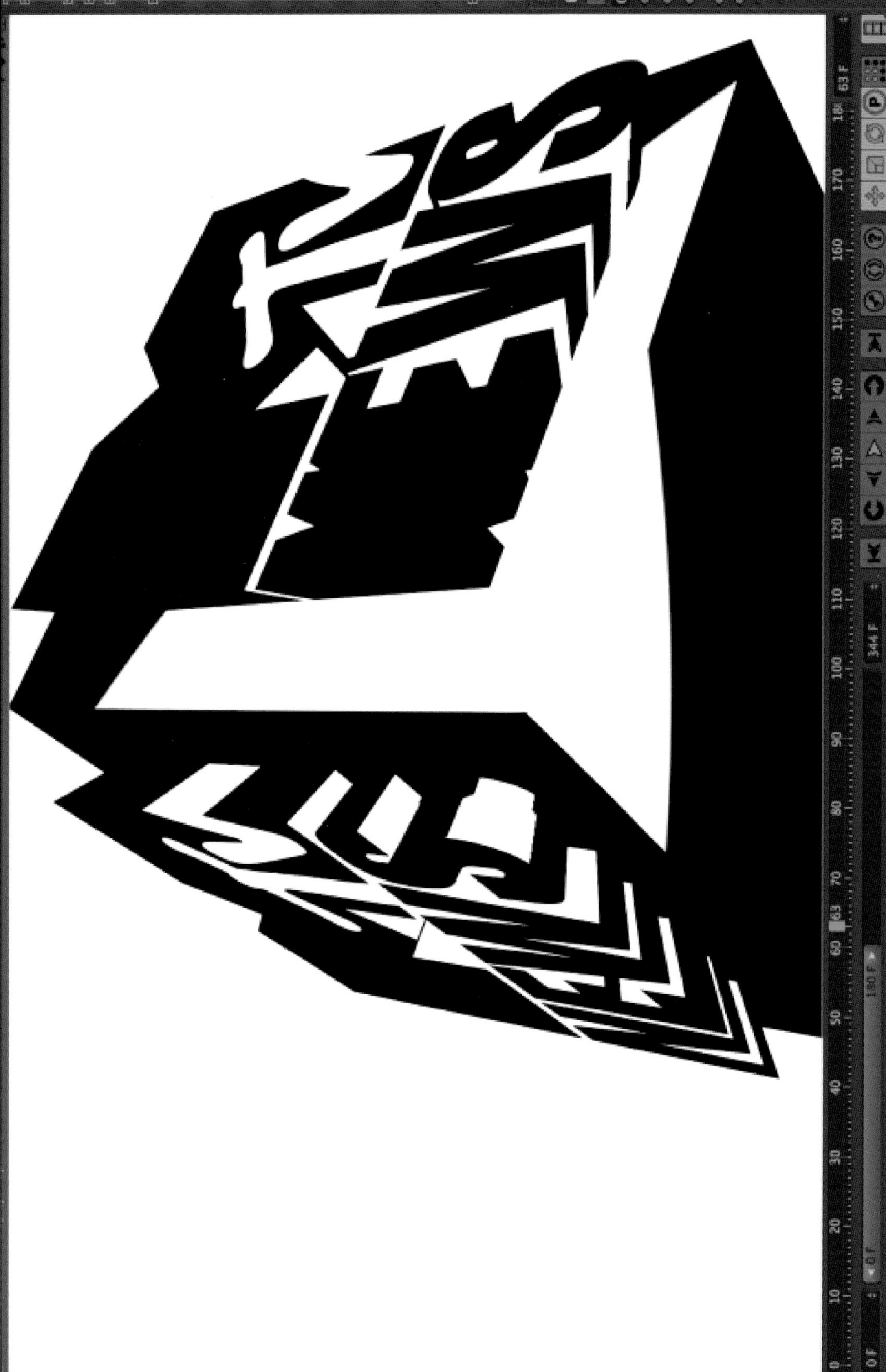

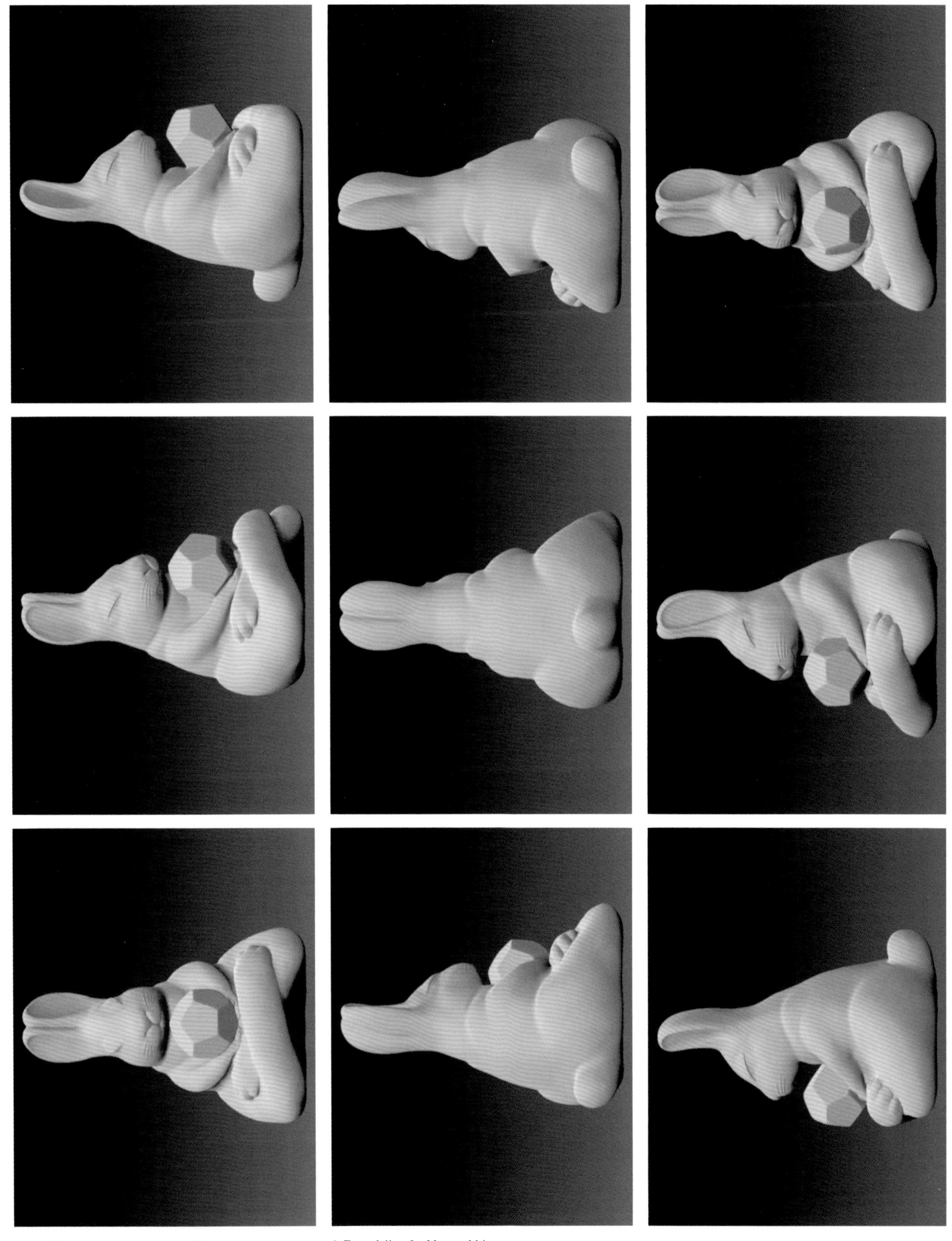

3-D modeling for Mysterabbit

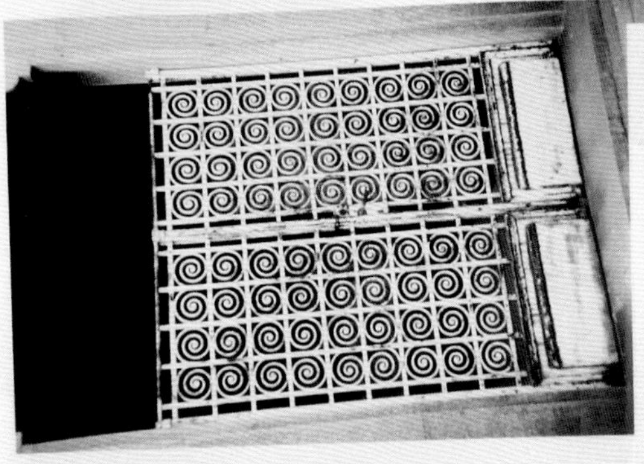

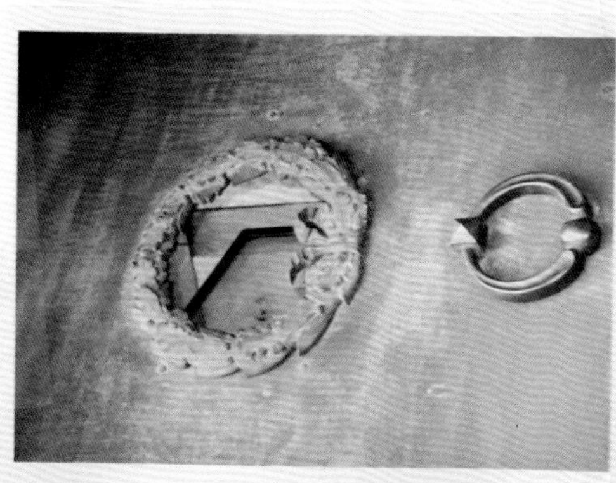

Photographic reference for Montreux Jazz Festival poster, 1976

Digital previsualization and set photography for Nationwide Insurance/IBM Big Data commercial

Custom typography and digital environmental graphic prototyping for Harrah's Resort

PIZZA
BAR-B-Q
CHICO'S
REAL PIT
ICE MILK BAR

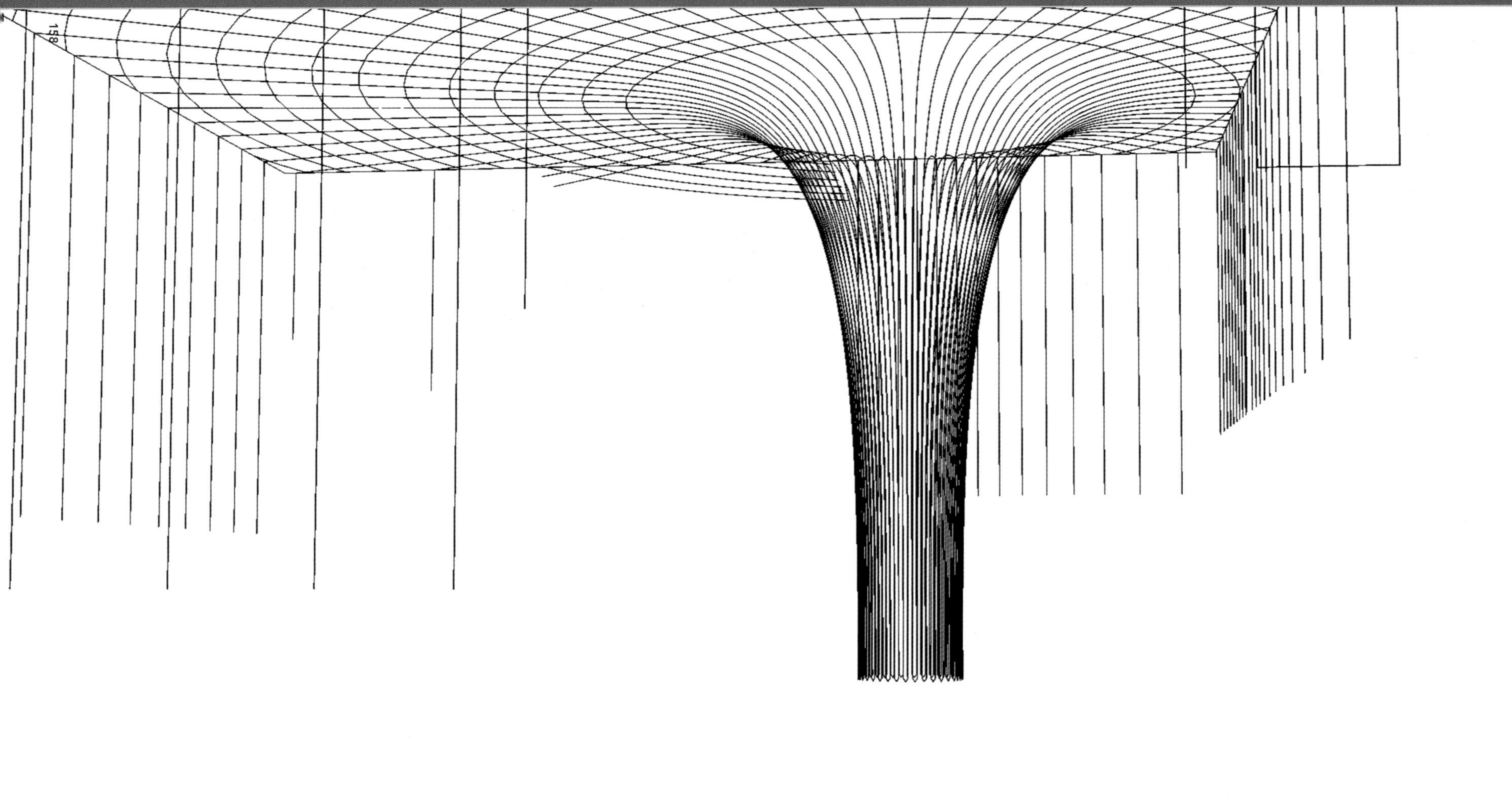

Freeform
Selection
19 / 100
Layer: LS Plaza01
Grid = 10.0

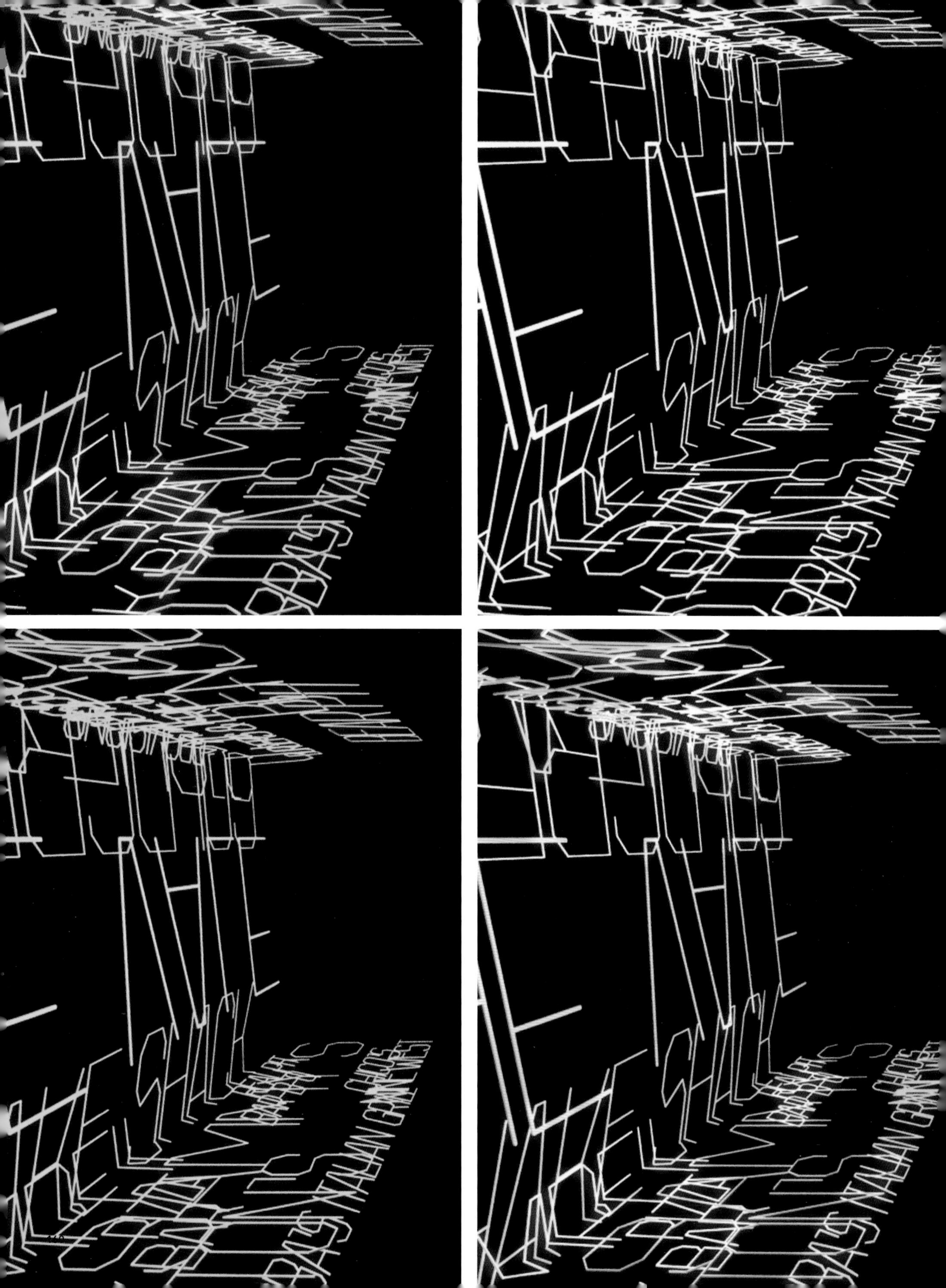

Elliot
t Earl
s

February 25, 2015

Classification

I'm a designer at my core, but if you queue up YouTube or Vimeo these days, you'll find pieces of cultural production that are unclassifiable. You'd look at them and think, "I have no idea whether this is made by a Madison Avenue advertising agency, a 16-year-old Chinese kid in some far-off province, or a performance artist." I find the most compelling forms of cultural production today are things that you have a hard time locating and classifying, so while I am definitely a trained designer and I think in those terms, when I'm making work I have a blatant disregard for whether or not it's considered contemporary art or pop music or cinema. I think that that has been a career challenge. I'm very happy with my career. However, when I position myself within specific boundaries it makes it easier for people to understand what I'm doing and therefore there's more commercial success.

Methodologies

Whether they know it or not, artists use design processes on a day-to-day basis. But design is both the history and a culture, so it's a set of institutions. Or, it's really three things—a shared history, a culture, and a methodology. Most artists probably don't have a very comprehensive knowledge of two of those three prongs. It's unlikely they have a comprehensive knowledge of the history or the institutions, however most painters do come up with a plan before they actually paint. The thing that I'm getting at is that I'm always very aware of design training, in terms of macro procedure as a way of generating ideas and a way of working through things. A lot of my thinking about design process has evolved over time and is quite a bit different from what I was trained in at RIT [Rochester Institute of Technology].

Prototype
Too
Photograph

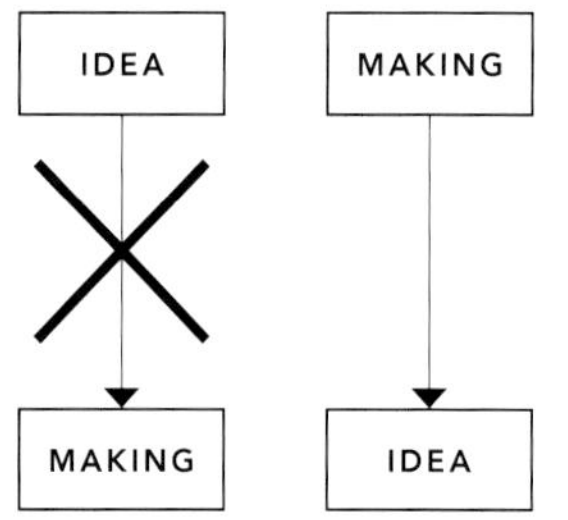

My understanding of the classic design process is that it has different phases to it. There's a research phase, then there's the thesis that develops, then there's an idea that develops, and then there's the implementation phase. That process can be organic, it can be thought of as linear or branching, but generally the thesis or idea often comes before the making. I have worked largely in opposition to that. I try not to come up with my idea before and then just go through the slavish process of making shit. I still consider it design but I think it draws more from contemporary art practice than it does from what you and I might have been taught in undergraduate design school.

Assemblag
Mechanica

Making Sense

It's the reverse or, more accurately, inverse. One of the things that I discuss with my students is the process of ad hoc or post-facto rationalization. On an undergraduate level that post-facto rationalization is all bullshit. A kid will come in and he'll show something in critique and you or one of your colleagues will say, "Why did you make that decision?" And then the kid will say something and all of his classmates will be like, "That's bullshit, you just made that up!" I think to myself, "What is the problem with that?" If you say something that has no correspondence to the work, then it is bullshit and fake—but the idea that I use my cognitive, intellectual, analytical power to look at a finished work and to come to a deeper understanding after the fact, then my understanding of what I've done is deepened by the process of making it. What we do is we make, and we're constantly revising what our understanding

Pleas
Mak
Th
Loo
Nic

of the work is so that after the work is done you can say this actually works because of XYZ. It's a form of post-facto rationalization without any of the hang-up that you're doing something wrong by post-facto rationalizing it. Turning the whole thing upside down.

First Idea, Best Idea

My students have this idea that one must begin with a fairly elaborate conceptual framework or construct to begin work and I always tell them to go back to something Jack Kerouac was famous for, which was relying on this Eastern concept of "first idea, best idea." I try to have an instantaneous, emotional, and instinctive reaction at the beginning a project. I ask myself, "What am I super interested in at the moment?" I try not to think it through or question what the motivation is prematurely. I begin getting material together, generating it, and, almost like a jazz musician, react to the material in the process of making.

Theory and Knowledge

I'm currently involved in a writing project about these issues, but I remind myself when I'm making work not to be theoretical or didactic or overly analytical. I try to separate those two processes, so for the writing project, I'm trying to break down the logic analysis, clarity of thought. I'm trying to inform myself when I'm actually reading, but when I'm making the work, I'm not saying, "Ok, now I need to rely on the gestalt principle of closure." I'm trying to bracket those things off. I always tell my students if they are doing a lot of theory reading, they don't need to try to push that shit through their work. It doesn't evaporate when you make work. It's in your brain, so don't try to make the work about that shit—it just informs the process.

Turning Point

I had a seminal moment in graduate school when a mentor of mine—the architect Dan Hoffman—was the designer/architect-in-residence at Cranbrook. I was really struggling with the didactic approach to trying to make work. Dan said, "I think you have this all wrong. When I take a look at a traditional, historical African mask, I have no sense of its meaning. I see these distortions of form—just a wooden mask with holes perforated in the surface and pieces of leather knots on it. I have no clue about the guiding principles behind making those masks and yet they carry a tremendous amount of power—both visually and spiritually—and are moving pieces of craft and art. Look at the people who are making these masks, they're not over-intellectualizing the work in any way."

That marked the beginning of when I slowly started to realize that there needs to be this leap of faith in the work where you realize that powerful work is ineffable—it has an inability to be contained by language.

Doubt

I have found that the decisions that I would initially be unable to logically substantiate or justify have often resulted in work that has had both critical and popular acclaim. So a feedback loop is established where you begin to trust yourself. After twenty-three years I still walk into my studio every morning and am confronted with the same problem, which is, if I continue to do the same shit, where I rely on the same strategies and techniques, then what ends up happening is that the doubt is no longer there and the work ends up being dead.

There's a project I did in 2008 for Cranbrook and when I was done with the series of posters I was like, "What the fuck is this?" I could not figure out whether they were beautiful. There was the same insecurity when I made them. They actually challenged my own aesthetic sensibility. In hindsight, they're totally cool. But when they were new, I wasn't sure.

Beauty

From the very beginning, I've been striving for this kind of aesthetic collapse that happens when ugliness collapses into a condition of beauty. In one of my lectures I talk about it in terms of Neil Young. As a fan of Neil Young, I am aware of this vocal minority of maybe 40 percent of people who think that his voice and nearly everything about his music is just grating and awful. I actually think that he has a hauntingly beautiful voice, but one that is not classical in any way. If you think about Neil Young with Crazy Horse with that proto-grunge sound as one that is typified by dissonance, so is a lot of my work, like those posters for Cranbrook. Something appears ungainly and awkward and really ugly in a way, but then collapses into a condition of beauty.

We often see beauty in other people that lies in these weird idiosyncrasies, and that's where the character comes from. For a long time I've been interested in issues of beauty and ugliness. It's been central to my work. I've been actively trying to make work that is, for lack of a better word, ugly and awkward, but to a point where it collapses over into a kind of beautiful condition.

Preconceived Ideas

You find students who come in deeply insecure and use a form of cultural anthropology as their primary method of creating. They're obsessed with graphic design culture, and they end up looking at the apex predators of the field and trying to make work that feels and/or looks like that work. I disabuse them of that notion quite quickly. That will relegate you to mediocrity quicker than nearly anything. Take painting as an example—it has a rich critical history and a rich material history. But graphic design, depending on where you draw the line, as a commercial art practice is maybe sixty, seventy, eighty years old. We don't have a rich history to draw on but we also don't have to bear the brunt of that. I tell my students to draw from life, literature, and art. I'm absolutely, unequivocally opposed to the notion of being studied within the microculture of design, knowing who the hottest and latest designer is, what's happening on blogs. I couldn't give a shit.

Kinds of Design

I've determined there are three different types of things that I do and that are happening in the Cranbrook studio under my leadership. In this taxonomy, the first is traditional design. I define that as work that has a form of communication at its core and the agency of the designer is downplayed in deference to the communicative strategy. In other words, transparency is a huge issue. I did a two-year project where I designed a new identity system for Cranbrook. There was a new logo and a whole new identity system. That was not about a display of my personality and my interest and my agency. It was about really trying to embody in form what I saw as the values of the institution. That, I define as traditional design—and I do that, my students do that. The second order is experimental graphic design work, when I take a look at fundamentals of the design field—assumptions of design history, process, or methodology, and make work that runs in flagrant opposition to those principles, but is still informed by it—"it" being the idea that the designer is a transparent vehicle for the transmission of corporate value. The third type of work is in a threshold condition, work that's pushing so far out of graphic design that it enters the contemporary art realm. That's where communicative strategy is completely suspended and the issue is not primarily about communication. It is based on other histories and other methods—the work largely becomes material in a way that it incorporates social practices, materiality, and strategy that are not from the design discourse. I don't go into a project thinking I'm going to do XYZ. It basically has to do with how much time I have.

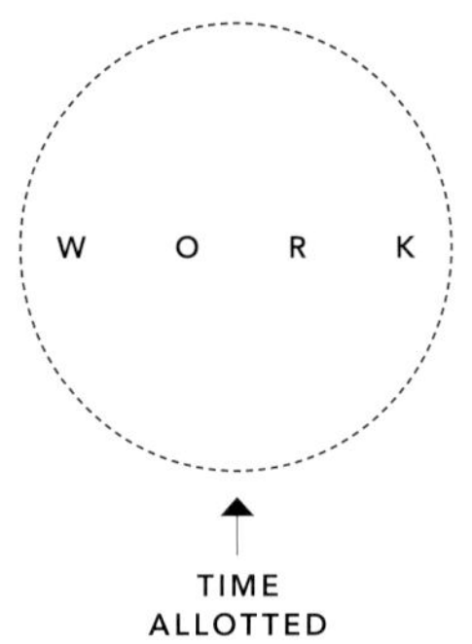

Time

I see deadlines as an inherently positive thing. There's this maxim that all work will expand to fill the time allotted and I fully believe that. So I have a number of different things that are happening in my studio and they're on purpose. I'm working on a publishing project that has a rough timeline of about a year to a year and a half. It's a self-initiated publishing project where I try to work about an hour a day and be disciplined about it. But then I'll have commercial projects that are super heavy-duty projects, like the cover for *MIT Technology Review*, which was creating forty-three different versions of the cover in ten days. Then I have these material projects that extend over years, like some of the performance work that I've done. I'm really conscious of trying to have different types of projects with different time frames going on in my studio at the same time. They satisfy different intellectual and emotional and financial needs.

For example, for *The Saranay Motel*, which is this feature-length digital film, I flew the collaborators to Detroit, got all the equipment together, and after a five-day period had terabytes of information, work, and so on. I set up a situation where I could work intensively—for nearly a week—producing as much as humanly possible and was then able to take a look at what the results of that were. It's a very effective way of working.

Imagined Audience

Much earlier in my career I had a very defined ideal viewer of my work. It was an amalgam of about five people who I have had the pleasure of meeting. I imagined that each one of those projects was speaking directly to this person, who was a mixture of five different actual human beings. When I was really developing as a designer, right after Cranbrook, I'd done a little bit of reading on method acting principles and one of the processes I use in design was that I did not look at specific designers' work because I was already familiar with it. Nor was I trying to make work that looked like their work, but I pretended to behave in the manner that I believed these people behaved in. Largely, the people I'd met were these famous designers who had floated through the Cranbrook studio when I was a graduate student, or who I had met in New York prior to going to grad school. So I tried to extrapolate the core personality of the people who had impressed me the most, and then I would make work with the same kind of confidence level and gestures that I imagined they did. I found it was a pretty useful project.

Initially, it was a guy named Brian Short, who was a fellow graduate student. He is a poet and has a number of advanced degrees—one in electronic music, one in poetry, one in photography, and one in graphic design. He had a huge influence on my use of language. So everything that I was doing linguistically, I imagined that he would be looking at it. The other people were some variation of Rudy VanderLans, [P.] Scott Makela, and Ed Fella. I had a problematic relationship with David Carson and I wasn't trying to make work for him, but when he came through the graduate studio at Cranbrook when I was a student, one of the things that he said really stuck with me. I asked him what was the single most important characteristic that he attributed his success to. He said very clearly, "Attitude." I was 25 at the time and this really resonated with me. From that moment, I tried to make work that had a kind of attitude or stance to it.

Technology

I had some visitors in my studio yesterday and I showed them this iPad drawing that I did that then became a painting. It has a central figure that has this kind of cyclopical head that is a bust that is actually in my studio, and then there's a woodblock print that I made from the oil painting. I'm always materially and intellectually looking at one thing and drawing it across a number of different social practices and material objects.

I consider myself a "future dude," like, wear a chrome jumpsuit, shave my head, and look like I came from the future. I've always been extremely interested in technology and, as a matter of fact, I went to Rochester Institute of Technology from 1984 to '88 so I remember when the Macintosh computer was released. They had a computer lab where I was working and one of the professors was like, "Give it up, typography is never going to work with these computer things." In the 1990s I was part of a loose affiliation of people who were considered "new media" artists and my current work is driven by very advanced technologies—things like CNC, laser cutting, 3D printing. Programs like Cinema4D, Rhino, or a number of other advanced packages. I'm always attempting to push that material. If you go into a 3D program and just simply render shit in 3D, fine, whatever. But when you're using these advanced technologies and cross-pollinate them with the hand processes, things get exponentially more interesting. So I would say that my work is as technologically advanced as it's ever been.

Studio Practice

I'm going to butcher this a little bit, but Frank Zappa was asked if he missed mountain climbing and all kinds of stuff outside of music, and in response he talked about how there's a universe within the music. I know exactly what he's talking about because nearly everything I do ends up blowing back through the studio process.

When I look at my work over a twenty-five-year period I see a real intellectual curiosity that has refused to be bound. As a career strategy that has worked to my disadvantage. If I had just simply done the same thing over and over again, the odds of me being fabulously wealthy and exponentially more powerful would be greater. But every time my curiosity leads me in a new direction, I follow it. The thing that has persisted is the making and being impassioned about the studio practice. But my work has been performance, music, digital video or long-form film, graphics, typography, two-dimensional work, painting—I see them all as the same, but I don't think that culture sees it that way. Culture says, "Do XYZ and stick with that."

Post Typography

Interview with Nolen Strals

June 26, 2015

Early Days

The name "Post Typography" came when my partner Bruce Willen and I were collaborating on a poster in college. That's how we got our start, making posters for our band or show posters for other people. We were making a poster for a show where the headlining band was Arab on Radar—a no-wave noise-rock band whose lyrics are about sexual dysfunction and stuff. The poster was all built from photocopies. We snuck into the MICA [Maryland Institute College of Art] campus mailroom where I worked and blew-up this photo of The Beatles with Ed Sullivan, and then cut all their heads off. We downloaded pictures of boners from gay porn using my boss's computer, collaged those on to where the heads were, and spelled the band names squirting out from the top. I forget who it was, but one of us said, "Whoa, that is so post typographic!"

So even our name was born from humor, or from a humorous situation. That level of fun, that undercurrent, has been built in from the start.

Mixed Media

A lot of our posters were screen printed. Bruce was actually a graphic design major so he was familiar with computers and design software but I wasn't. I didn't ever complete a full design on a computer while I was in college—it was all photocopies and Rubyliths or a combination. Bruce was also doing a lot of handmade design back then which, in the late 1990s, not a lot of people were doing. I actually feel that these days a lot more people are making work with their hands.

That mixing of all those elements—the human touch composited with the digital—is also something that we've been doing for as long as we've worked together.

Serious and Fun

Double Dagger once played a show where our bandmate Brian Dubin got frustrated with his gear and threw one of his drums out into the crowd. It actually hit somebody in the head and got us in a lot of trouble. The next year, the organizer said, "Don't throw any fucking drums." So before the start of the show we ordered and blew-up a couple dozen inflatable drums. We went on stage and said, "Now we were told we couldn't throw our gear this year," and started hurling these small, air-filled drums at the crowd.

I mention that because I think this idea of bringing humor and a lightheartedness into our work—even if we're doing something that's serious or even a little dark, is important. It makes it more engaging for the audience—in music or in design—as opposed to just being presented with this thing. It adds more depth and texture to what we make. Today we bring this sensibility through in the imagery we make and the copy we write for a project, but it really extends back to when we had the band. In saying this, it makes it sound calculated but it's totally not. Working that way is more fun for us and the client and audience get something positive out of it too.

Language

Writing lyrics for a band and writing for a design project are pretty similar, I think. With a song you've got your core idea but the musicians in the band have only given me a certain space to fit it in. It's similar to writing copy for a website or for an ad in a magazine, except in that instance the restriction is mostly visual. The question is—how can you get the right information to the listener or viewer? What words best express the appropriate sentiment or core idea? With both lyrics and copywriting you have to determine the impact that word choice has on the audience and how they're going to respond to the language.

I was raised in a very religious family—both of my parents are Methodist ministers—but from a pretty early age, I was not into the church idea. During the last year or two of Double Dagger shows, from time to time, at a really stand-out show, I'd find myself saying to the crowd, "How I feel right now, thanks to the band and thanks to you, is how I think my parents always wanted me to feel at church." And so, as a nod to that and to the power of religious language, on our last record one of the songs very blatantly uses language drawn from the church. This co-opting of language was used to express how deeply spiritually felt making this music was.

That idea of repurposing to give emphasis or express a sensibility is very closely related to what we do design-wise. We have a brewery client who comes from a blue-collar part of southeastern Pennsylvania. As we were developing their identity, because of the area they're from and the background and attitude of the founders, we drew from the design style of old oil cans and other industrial packaging and Americana from the early to mid-twentieth century. We're playing with a visual language that was once used to describe industrial products and when used in the context of beer, communicates a certain point of view or attitude.

Gail Anderson

June 24, 2015

Early Days

I was the creative director of design at SpotCo, a theatrical ad agency, for about eight years, and that's where I really learned about process. I'd been at *Rolling Stone* for over fourteen years prior to that, and we worked very quickly since the magazine came out every two weeks. While the pace was less frantic at SpotCo, my department was responsible for generating an abundance of ideas for each Broadway production that we worked on. We juggled several shows at a time and had to come up with multiple unique design directions for each client presentation, not just variations on a theme. We all learned to get comfortable with just throwing stuff out there to see what stuck, and not to be too self-conscious or territorial about the work. Even the "bad" ideas were up for discussion.

Designers were encouraged to sketch on paper, rather than to get too caught up in the technical details of Illustrator or Photoshop. And while the final comps that were presented to clients were extremely tightly rendered, the greatest focus was put on the ideas behind those polished posters and ads. Over the years, I learned that sometimes your sixth or seventh idea is the "brilliant" one, even though, of course, I'd love for it to be my first or second.

Sketching

My partner now, Joe Newton, and I work on multiple executions for most of the projects we create together now, though we're experimenting with reeling it in a little. Every now and then, we feel so strongly about a direction that we'll send—gulp—one sketch and try to convince the client that we're certain that's the way to go. Of course, that doesn't always work, but it occasionally does. When I worked with Fred Woodward at *Rolling Stone*, his pencil sketches were so precise that you could just blow them up to magazine size and add the copy. Done. Joe's pencil sketches are so beautifully drawn that they're almost camera-ready, so I'm definitely working with the right people because mine are pure chicken scratch.

Back when I was working for Lynn Staley at *The Boston Globe Sunday Magazine* in the mid-1980s, Lynn sketched and I fleshed out ideas based on her drawings, and over time, she encouraged me to sketch, too. I was part of a team, and knew that someone had my back. That was invaluable to me, and I built on that lesson over the many years I worked with Fred, who was also a generous collaborator.

Trust

Awhile back, Joe and I worked with a client who clearly didn't see the design process as something malleable and that we needed a little time to get a stronger sense of what would best suit his needs. The client clearly saw design as more of a transaction, and after two short rounds of sketches, cut bait angrily and with the notion that he owed us nothing—like money—in exchange for our efforts. Were we not listening to his needs, thinking that we could get away with not immediately executing the awful idea he came to us with? Maybe. But from the beginning, the trust just wasn't there, not in even one of our exchanges with him. We're more careful now about choosing clients.

Technology

Technology has definitely made the work process easier, in obvious ways like being able to test color combinations and multiple typefaces. I think back to my early *Rolling Stone* days, waiting for type samples to be set on the Typositor, and using a Rapidograph to draw picture boxes. We had colored pencils and Prismacolor markers, and we were always in search of that perfect shade of putty.

Technology has made aspects of teaching harder, though, since I find that students don't always give enough thought to the typefaces they're using. They scroll through what's open on the machine they happen to be using, or search dafont.com for often poorly drawn or badly spaced fonts. I'm extra sensitive to what sometimes feels like negligence since I love letterforms.

Doubt

I both love and fear the thought process intrinsic to good design—or even mediocre design, I suppose. Will this be the time when I'm exposed as the fraud that I am? Will Joe pack up his laptop and find a collaborator who comes up with ideas more quickly? I always fear that I'm not fast enough.

Once we actually get our ideas in motion, I'm ready for the next one, while Joe really digs in deep and revels in the refinement and execution of every nuance. He can focus for hours on creating perfect textures or curves. I still have a bit of SpotCo in me, where I think we need to have a dozen versions and six back ups ready tonight just in case.

I love chewing on ideas while riding the subway or staring at a blank piece of paper. But that love is definitely coupled with a genuine dose of fear that the sheet of paper will always remain blank, or that we'll just keep talking about ideas without ever actually getting anything done.

I do think that some designers brush off the struggles inherent in problem-solving, leading you to believe they're able to rattle off brilliant solutions effortlessly with complete client buy-in. Maybe it was easier back in the day before focus groups and before the Mac made everyone's nephew a designer. I just don't believe it could have been as effortless as some would have you believe.

I'm actually okay with the client knowing that there's some nail biting involved in the process. My experience has been that it helps make the client an ally and partner.

A Good Client Is One With Vision

Joe and I worked on an installation for the Pennsylvania College of Art and Design [PCAD]. They had recently purchased a piece of land across the street from the school and wanted to put their imprint on it with some sort of "art." We had never done anything like that before and spent time at the college to hone in on what the school's message was. After a bit of hand wringing, we presented two sculpture models that were initially liked and then rightfully rejected. After that we went back to the drawing board in search of a new direction.

Joe and I were chatting with the president of the college on our next visit, and in conversation, mentioned some copy that we thought kind of summed up PCAD's mission. The president was intrigued, and she encouraged us to explore working on typography with the text we had suggested—which was something we were infinitely more comfortable with.

We presented a paper model of a new idea that would utilize the back wall of the property—a piece of typography that spanned over sixty feet in length and would stand about five feet tall. It would be made of powder-coated aluminum and fiberglass and would require city approval and a lot more money. We were so enthralled with the idea of our fancy type solution that we even offered to cut our fee since we knew we were proposing an idea that was beyond the scope of the original project. In the end, the president was so excited that she raised the money to make it happen—and though it added months to the project, she was determined, resourceful, and completely gracious.

Our inexperience led us to initially think too conventionally. It was the genius of a client who knew what she wanted and saw something special in us that led to an innovative idea.

Handwork

Joe is happy drawing on a piece of crumpled paper, but I need some sort of small journal, preferably with lines, but definitely not graph paper. And the pencil has to be just-out-of-the-sharpener sharp. The importance of getting off the computer and drawing can't be stressed enough. I actually wish I could draw better and regret that I've lost what little skill I initially had in my youth. I think that any kind of handwork only makes you a better designer and connects you to the materials you're working with, whether it's drawing, painting, or collage.

Nicho las Bl echm an

January 8, 2015

the wit and imagination of Gill's solutions to the graphic problems in this unique collection are remarkable.
But the most remarkable thing is that although 30 years of his work is represented here, you won't be able to tell Gill's early designs from his most recent ones.
Forget all the rules you ever learned about graphic design. By Bob Gill.
Forget all the rules you ever learned about graphic design.
Including the ones in this book.
Forget how good design is *supposed* to look. What you think is good design, is what other

Oddball

I haven't really had the luxury of time to look at how I operated. I was putting out fires each time. There's a deadline and I have to come up with work that is of some quality that will make the deadline—work that I'm not too embarrassed by, that is publishable. That's really all it was. I was never aware of any kind of system. I'm such an oddball in the sense that I do so many different things—some people think of me as the Art Director at the *New York Times* who does this thing called the *Book Review*, and other people think of me as the guy who did that magazine called *Nozone*, and others think of me as someone who does illustrations. Depending on which project, I have a different system.

Inevitability

I think panic and deadlines just get it done. There's a guarantee that it will actually happen, so I believe in them. I think with all good designers, there is a certain way of coming to a solution and the kind of solution that it is, somehow that will manifest itself in the end result. I like to come up with ideas because I can justify a solution if there's an idea behind it. If there's not an idea behind, it, I can't justify the solution. So I do always find myself asking "Why?" as a habit and as a way of answering the problem. In that way, Bob Gill was a huge inspiration, particularly his book *Forget All the Rules…*[*You Ever Learned About Graphic Design: Including the Ones in This Book*].

Early Days

I came to design by starting my own side projects before I had real clients. Among them was *Nozone*, which actually started as a college project.

When you're starting out, you're just looking for assignments. When you're younger, you're just hungry and inspired by everything. I was passionate about underground comics and politics, so I decided to bring the two together through this magazine. Doing a magazine was always a dream for me. It was part of this whole DIY culture that was happening at the time. I was also buying a lot of zines, photocopied zines that other friends were doing, so it seemed very possible to put it together myself.

I went to Oberlin [College & Conservatory]—a liberal arts college—and studied art history and studio art. There wasn't really a design class, per se. I loved being in a liberal arts college, knowing full well I wanted to go into design afterwards and that all the history and politics classes would somehow fuel my interest in design, providing content or a framework through which I could later design.

That's the great thing about not going to an art school and wanting to be a designer and an artist. Even though you're taking an English class, it's a design class in a sense because it fuels your sense of design. Learning about post-modernism and post-modern theory and writing papers allowed me to be a better editor and allowed me to write my own rants and come up with my own personal manifestos. My education was word-based but what is design except for words and how they combine with images?

My father had an animation studio, so I used that as a home base, as a sort of headquarters, and I'd work on various animated projects. At the time there were no computers, so there was a lot of manual work involved. I'd do that as a side gig and I'd use the Xerox machine and whatever equipment I could off hours. I spent one summer as an intern—the "photostat boy"—at Paul Davis's studio at *Wigwag* magazine, so that was my training ground for design. And trying to launch the magazine myself. Trying to make *Nozone* was a huge learning experience.

Technology

I think it would be naïve to say that my process hasn't been at all influenced by technology because technology is this pervasive force that has impacted almost every facet of our lives. I'm sure it has influenced the way I go about coming up with or arriving at a solution. It helps me kill ideas because you can see what everyone else has done that you thought was an original idea. It's also great for visual reference, especially as an illustrator. It's also a hindrance because it's too easy to copy or be influenced by other images and other people's work. I think that when we were surrounded by fewer images before the Internet, maybe my own work had a little more soul. It was just me doing it, just me working on paper. It was less channeled through these other influences that are inevitably in my bookmarks and my browser. Especially as an art director, I'm surrounded by so much different work. Also in terms of execution, people really like to categorize the difference between what something means and what something looks like. It's very slippery. It's a very gray area, the way something looks, the way it's rendered changes or alters the meaning.

Ultimately it all gets filtered through a screen, but usually the progression is from the head to the paper, and eventually somehow it gets to the computer. Either I render a scan, sketch into the computer, or draw it on a tablet or a computer. Sometimes if I'm bold I'll just come up with an idea and execute it directly in Illustrator.

It's really a subtle thing that's hard to quantify, but something like a drawing of a shoe won't have as many laces, won't be as intricate, won't have as much detail, or it won't be from the same point of view or angle. In drawing a shoe I could either just quickly draw something on the computer, but if I draw on the computer, am I trying to replicate a hand drawing but doing it with a machine? I feel like that's a mistake. In a way, I should draw it as stupidly as possible, like the way the machine works. If I'm going to draw the shoe, I could do one line for a leg and one line for a shoe, and maybe add a little heel if I wanted to be fancy.

If I were to draw a shoe in Illustrator and another on a piece of paper, there would be two complete iterations, but sometimes I confuse the two and I try to draw on the computer as if it's my sketchbook, and then it comes out awkwardly. There's this whole idea of how it's important to make mistakes and how when we make mistakes, other ideas present themselves. I try not to get too hung up on a certain way of drawing.

The Hard Way

Within a certain design problem, if there's an aspect that's more difficult and a part that is more easy—let's say with multiple illustrations—I usually like to go for the most difficult one first because I know if I can do that then the rest is going to be a piece of cake. So there is this certain kind of anxiety at the beginning of each job that spurs me on.

I spend a lot of time sketching different ideas and coming up with the idea that I like best. I always get stuck in the usual clichés, like everyone does. The clichés surface to mind and you want to peel those ideas away to get deeper. To do that I have to force myself to think about it often during idle moments, like while waiting for the subway or taking a shower—these are times when an idea can slip in if I keep something percolating inside my head.

I try to define what the problem is. Once it's understood and I've defined it on my own terms, then I visualize it and find an approach or an angle into it. Sometimes I feel like I have to sketch out a lot of bad ideas. A lot of people just do one sketch or drawing, and I'm always impressed by that because obviously they had many, many other ideas before they came to that one, so how do they know that one is the one that's right?

One or Many

It's modern versus postmodern. The modernist says there's one idea and that's the idea. I came up with it. The post-modern approach is more process-oriented, more meta. I don't think it necessarily leads to better solutions, but that's just where we are right now.

There are certain people or clients who you trust so you want them more involved and engaged in the process, and some you don't, so you'll say, "This is just how it's going to look." I also think it's very personal. Different people have different styles and methodologies. Recently I did a job where I presented four ideas and I wasn't sure—there were two that were really good and the other two I couldn't tell. We finally chose one and in the end, I felt like I really didn't like any of them. I think it's much better to be Vignelli-like and say, "This is the way it's going to be." When designers do that with me, I always admire that so much. I think that's classy and shows a lot of discipline.

Ideation

I like coming up with the idea that somehow works, and then watching that idea like a little child to see if they'll make it through grade school. Are they going to survive and graduate to the next level? And then presenting to the client and seeing how much is going to get destroyed or remain intact. That's always fascinated me.

I used to be an obsessive sketchbook chronicler. Every now and then I indulge myself and look at those books and there's so much really nice work. Ever since I had a kid all my old beautiful work habits have gone to rot, but that used to be my platform for ideating. The thing that's important is to do some work very quickly to get the ideas done and then not look at it for a day or two. It's so hard to be objective when you're in the creative moment. You're like, "Yeah, definitely red," but you don't know anything. It's not until you can look back on it that you can actually see it freshly, almost through the eyes of someone else. I find it hard when you're in the creative process knowing whether you really like something. If you like something, is liking it enough? Maybe you have to love it. How hard do you push yourself?

Presentation

I try to look and see as much as possible, more illustration than design—and magazines. When illustrators come to show me their portfolios, as soon as they reach into their bag and pull out an iPad or laptop, I don't want to see it anymore. I know it's going to be slick and glossy. I know that it's going to look good because it's on screen. You're going to be swiping something, you're going to be interactive, zooming in, and the colors are always going to be bright. I look at a screen all the time and I'm pretty good at judging what looks good or not, so when I'm looking at the portfolio of a designer, I want to see the real thing, unless it's for a website. With Google Images, you almost don't need to look at designers' websites anymore. I'll just search their name and see what comes up. So all the thought and time and effort that goes into designing a website is just out the door. Especially working with editors, I might just give them a name and they do an internet search and whatever comes up, someone will get the job based on that. In that way a computer algorithm becomes your portfolio—which is a really scary thought, but chances are, if you're good, lots of nice stuff will come up.

John Gall

November 23, 2014

Early Days

I graduated from school in the mid-1980s and started working when design was still an analog process—stat machines, light tables, Lucigraphs, all that. For me, it wasn't all that difficult to turn to the computer. In fact, in many ways I found it freeing because everything you did before the computer cost money. Typesetting cost a fortune, so you couldn't really experiment *that* much. Any time you had to make even the slightest color change for a comp, it was a twenty-four-hour turnaround plus a rush charge. For art you had to order a bunch of C-prints in different sizes, just in case. Computers changed all of that. They opened doors and closed doors.

Empowerment

The work I was doing in those early days wasn't all that interesting—it was more "foot in the door" kind of work. I left publishing for a bit and then drifted back at about the time computers started. With the new technology there was a new way of working for designers. I decided that if I was going to do this, I wanted to see how I could make books and book design work for me.

There was a point early on when I realized that I could make my own thing, as opposed to following standard book-cover design rules—big type, small image, title at top, author at bottom, art in the middle, no green covers, and so forth.

Different Paths

There are two ways I typically work—the first is where very early on I have a pretty clear path of how it's going to be—even though I never really know what it'll look like. I'll say, "Oh, there's going to be a mountain and a bobcat. Those are the things I think will work and I just need to see how they're going to fit together." The other way is where I don't know at all where it's going. I might be gathering information and start playing with different elements in order to make them into something through just sketching or playing—creating variation after variation to see where things go.

I will go to my immediate sources and find the crappiest picture of a bobcat and the most beautiful picture of a mountain and when they're put together something unique will occur because of certain contrast or texture.

This is where the exploration that occurs during the making of the thing comes through—where you make mistakes or discover new paths to follow. If I do sketch something it tends to be an exercise to get the clichéd ideas out of the way. Get rid of the stuff rattling around in my head. Mostly things I've seen before, but even those clichés can actually turn into something else depending on how you go about it. For me the process of going from head through hand onto paper or computer is where the interesting things happen. I've never been one of those people trying to recreate the thing I see in my brain. And when I do it's usually terrible. It's all in the translation.

Book Covers

Designing book covers is not a very elaborate or complex process. It's reading a book and jotting down lists and notes and then, at some point, an idea is going to gel. Sometimes it happens on the first page and sometimes it doesn't until weeks after you've finished the book. Next it's a matter of how you visualize this idea, which can take many, many forms.

At this point in my career, I get to the visualization point quickly and just start doing. There's not much physical drawing or sketching, although I will make little sketches so I don't forget something or if I'm trying to explain something to someone else. I use these little Post-it notes that are just the right proportion for a book cover.

Collage

I've always been interested in collage. Even when I was in school my work had a real collage-like quality to it. I think that that is something that speaks to me in the way I work. If I had to make something up myself it's just going to be a mountain with a bobcat standing up on top of it. With a collage technique, I can get to all these other forms and relationships.

I look at design overall as a collage-like experience. It's almost always working with things that already exist in the world—a photograph, a typeface, even a commissioned illustration. For other projects I do make that material myself and may have to draw or physically assemble something and then photograph it.

In fact, my original entry into collage was an attempt to get as far away from design thinking and design making as possible. Away from metaphor, analogy, concept, layout, and ideas of beauty and visual connection. It means checking—or at least trying to check—all your pre-conceived notions about good and bad, beauty and ugliness, and what looks good on a page at the door. On the downside I am rarely ever successful at doing that. It is rather difficult. The hope is to discover new forms and thoughts and ways of seeing the world that won't necessarily happen through the normal "problem solving" design process.

Like I said, the thing that took me a long, long time to come to terms with was giving myself permission to make something just to see what it looked like. Normally everything I make is in service of something else: a book, a record, an editorial. I can't tell you how freeing it was to just say, "I wonder what that would look like on top of that," and then actually do it.

Approach

I really have two very distinct ways of approaching work. One is purely concept-driven. I don't like to completely define what it's going to be because something will happen between here and there, but it's definitely going to be in the zone that the concept has set out. The other method is to have a very rough idea but rely more on play and exploration. It's like grad school versus kindergarten. Coming up with a good concept is always very hard, as is coming at it from the other end—the other extreme. You can be going for days without anything really happening. These two ways of working made sense for me as soon as the work that came out of them started to be accepted.

Today, the computer can make the process almost too exacting. I try to leave space for accidents to happen. There are ridiculous things I do where I might be working on two projects at the same time and neither one is working, so I'll take the type from one and put it on the other. I also turn things upside down, sideways, reversed, and so on—just to get a new perspective.

I think some of that is intuitive. Sometimes you do things and you don't know why you're doing them, but they reveal themselves later, which is so different from the method of, "I'm going down this path and just doing things on this path."

Put another way, I am sometimes in pursuit of the wrong answer as a backwards way of getting to the right answer and this is really where the collage stuff I was doing on the side—even before the computer—comes in. I was making things that had no meaning but just exploring the format, the form, the physicality. The big thing for me with collage was getting out of the design mindset where one needs to have an idea to execute, as opposed to, "I'm just going to see what this looks like." Giving myself the permission to do that was really a big deal.

A lot of these things also have to do with taking ownership of a project. In publishing you are never sure exactly who your client is—it could be the editor, the publisher, the author, or even someone in sales. But to really make something worthwhile, you need to put all that aside and take ownership over the work. Not that you're making selfish work, but you're taking it all into account, all the considerations, including yourself.

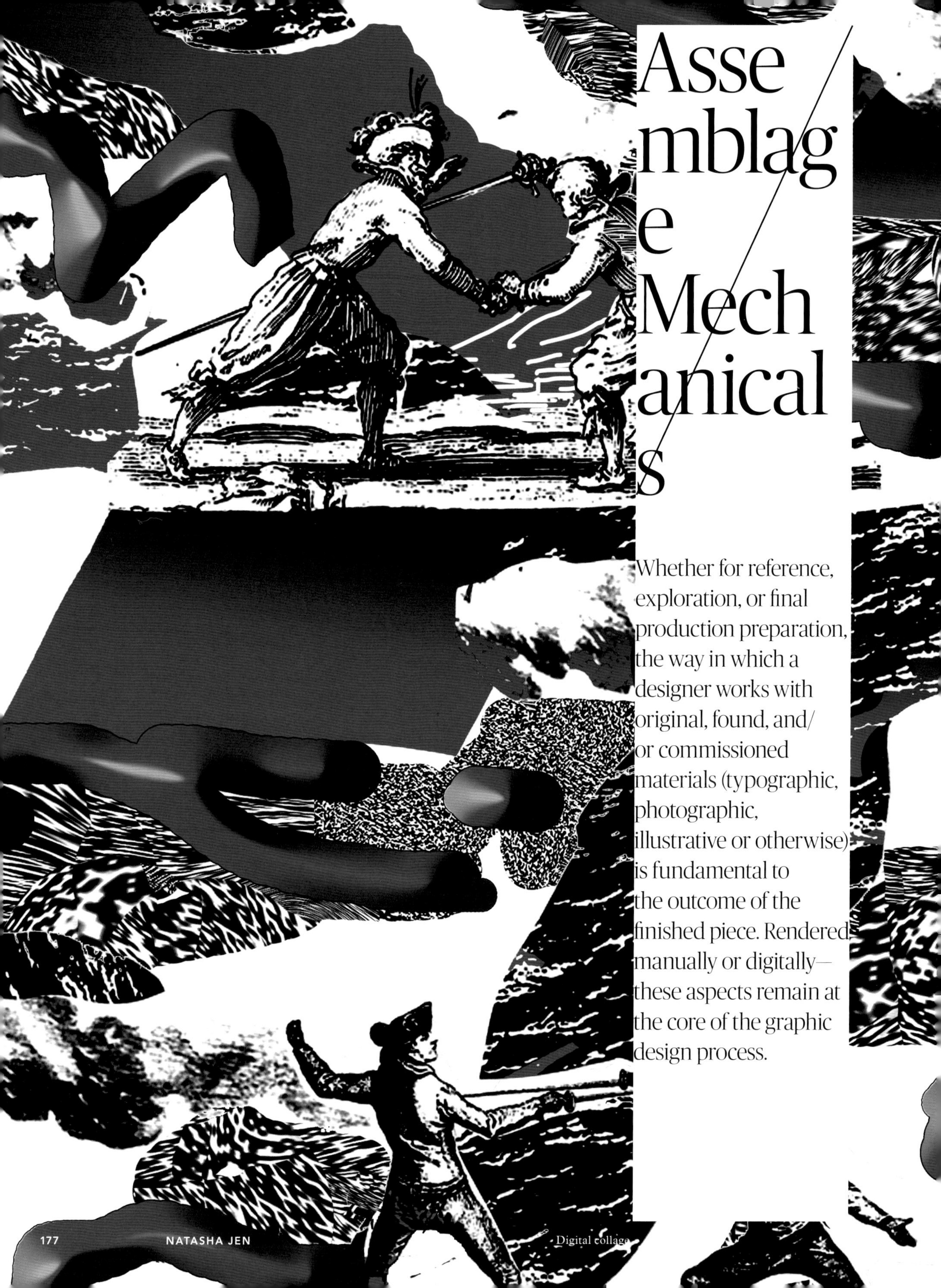

Assemblage Mechanicals

Whether for reference, exploration, or final production preparation, the way in which a designer works with original, found, and/or commissioned materials (typographic, photographic, illustrative or otherwise) is fundamental to the outcome of the finished piece. Rendered manually or digitally—these aspects remain at the core of the graphic design process.

Digital collage

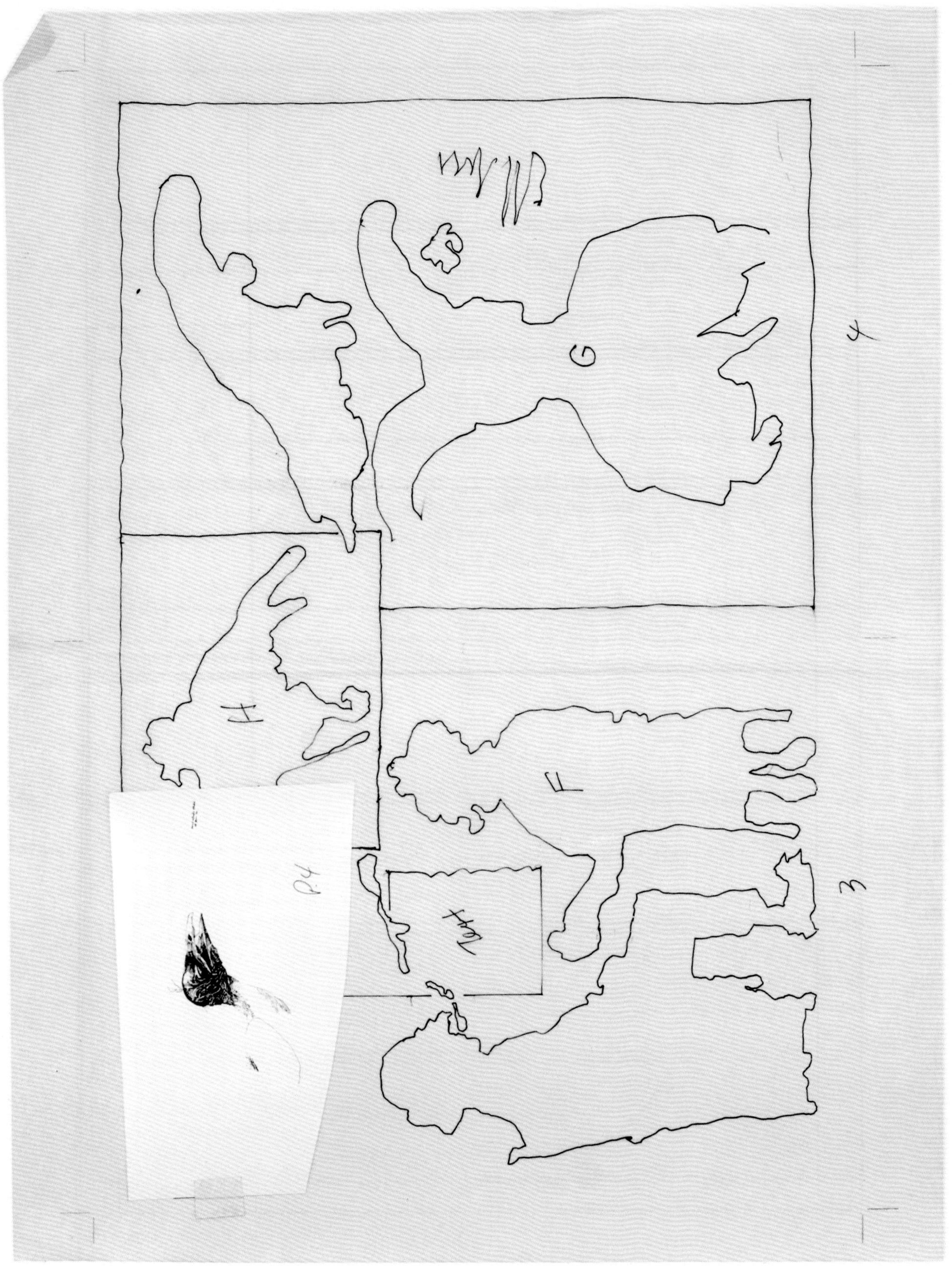

Tracing paper page layout sketch with affixed drawing

"Fantastic Alphabets" negative

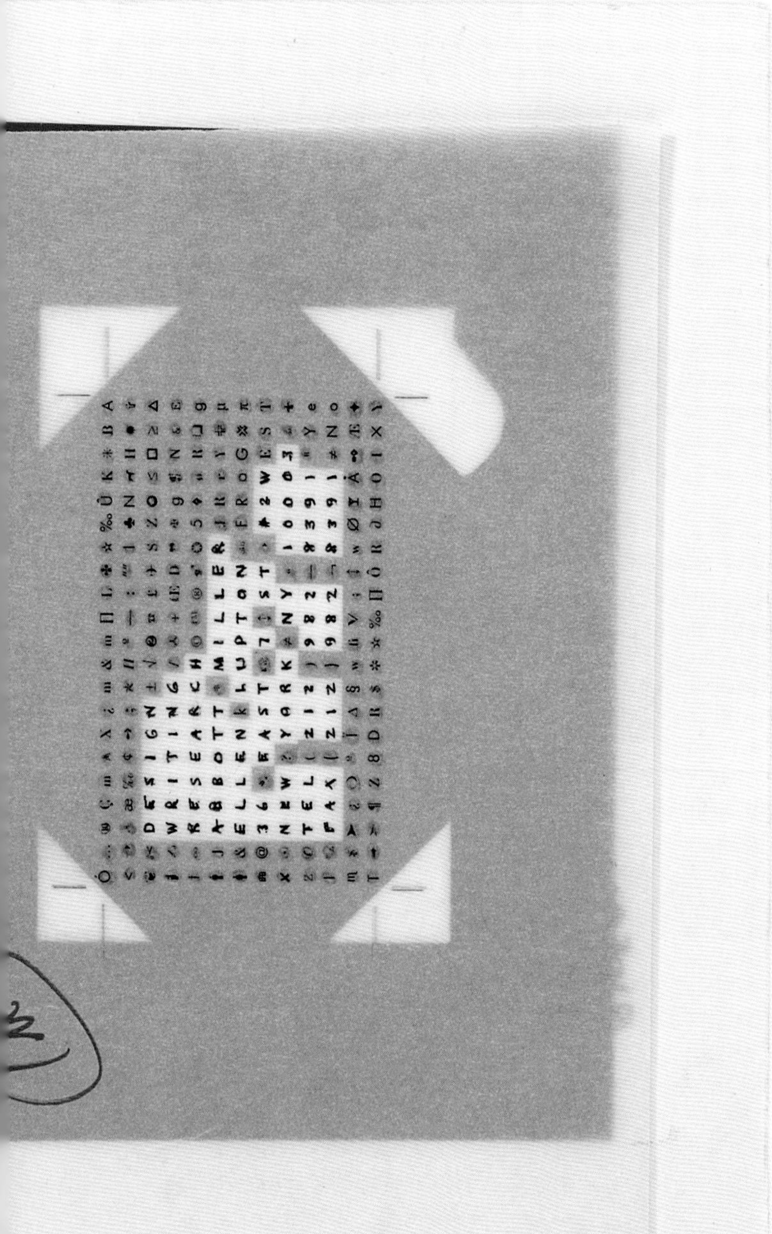

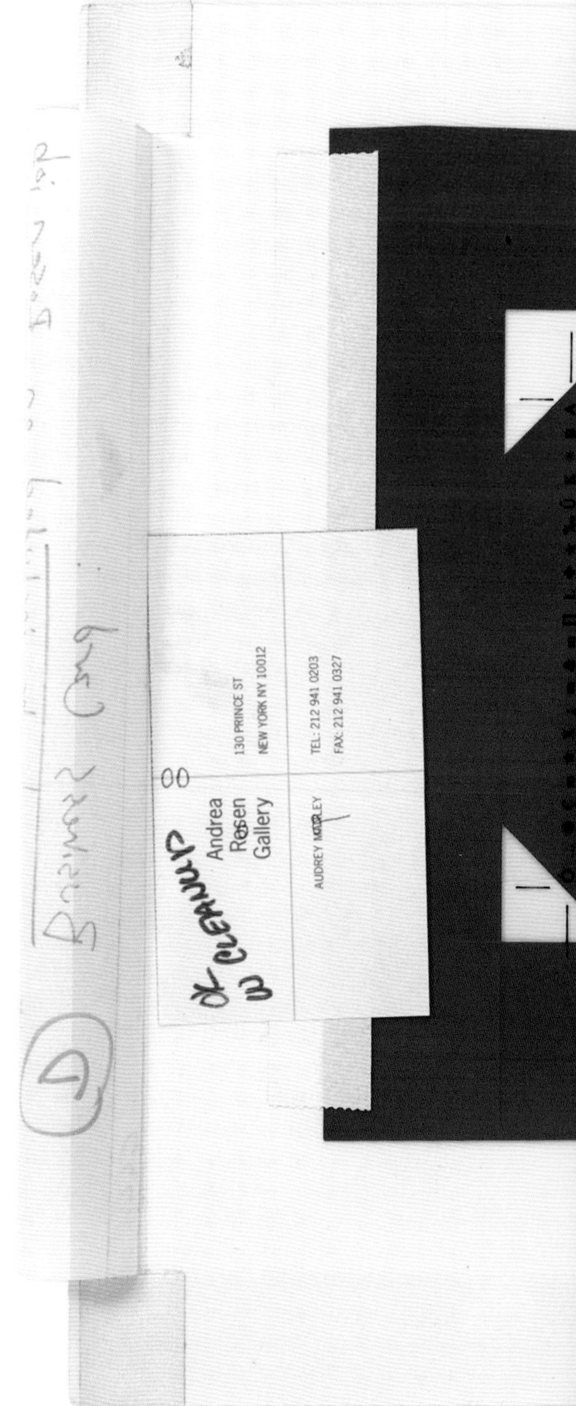
Andrea
Rosen
Gallery
130 PRINCE ST
NEW YORK NY 10012
TEL: 212 941 0203
FAX: 212 941 0327

 Design, Writing, Research business card mechanical with Rubylith

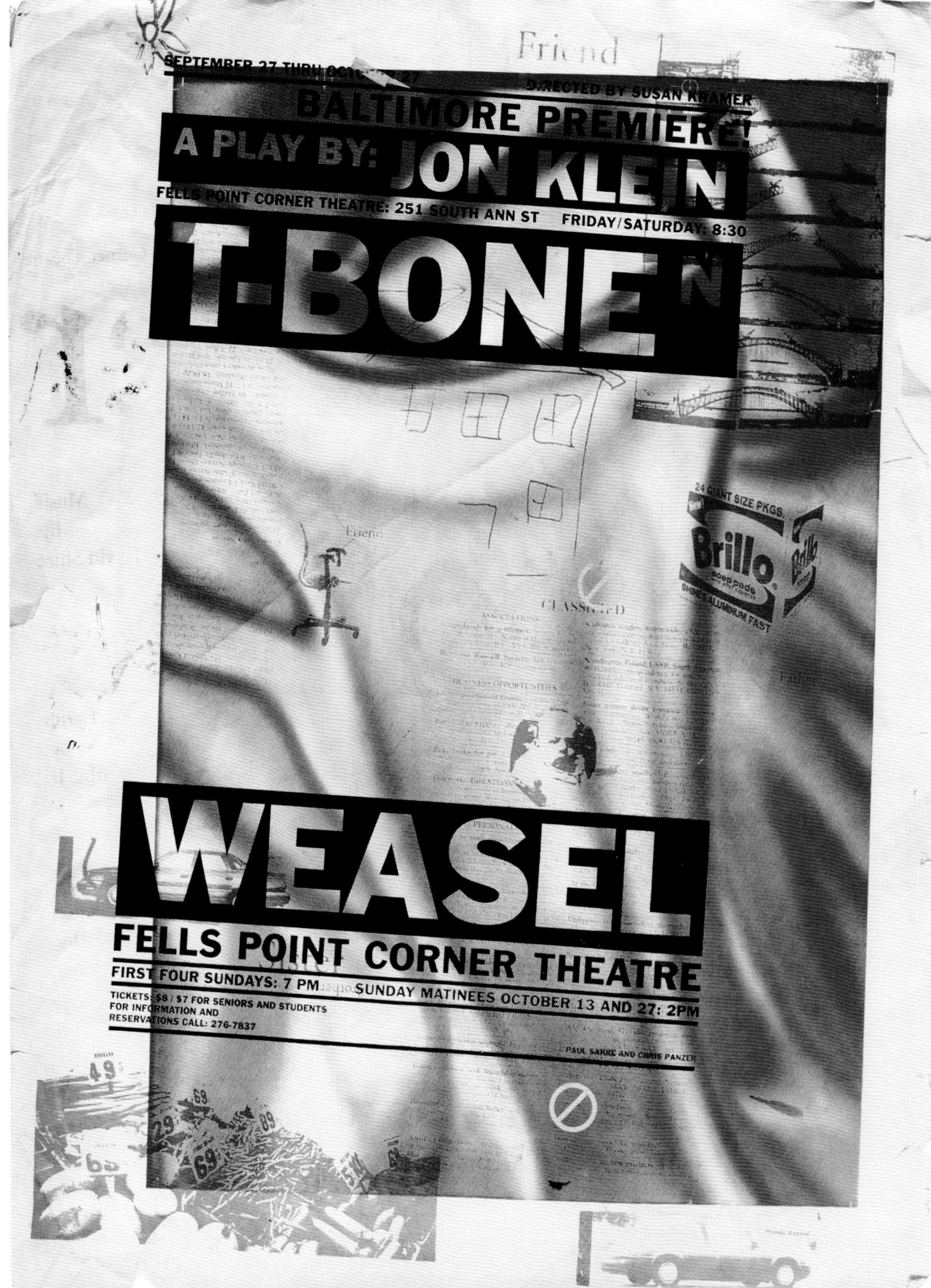
SEPTEMBER 27 THRU OCTOBER 27
DIRECTED BY SUSAN KRAMER
BALTIMORE PREMIERE!
A PLAY BY: JON KLEIN
FELLS POINT CORNER THEATRE: 251 SOUTH ANN ST
FRIDAY/SATURDAY: 8:30
T-BONE N
WEASEL
FELLS POINT CORNER THEATRE
FIRST FOUR SUNDAYS: 7 PM
SUNDAY MATINEES OCTOBER 13 AND 27: 2PM
TICKETS: $8 / $7 FOR SENIORS AND STUDENTS
FOR INFORMATION AND
RESERVATIONS CALL: 276-7837
PAUL SAHRE AND CHRIS PANZER
Friend
CLASSIFIED
24 GIANT SIZE PKGS.
Brillo
SOAP PADS
SHINES ALUMINUM FAST

PARTNERSHIPS IN MANAGEMENT AND DEVELOPMENT

Fells Point Corner Theatre

closer than ever

Music by: David Shire

Lyrics by: Richard Maltby, Jr.

Musical Direction by: Tim Delaney

Directed by: Terry J. Long

Screen print make-readys for Fells Point Corner Theatre posters (recto/verso)

Balance collage word game

Rain
22

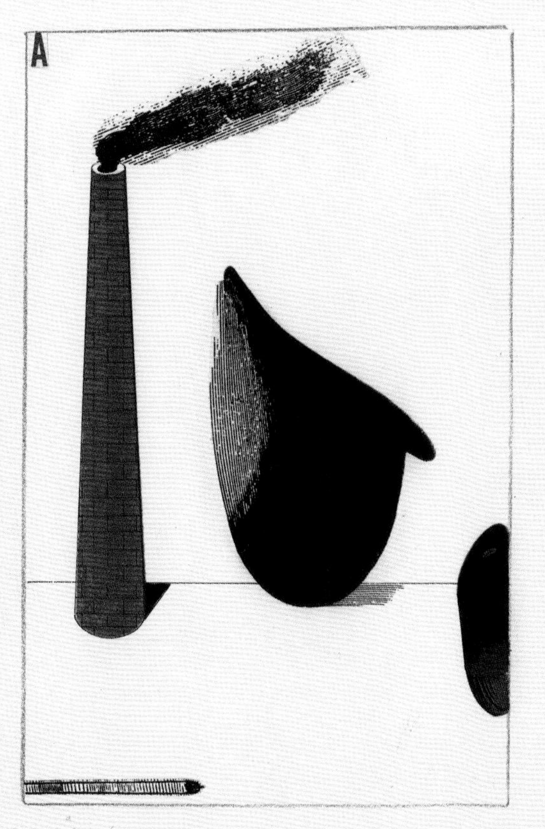

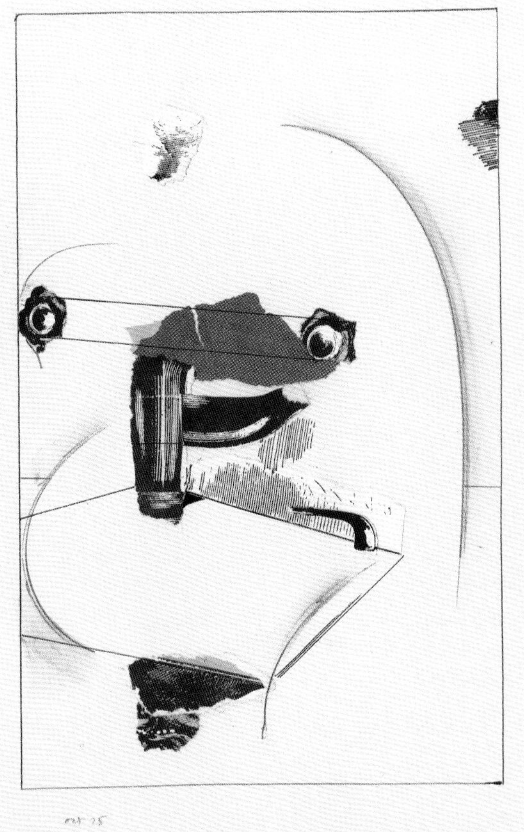

Preparatory collages for "Fat Face" (Aggravate) poster, October 1986

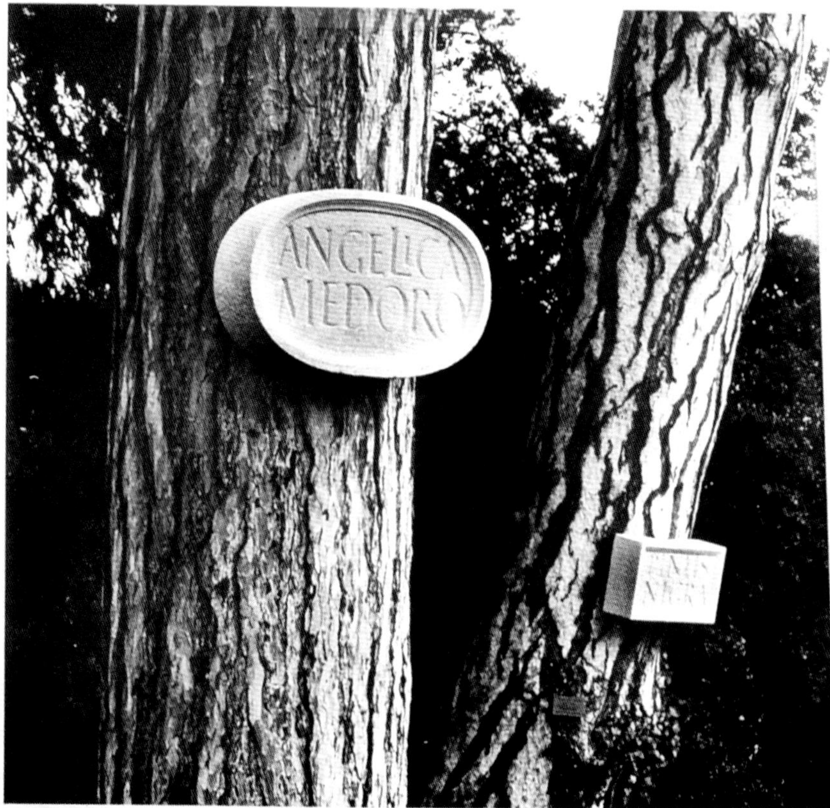

Plaques on trees, 1984
with Nicholas Sloan
Bruglingen Gardens, Basel, Switzerland
Five oval plaques are inscribed with the names of classical lovers, and five rectangular plaques identify particular species of trees

Performance of Wilma Paterson's Bruglingen Suite, 19
Bruglingen Gardens, Basel, Switzerland

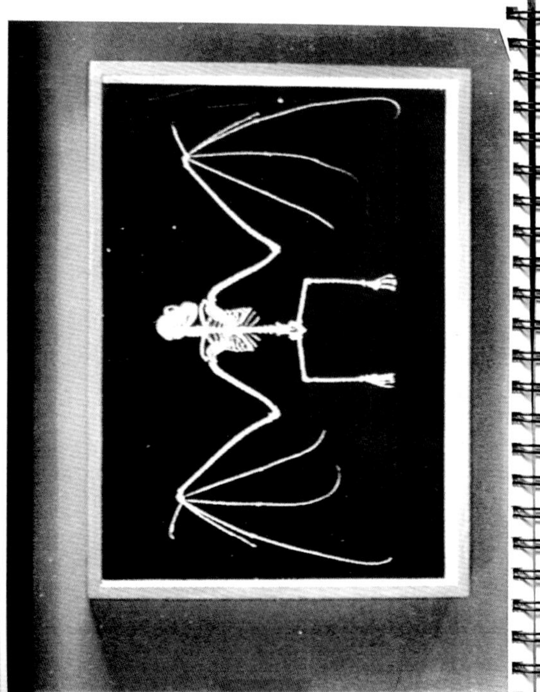

Best wishes,
Eliot Weinberger

BALTIC SHIPPING COMPANY ● USSR

ZEITGENÖSSISCHE
KUNST IN ESSEN
20.10.06
BIS
MUSEUM FOLKWANG
RWE TURM
07.01.07
EINE
KOOPERATION
RWE

G. Jouve, S. Mouille, A. Noll,
Ch. Perriand, J. Prouvé, J. Royère
5, rue des Taillandiers · Paris 75011
Tel. 1 4700 3235 · Fax 1 4021 8295
GALERIE JOUSSE SEGUIN

Coffin Ignites at Funeral
BATON ROUGE, La., June 4 (AP)

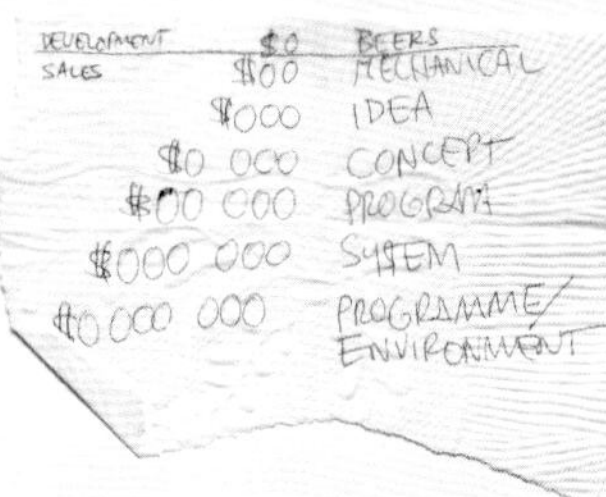
DEVELOPMENT $0 BEERS
SALES $00 MECHANICAL
$000 IDEA
$0 000 CONCEPT
$00 000 PROGRAM
$000 000 SYSTEM
$0 000 000 PROGRAMME/ENVIRONMENT

The parallel universe from the Châtelet production of Richard Strauss's opera "Die Frau ohne Schatten."

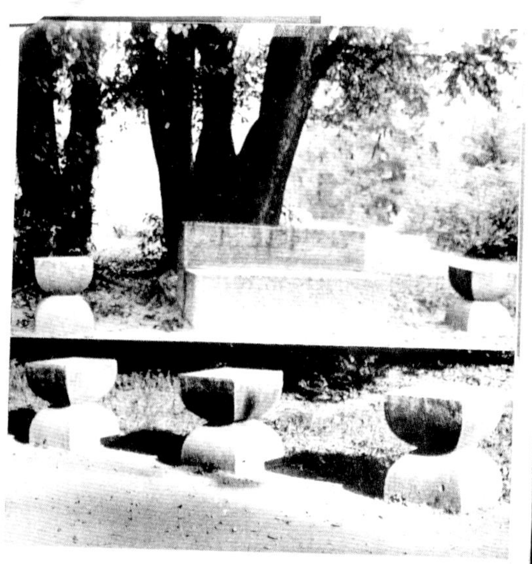

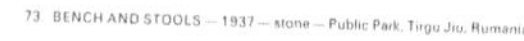

73. BENCH AND STOOLS — 1937 — stone — Public Park, Tirgu Jiu, Rumania

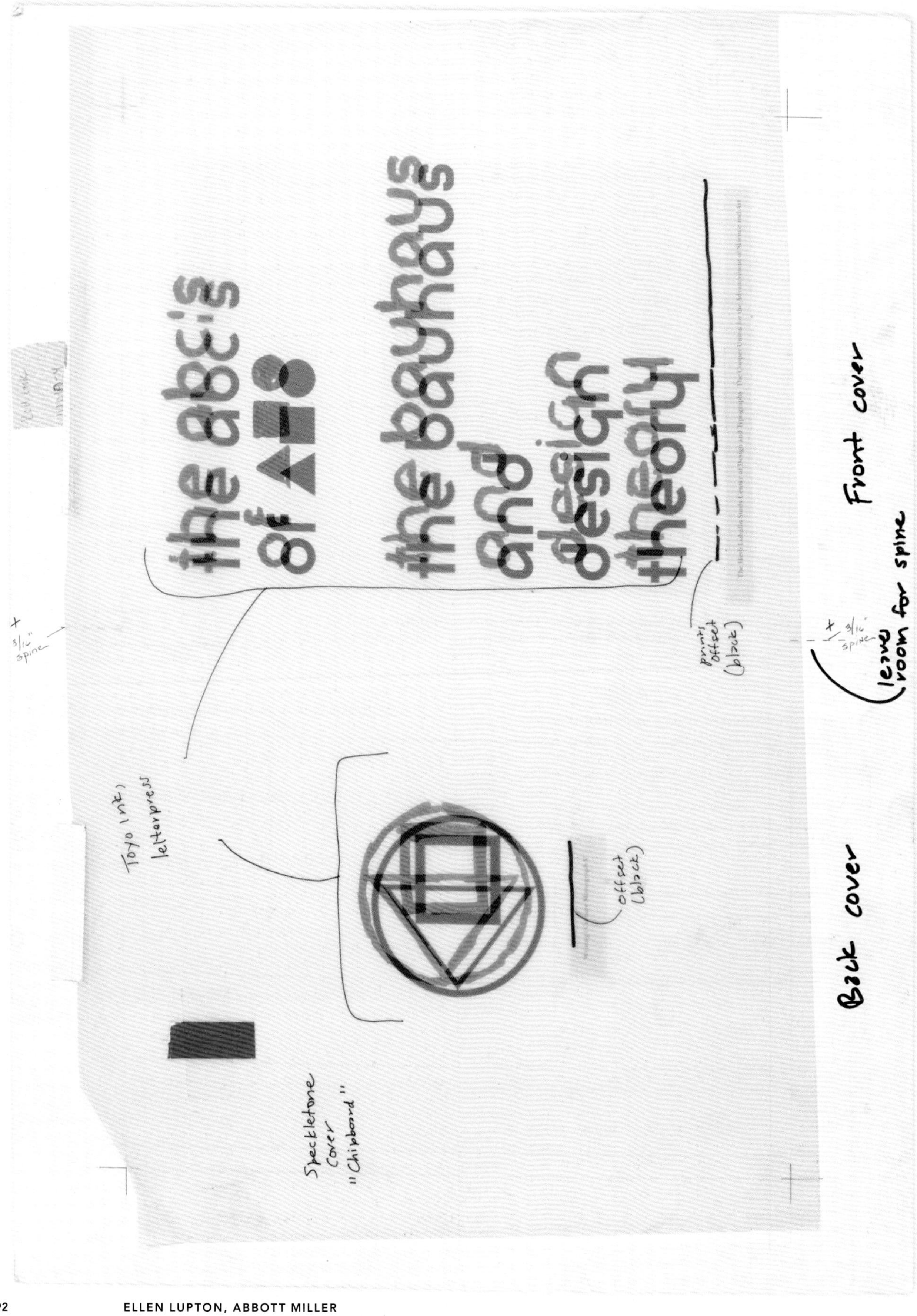

the abc's
of ▲■●

the bauhaus
and
design
theory

Front cover

leave room for spine

3/16" spine

print offset (black)

Toyo ink, letterpress

offset (black)

Back cover

Speckletone Cover "Chipboard"

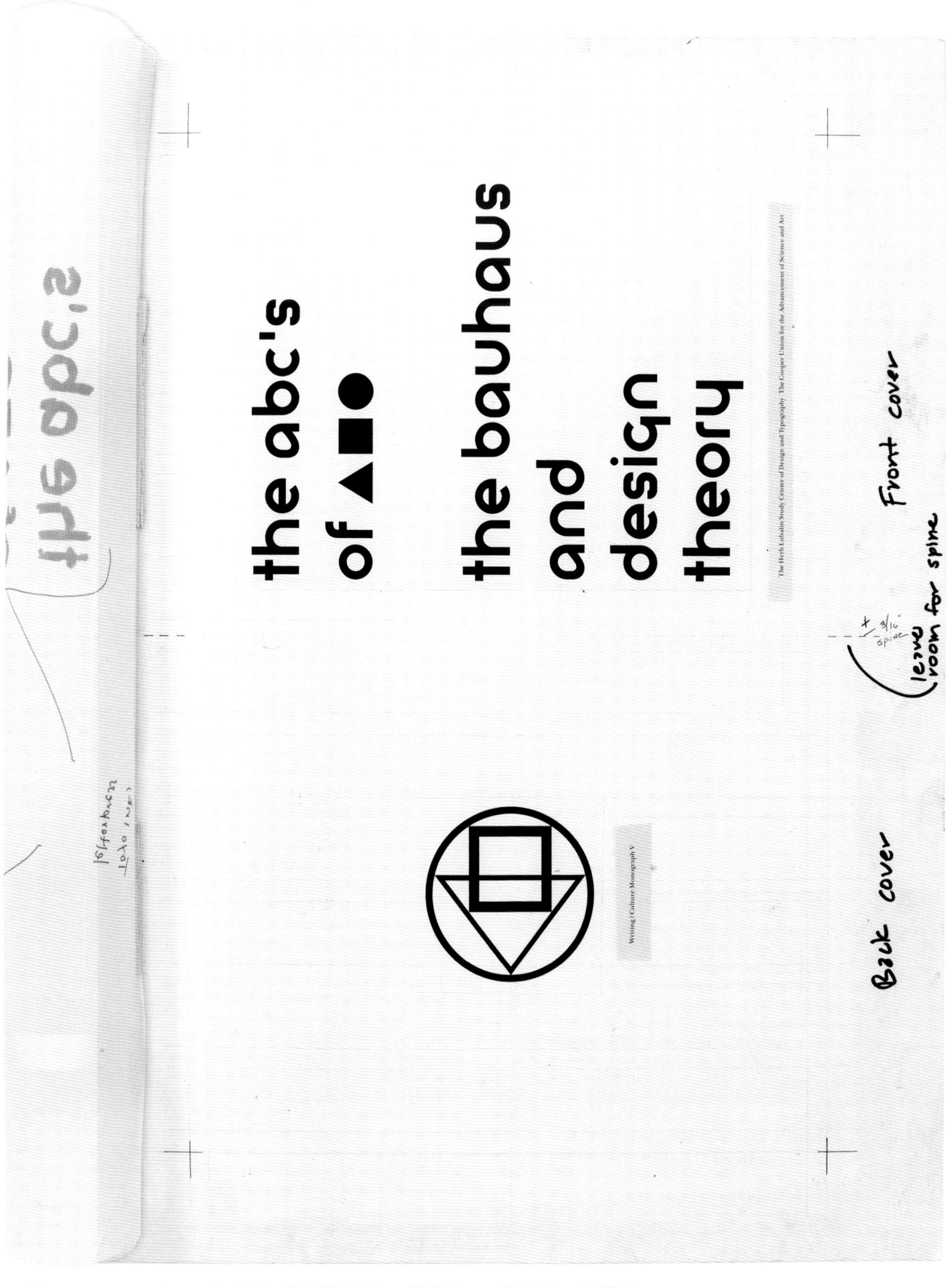

the abc's
of ▲■●

the bauhaus
and
design
theory

The Herb Lubalin Study Center of Design and Typography The Cooper Union for the Advancement of Science and Art

Writing / Culture Monograph V

Front cover

Back cover

leave room for spine

3/16" spine

Cover mechanical for *The ABC's of Bauhaus: The Bauhaus and Design Theory* by Ellen Lupton

NATASHA JEN

Digital collage

 Digital collage

Bridges
a Liberal/Conservative Dialogue
with Larry Josephson
A Co-Production of WHYY, Philadelphia and the Radio Foundation.
Funding in part from the Corporation for Public Broadcasting.
Distributed by American Public Radio. Call Ken Mills (612) 339-9242
©1993 The Radio Foundation, Inc. ALL RIGHTS RESERVED
Bridges
a Liberal/Conservative Dialogue
with Larry Josephson
©℗ 1993 The Radio Foundation, Inc. ALL RIGHTS RESERVED
Distributed by American Public Radio.
100 North Sixth Street, Minneapolis, MN 55403
For more information, call Ken Mills at (612) 339-9242
Demo
Cassette
BOB
RAY
1.
2.
1. Bob 2. Ray

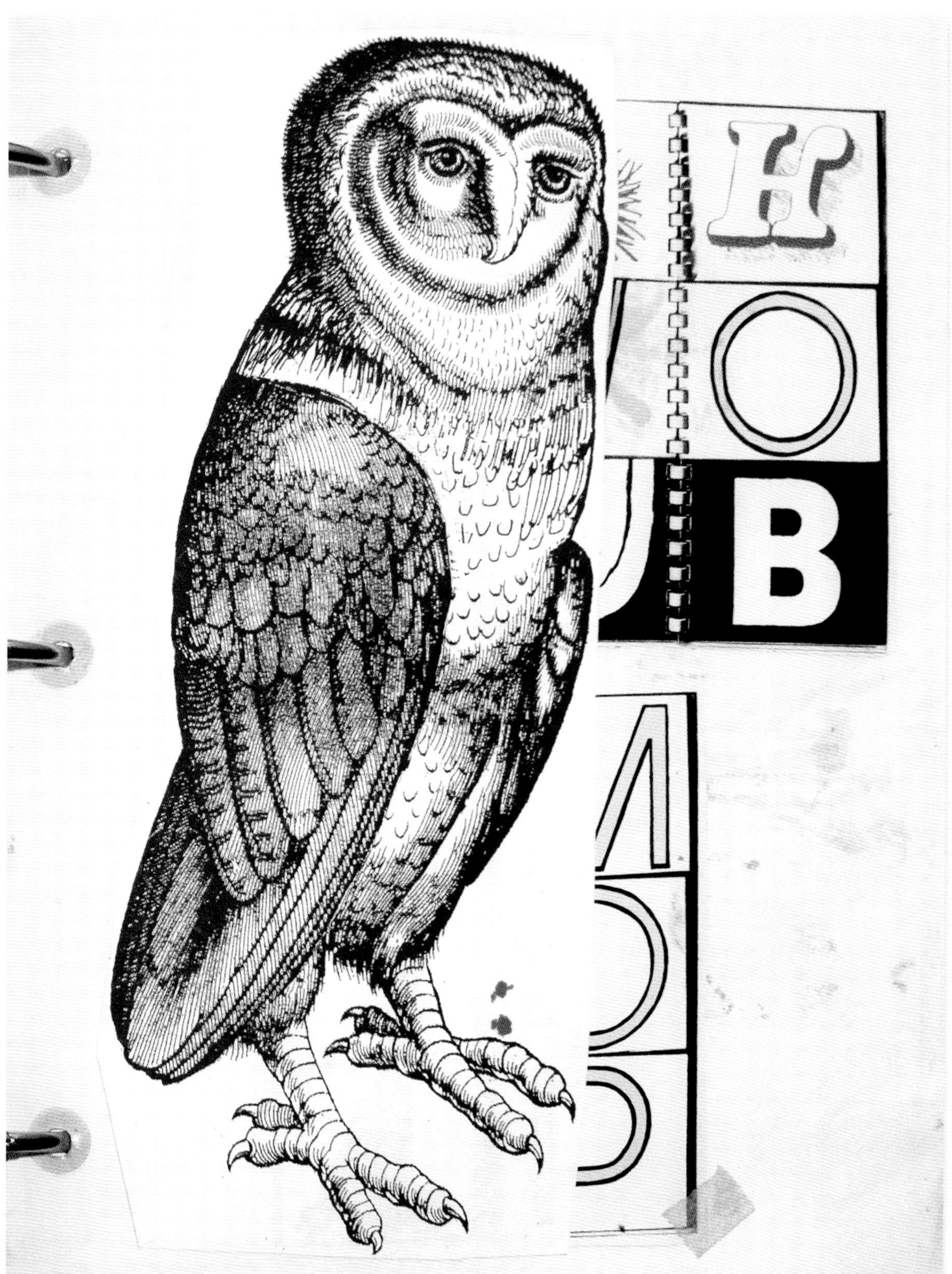

Pages from reference material project binders

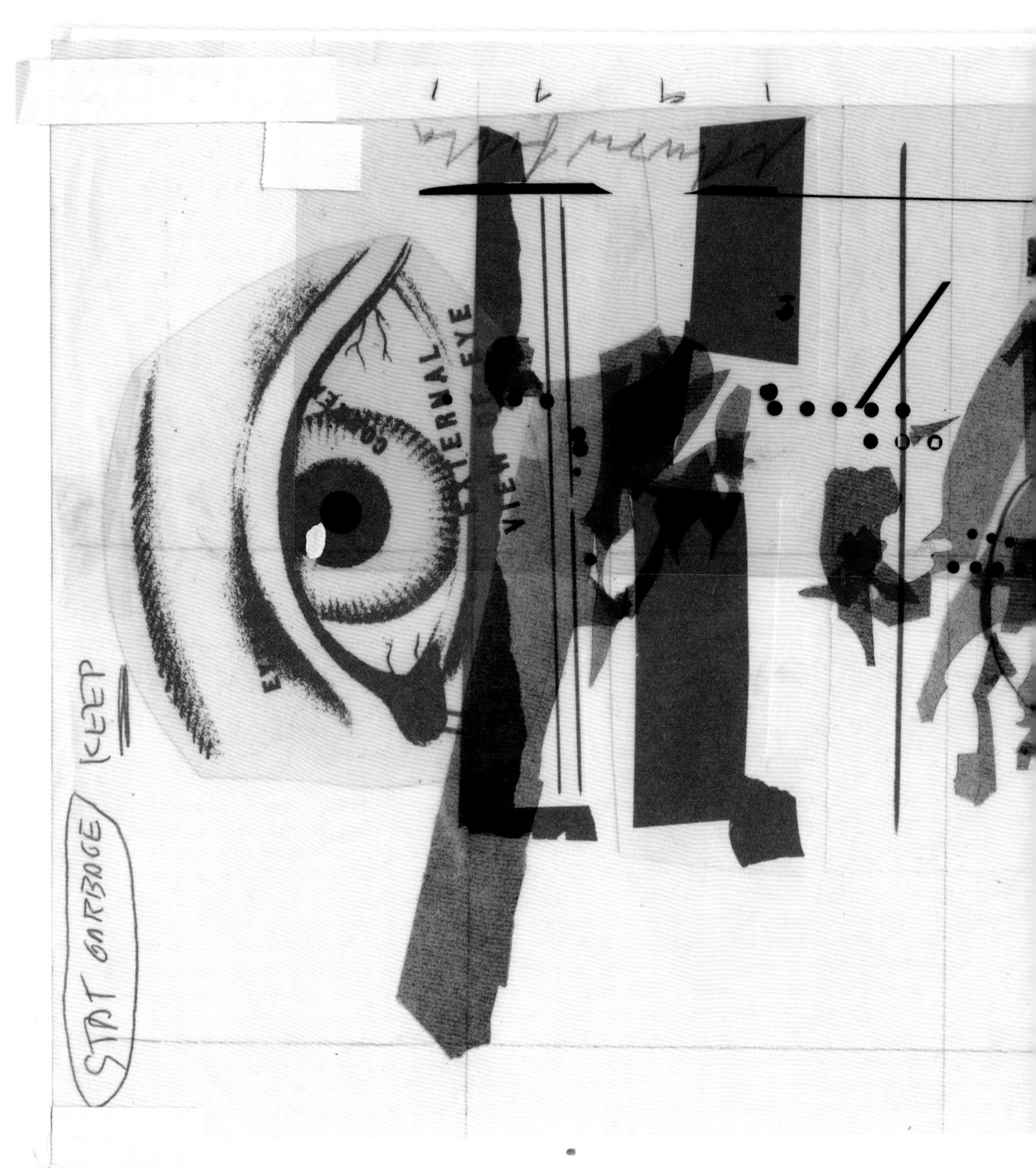
EXTERNAL EYE
VIEW OF
KEEP
STAT GARBAGE

THINGS I GOTTA DO
TODAY
DATE
1.
2.
3.
4.
5.
6.
7.
8.
9.
10.
11.
12.

PHOTO EXPERTS, INC.
NEW YORK, NY
1981
SINCE
NW
W
SW
NE
S
E
SE
8

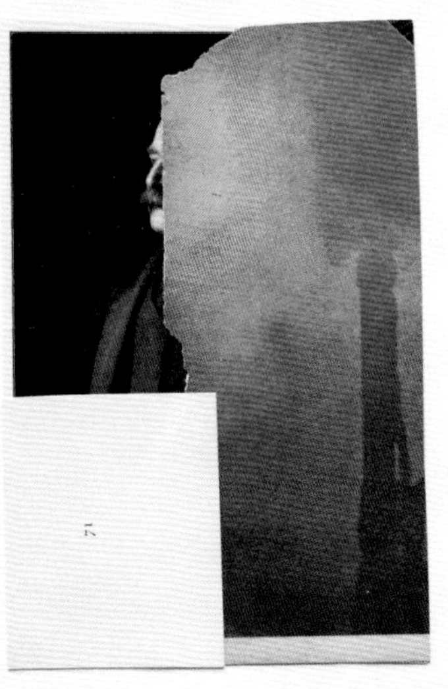

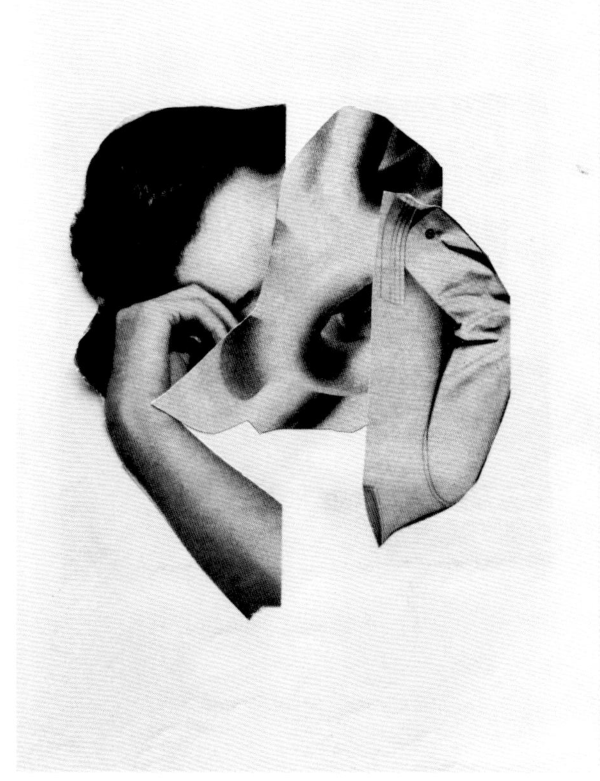

ELEMENTARY
GEOGRAPHY

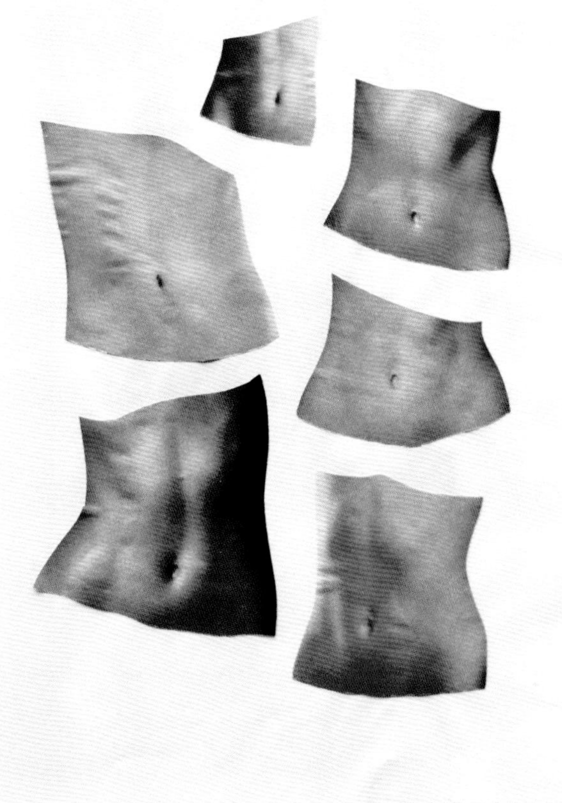

Digital collage

Digital concept collage for event

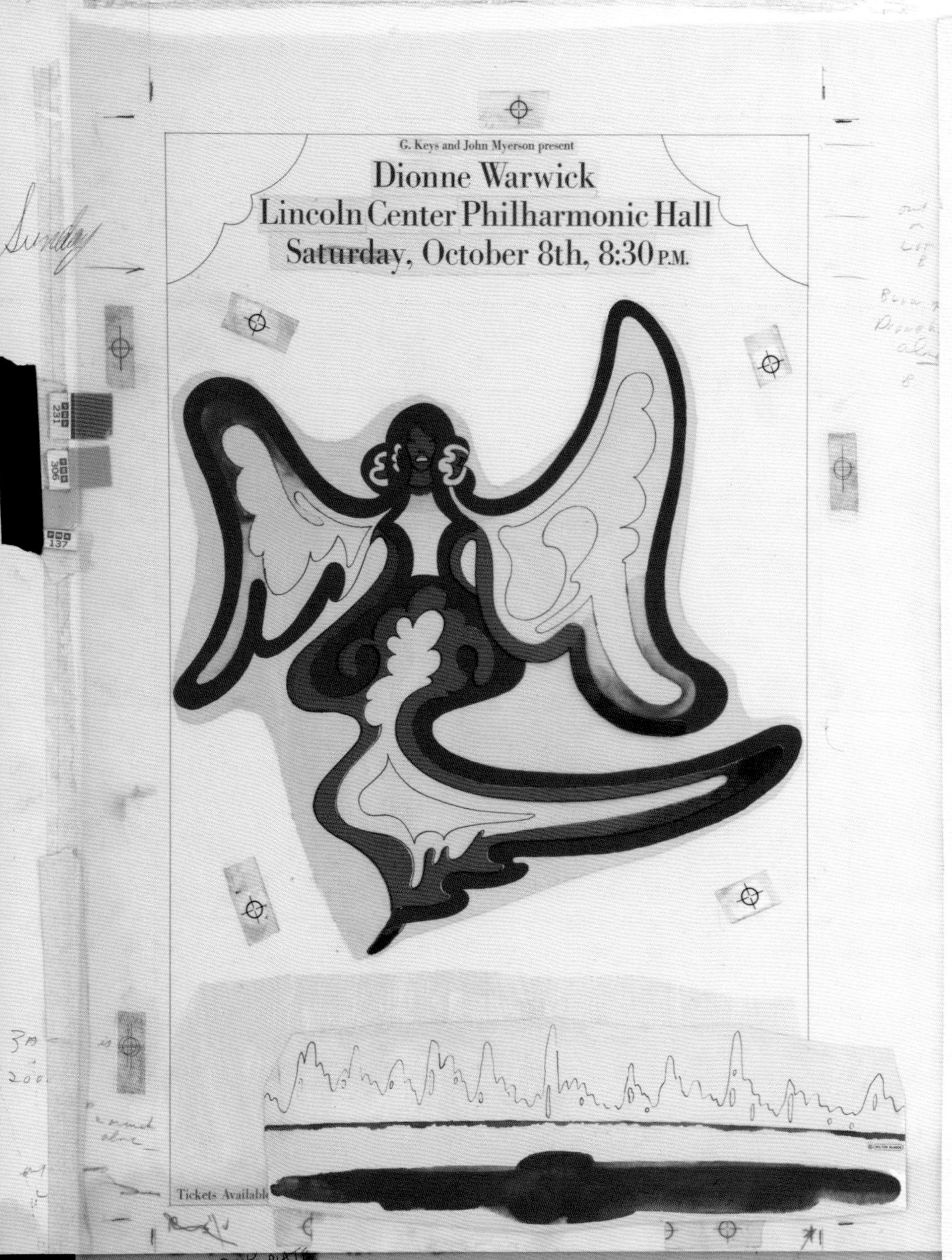
G. Keys and John Myerson present
Dionne Warwick
Lincoln Center Philharmonic Hall
Saturday, October 8th, 8:30 P.M.
Sunday
Tickets Available
PINK PLATE

Mechanical for Dionne Warwick at Lincoln Center poster, 1967

"Castro" Mechanical

C. San Antonio
I. OF PINES
Broa B.
Bahia Honda
HAVANA

Celebrate Columbus
1492-1992
F.P.O.
América hoy, 500 años después / America today, 500 years later / L'Amérique aujourd' hui, 500 ans plus tard
50% MECHANICAL
PANTONE® 449U
1,500 PIECES

50% MECHANICAL

1,500 PIECES

C·H· MUSEUM

9-10. David Farey's restoration of a little-known Cooper display type called Cooper Fullface has recently been released under the new name of ITC Ozwald. Cooper's intention was to create a modernised version of Bodoni by combining the face's sharp contrasts of line with the "free rendering of pen-drawn characters".
ABC
abcd
DEFG
efghij
HIJKL
klmnop
MNOPQRS
qrstuvwxyz
Nat

Signage study collage for Cooper Hewitt, Smithsonian Design Museum

Stephen Doyle

March 13, 2015

Pinnacle

What was the turning point, when I started to become me? I know exactly when it was. I was working here. I had a friend who was dying of AIDS and I was asked to do a poster. I thought, "Well, I'll do a poster to my friend Chris." So I took a glass and I put the word "live" on one side of it, and "a little" on the other side of it, and I poured some water in it and tried to photograph it beautifully, with light refraction or upside down just to see what the water would do to the type on the far side of the glass. And it wasn't very good at all but I sent it to myself first and him next. I said, "This is where I'm starting. I'm going to go from here. I'm going to get type off the page and I'm going to bring type to life. It's going to live in the same world as us and it's going to cast shadows and that's going to have more power." It was just this inkling that I had. I had tasted what happens when you don't do messages the way everyone else does them. It has led to this blossoming of being able to create images or messages. That's when my voice started. I love doing stuff for the Op-Ed page because the audience is huge and it makes you feel like you're part of the intellectual dialogue of the city, which is really fucking different from being a graphic designer who works in New York.

It's curious to call the stuff that I'm doing now graphic design because it's way off track from what I think other people are doing. I'm doing an awful lot of illustration and sculptures, but it's a sideline that reinforces the design. It's something that propels the design we do in a profoundly different way than how other people engage audiences, let's say.

The Nature of Design

Communicating something is what advertising does. Engaging is what a good designer can do, because it's about a dialogue rather than just sending an arrow with a message strapped to it—"Here's what I want you to know about my brand." The work that I'm trying to get better at doing is about trying to make something unforgettable and also letting it be a little ambiguous and a little bit crappy and a little bit handmade—a little bit made in the basement, as you see evidenced here. We're not making polished computer graphics because I don't think they have any soul. A little explosion of delight or wonder or mystery so that other people are intrigued or drawn in.

For me design is about seduction. People will argue that advertising does it too, but they're doing it with a very different goal. The projects that we work on are inevitably for the well-being of society and New York and mankind. We're committed to only selling good stuff, if what we're doing is selling. We're selling ideas, we're selling the debate in the *New York Times*—"Here's a point of view. It's worthwhile considering it."

Early Days

I don't want to start at Cooper Union because a lot of who you are comes from where you come from. Especially since I have grown kids now and have been able to observe the full process of raising somebody and sending them out and seeing that who they are is such a reflection.

My upbringing was very Catholic. I went to Jesuit school and the Jesuits are all about intellectual debate and questioning and your responsibility to society. Then I got another dose of that at Cooper with Milton Glaser who was so much about the ethics of design and the commitment of getting a full scholarship to Cooper Union—time to give something back. That's a really

Assemblage
Mechanical
Object
Work
Studio

powerful part of my whole educational experience. My dad was a psychologist. We didn't have any *Playboy* magazines around the house. I had to read Freud looking for stories about sexuality and, believe me, they're pretty fucked up, but that's where I got it. They were they only thing available to me.

The People

I'm such a mainstream guy. I think Michael [Bierut] is designing for people who are shopping at Prada and he's designing to seduce them. I'm designing to seduce the people on the street. When I won that AIGA medal they said, "Stephen's really the designer's designer." I'm so not. I'm a people's designer, not a designer's designer. I'm not doing stuff to win awards or get in annuals or be over anybody's head or aloof or elite. It's really more about grabbing somebody with an image or a package or environmental graphics, and putting some smiles on some regular people's faces. I'm very democratic but I don't want you to think I actually like people that much or anything.

Idea vs Form

It never occurred to me that idea and form are two different areas. For me they're really the same thing. A lot of the work we do is about tactility. It's about how badly these initial caps are carved that makes them more enchanting than a nice piece of type on the computer. So the form is the content in so many ways.

How Do You Know?

I would never work just for a client. Why get up that morning? We're working on titles for Stephen Colbert's show and we have this vastly different collection of approaches. We had no information about the show whatsoever, so, "What smells right? Which zone should we chase?" That was a really effective presentation. They were thrilled because they felt, "Oh, we could do this or we could that." It's not about one thing, because the content and the audience are so undefined. For us it's a question. How sophisticated, how playful, how funny, how late night? And how do you distinguish yourself from the competition?

The Process

It's not linear like people want it to be described. It's more organic. Everybody always wants to have the process explicated and it's fascinating to me because it's not like there's any secret that I'm hiding, but it's a real alchemy when you have a pile of books or a file on your computer and memories of something that you saw in Turkey on vacation or architecture in China or South Africa and then you go, "I'm going to take this and pair it with that one and it's aha!" I read this article yesterday and went out to get lunch and was walking along the street thinking, "How the fuck am I going to make automatic regulation be interesting to anybody?" Then just by thinking about it and not thinking about it, you surrender. You have to dive in the water and clear your mind and let something land. It lands, everybody goes "Yay!," and then you just make it. Am I being evasive? It's an evasive topic. What leads to eureka?

Subjectivity

I've got a son who studied engineering and in a rare moment of articulation, he said to me, "I don't know how you and mom can do what you do because you never know if it's right or wrong and the reason I like math and science is that I can prove that I'm right. With you guys, it's all feeling and instinct." And that's why I love it—because there aren't any rules. One of my best classes at Cooper was with Henry Wolf and Milton Glaser. They taught a course on magazine design and for three hours in front of the class they would just argue. It was so liberating to see that. Here are guys who are out there doing it professionally—Henry was *Harper's Bazaar* and *Show* and Milton was *New York*—and all they did was fight and it was like, "God, there are no rules! You can really take it as far as you can take it. This is a cool field of work."

Finding Your Voice

Before I had the eureka moment with Chris and the glass, another eureka moment was at Cooper. There were a bunch of kids who were "designer's designers." They dressed the thing, their desks were clean, they could draw perfectly with their Rapidographs with the straight edges and do all this stuff that was really impressive, stuff you were supposed to do. But I just didn't have the facility for straight lines. It's not my thing. I had to learn early on to embrace it, and then I was free to feel ok about not being the designer's designer. They all got jobs out of school like that [snap, snap] for CBS and Herb Lubalin and I was making my wiggly stuff and learning to trust my inner wiggle and let that become part of my walk. That was really important for me in terms of being where I am now, making rather strange stuff on the periphery of the profession.

Multidisciplinary

That's where those sculptures that I make come in. That's my form of meditation. Doing stuff that's not problem-solving. It was to get away from all this and curiously it's circled back into my work and led to this whole other, second line of being an image-maker for magazines. Funny, it's where I started out, so now I've got a foot in both camps and can do motion graphics for Amex and *Wired* at the same time that we're doing environmental graphics for Rockefeller Center. It's really fun to dabble in all these worlds at the same time.

The graduate class that I teach at SVA is called Commercial Art and I think that those are really good words for what you're talking about because it has to be commercially feasible, yet it has an aspect of art in it that is that special alchemy that actually makes it lift off. But you've got to lift off by a certain deadline and that's the yin and yang of what we're doing.

I never really do shit until the very end though. I'll clean my office for days before a project is due and the day before, I'll nail it. I'm ruminating. It's not like I'm not industrious, but I'm a real procrastinator. Maybe it's like getting your adrenaline together before you go on stage. I'm a real right-before-the-deadline-get-it-out guy.

I like dimension. I'm a builder. When we go on vacation I do little watercolors and stuff like that, but I'm not passionate about the two-dimensional form or as good as other people are. Because I can move around comfortably in any medium, I'm really not scared to make stuff. It's fun to watch these kids who work in the studio here who have grown up in a design world with computers. They'll watch me carve something or build that shirt out of paper and glue. To see these things puff into a three-dimensional existence and cast shadows is a real revelation for them. It's really a delight because our profession, in particular, lives on a screen. So when it gets off the desk and it's bigger than a drawing—not disparaging drawings, but it's a different thing because of the edges and the surface and the material—all of that endows it with a little more soul.

I lost fear early on in the non-digital world of experimenting and using different media to make things or to tell a story. I'm just telling stories.

Technology

The process and technology are so intertwined because I jump back and forth between this card and that computer and that's where the dialogue happens now—ricocheted between the computer and the camera and my hands over here. This desk is a mess because I build here. It's a studio—like those pictures of those guys who used to wear white lab coats over their jackets and ties.

I also like that I get away with being a crappy photographer and still turn this stuff into beautiful things thanks to new technology. And I've got a staff that's incredibly helpful doing that too. You've got smoother, slicker tools that you can use to make even the handmade stuff look rawer. You can use technology to unslick things as much as you can use it to slick things.

My sculpture is definitely a reaction to the computer. It's like the industrial revolution and the craftsman. People needed the reassurance of the handmade and the particular. When you can alter photography as easily as you can now—like the Israeli press taking women out of a march after Charlie Hebdo—people don't trust the medium. But if you put something here and it's casting a shadow, even if it's a picture that's still on your computer or you're reading the *The New Yorker* on your iPad, you trust that more than you trust pixels in planes and vector.

Signage is completely related to my three dimensional work. Like that glass prototype I showed you. Nobody's making glass numbers out there because why would they? It's so easy to make them in steel. Who's going to go get somebody to mold this address in glass? But it's gratifying because it's magical. For 300 Park Avenue South, we made the address out of 300 polished stainless-steel cubes glued onto the transom. That thinking comes out of the sculpture stuff that we're doing and you saw the pixels right there that we photographed in front of—taking the computer ideas off of the computer. It's a pixelated number, but it's a sculptural idea.

Doubt

Failure? Oh sure but I also have a lot of people around me to check in with and see if I'm going too far or not far enough, including my wife and my partner Tom and the studio. I often ask people if I'm losing it. I don't know what to say about failure because we don't fail at what we do, we fail at getting the stuff that we don't do. We fail when Pentagram gets the project instead of us—that's my failure. Maybe it's deserved. I only have the capacities that I do. I can't do the big brand talk or give a lecture about brand architecture and stuff like that, and maybe I lucked out because I don't do that, and maybe I get to work with the clients I deserve and not the ones I don't deserve. I don't know.

It's interesting how being able to go home and make sculptures and meditate assuages a lot of my feelings of inadequacy or vulnerability because it confirms for me that I have a certain kind of power that is unique to me and that people are responsive to these things is really wonderful. Who knew that people would validate my little chance at getting away from solving problems? It feels really good to make it and it feels really good to sell it. I didn't expect the sculpture to come back and infiltrate what I do here as much as it does, but it really does. It's really a full circle.

The Culture

The people who are really impacting the culture are those who are putting up all the crappy buildings on Sixth Avenue and the towering, sparkly new skyscrapers along Fifty-Seventh Street. They're the ones who are really changing the face of the city and contributing to the enormous amout of mediocrity that's shaping our culture.

I think most designers are working from the other end and we're trying to have more control and say in the culture, but how effective is it really? We're kidding ourselves if we don't admit that we're working on the fringes.

Gratification

The most gratifying part of a project is when the checks come in! I'm just doing it for the money.

I'm actually thrilled every time I make something and it feels new to me. It's validation that I'm still alive, that I'm able to make a thing—maybe even an artifact. It's why I'm not an accountant—that, and I'm bad with numbers.

The making makes me feel alive and powerful. When my kids come by asking what I'm doing when I'm working on a sculpture I can't really answer them because I don't really know. Everything starts as a question. It's hard work to get from here to there and to pull it off because you don't know if it's going to work until you do it.

Most work is an experiment until you get to the other end of it, but that's when the craftsmanship comes in and that's why going to the Armory Show can be so disappointing because there are lots of questions that are started, but there's not the commitment of the craftsmanship to see it through. This year, the craftsmanship was much better and it was much more fulfilling as a show, but still there's stuff that seems rather lazy. Sometimes there's stuff where the craftsmanship is perfect and you're just knocked away by the sheer scale and commitment of something. Some of my sculptures are like that.

Alchemy

Knowing what to do when—and understanding the context of the work we're making is all instinct and experimentation and practice. If I do something where I think the form is right and the color is right—color is really important to me—and you show it to the client and they go, "Oh," you've obviously missed or you've got the wrong client. My clients don't say, "Oh," they say, "Oh my god." So why is it right? I don't know. I can't prove it until I try it out on people and when they react positively in numbers, then you know you're onto something. Best is if they laugh. If they laugh then you know you're right.

Color is also a huge part of my toolbox—my vocabulary, my way of communicating, my way of making people like me. It's another thing that can't be defined. It's got it's own alchemy too and people have different takes on it and I think that people see color completely differently from one another. I don't think there's a standard. I think that it's a really powerful communicator. I think there's something synesthetic about color that makes people feel a certain way or associate with certain things or adds comfort or discomfort.

It's certainly finessed, but I don't know if it can be learned or taught. And I don't know if it's a sensibility or an intelligence. Being good with numbers is an intelligence, right? People are good with numbers. Is being good with color an intelligence, likewise?

I think that my travels throughout Europe had an awful lot of effect on my color sensibility. Getting things to be grayer and quieter like the painted houses in Salzburg, or Italy, or look at this carving of a squid here. Look at those colors, look how gray they are, how beautifully they go together. Americans don't have enough gray in their paint.

Words

One of my favorite hobbies is language. Being able to try to speak other languages in other places changes your sensibility. It's really frustrating, for instance, to not be able to be funny in French or German or Italian because my language is not that good, but it really changes everything. So that's why a lot of my work is about language and that's why it's dimensional, that's why it casts a shadow, to validate the power of words. I used to be into typography, but I was mistaken. It was language I was interested in. It's the words, not the letterforms.

Bob Gill

November 12, 2014

The Process

The process is very simple.

The culture is so pervasive that it's nearly impossible to free yourself from its dictatorship—which tells you how to make every single decision. If you're going to do something original, going to try to have an idea that nobody has ever seen before, how can you do that if the culture tells you what's good and what's bad?

Say you get a logo for a dry cleaner—a typical dopey design job—what's the answer? The answer is, you can't sit at your computer because the computer is going to belch out what the culture has already put in people's minds. You can't look in a library of design books because they already exist—they're not original. So what's the answer? It's obvious! You go to a dry cleaner and you sit there. I have no idea what you do there except I know you must go to the dry cleaner. You sit there and you watch what's going on, you listen to customers talk to the guy at the counter, you go in the back to look at the machinery, and so on.

You cannot think of an image because everything in your head was put there by *Seinfeld* or *Vogue* or whatever. So when you're at the dry cleaner what you have to do is make a statement, one that you honestly feel is interesting. If you know it's interesting and you listen to the statement, it designs itself. It's outside of the culture because you're looking and you're having a new experience. Even if you think you knew what dry cleaning was about before, you now have a new experience. It's so simple.

This is the process I go through in order to get an idea, because I get one for every job I do.

The Culture

When I talk about having a statement or idea, I'm not advocating that it shouldn't be nice looking—whatever that means. Of course the culture tells us what's nice looking and the culture is important. It gives us something in common, otherwise we're all strangers to each other. So I'm not saying we shouldn't observe, and be part of the culture, but the fun is to use and make images only after we've listened to the idea.

Early Days

I went to school in 1948, which was a long time ago. At that time we were taught what "good design" was. Good design was a particular layout with white space—a tasty photograph—et cetera. When I graduated, I needed a letterhead because I started to freelance. So what's good design? Flush left and right typography? A miracle happened—I had:

BOB
GILL
47W
48ST
NYC
PL7
6136

I had the "best designed" letterhead. It was all flush left and right in the upper left corner. I twisted the type so it all aligned. What a dopey letterhead that was! But it was also inevitable—it designed itself.

Then I noticed Doyle Dane Bernbach, the advertising agency who did the Volkswagen ads. They didn't know what good design was but they knew they wanted to say something about the Volkswagen that was interesting. Their process seemed to come naturally—like it did for me. Look at the "Think Small" advertisement—it's so obvious. This way of thinking is not the province of advertising alone. We all have the same problem, which is that we want someone to look at what we do and have him or her think, "Wow!" Advertising people don't have a unique problem. Every job we do is really an "ad" of one kind of another.

It was at this point, still fresh out of school, that I realized that I didn't just want to make good design. I wanted to make statements, which you could also call ideas. Obviously I want to make it as interesting and nice looking as possible, but never at the expense of the idea. If the statement isn't interesting, the visualization isn't going to be interesting either. But if the statement is genuinely interesting, you can't miss—it designs itself.

So for me, my evolution as a designer happened only once—six months after I graduated art school in 1951. I've been doing the same thing ever since. It has never changed. You can look at any of the nearly one hundred logos I've designed, and something I did in 1960 is no different than what I did yesterday—they're both executed at the highest level. My education at the Philadelphia Museum School was perfectly acceptable, and it taught principles of good taste and so forth—but it was only half.

"Noise"

I once found myself in Ulm in the 1960s—which was the new Ulm, having been thrown out of Germany when the Bauhaus started and all that. I walked through the park and there was a design student from Ulm with a pad. He had made a grid of boxes, which corresponded to the lines on the pavement.

In the grid there were a bunch of dots and he explained that he was charting the pigeons. Of course the pigeons are too dumb to know about grids so they land anywhere they feel like. The dots didn't correspond, they made no sense at all, except they were very interesting because of the sheer variety—one dot was close to another and another was very far away. It was very interesting and actually appeared in one of my books. I call it a "non-grid" because, while I'm not saying that's the way you should always work, once in a while it's fun for it to not conform to some neat scheme.

While I was there I went to see the director of the Ulm School of Design school who was a South American architect. He looked at my portfolio (here we are the hottest designers in Europe), which I had because I was visiting a client, and he said, "Ugh, this is awful!" I said, "What!? Isn't this exciting?! No one ever told me I was terrible!" First he said, "You have drawings in here. Drawings are old fashioned—they're not twentieth century." Then he said, "Also, there are three ways of doing a poster. The first is called 'Image.'" We all know what that means. If it's a poster about the life of Winston Churchill, the image is Winston Churchill and it communicates perfectly. Then he says, "The second way is 'Icon.'" And what's an icon? It's a symbol. Well, what's a symbol for Winston Churchill? A cigar or a Union Jack. Then he says, "The third is 'Noise.'" I said, "What's noise?" and he pulled out a portfolio of posters by Otl Aicher—who did a monthly poster for a kiosk in town about what was going on at the university—and shows me one that was about evolution or something. It was a blue background with pink dots and the director says, "This is noise." And I said, "How do you evaluate it?" He said, "If it makes people look at the poster, why not?"

So when I went back to London, I said to myself, "I'm going to make 'Noise.'" So the next job came in and I said, "Ah! I'm going to use a green triangle with red lines going through it." Which of course had nothing to do with the subject of the poster. And then I said to myself, "Should it be a green triangle, or a purple triangle, or a yellow triangle?" I didn't have the confidence that Aicher had for choosing a green or yellow triangle. I tried a bunch of colors and triangles but in the end I couldn't make up my mind and I couldn't do "Noise." But it's a perfectly valid solution. So not only am I not condemning designers for not having an idea but I'm not even condemning them for making purposeless blue triangles. It all makes the world more interesting but for me—I'm not capable of making "Noise."

Robert Brownjohn

He also knew how to have an idea—he really did. He used to call himself the "Second Best Designer in New York." Brownjohn, Chermayeff, and Geismar was the hottest thing in America while Fletcher, Forbes, Gill was the hottest design office in Europe. But he became so addicted to drugs and alcohol that Ivan [Chermayeff] and Tom [Geismar] threw him out—and rightfully so.

But he was also an absolutely brilliant, fearless man.

Let me tell you about a commercial he did—maybe the best ever: The screen is black, and the door opens and there is a sliver of yellow light coming from the other room. The door opens a little more and the most beautiful six-year-old, blond English girl walks into this room. As she comes in the light fills the room so you can see it's very brown, leather—it's obviously daddy's studio or office. She walks over and sits at daddy's desk, and you can barely see her because she's so small. She opens the drawer and takes out a pack of cigarettes and she takes a cigarette out and puts it in her mouth—this six-year-old beauty—and lights it and starts smoking. And this is all in silence. A voice, in the last five seconds of a thirty-second spot, says, "Now don't you feel stupid that your kids are seeing you with this disgusting habit." And you know what, they never produced it. It wasn't allowed on TV. It was too strong. It was too good. That was Brownjohn.

Career

For more than fifty years I've talked about how to get an idea and for fifty years people nod, they say, "You've changed my life," they say, "Isn't this amazing!" but they can't do it—they just don't get it even when they think they're doing it. It's the tyranny of the "good design culture" that keeps people from getting "it"—from being able to have a great idea.

Chermayeff & Geismar

May 22, 2015

Ivan Chermayeff and Tom Geismar

Where To Start

I/ We spend a fair amount of time finding out who our clients are and what they want, which sometimes may not be what they need, and that means we have a bigger job. Most of the time people come to us because they have some recognition of what has worked and they see our track record, but that's not the way it necessarily started in terms of the design process.

We need to know a great deal if we're working with a corporation. We like to talk to the people who have the responsibility for doing it—not necessarily the man who owns it or is at the top of the pile—to really understand who their audience is, and who they want their audience to be, which is not necessarily the same. All of these things have a certain amount of variable in them. We, unlike most people in the field, cooperate and don't divide up into teams. We are all involved with everything that comes into the office. We develop a lot of alternatives and talk about them and narrow them down but rarely do we feel that there is one answer to the problem. This is something we haven't encountered in recent memory because our clients are usually too complicated for that. Then we argue with each other and winnow down a lot of ideas into a small number, half a dozen at the most, three is better. If asked, we tell our clients what we think is the best of what we're showing them.

T/ In spite of what Ivan says, the thing that's always amazing to me is that we are so different in terms of process. Ivan usually has a solution very quickly, whereas I want to stew and go through lots of things and have a lot of time. We'll come out in a similar place in the end, but Ivan's too impatient to do that.

The Office

T/ It's always been a very open, non-hierarchical office and we've also had many partners. Our office was much bigger for many years and we were doing different kinds of projects, which we don't do now. We purposefully decided to concentrate more. But I think the character of the office has been pretty much the same. When we were bigger, we had more separate projects that we were working on, whereas now we're all pretty much working for one.

Assemblag
Mechanical
Bo
Gi
Object
Work
Studio
Pleas
Mak
Thi
Loo
Nic

Home Away From Home

T/ The thing that I need, which is very hard to find, is peace and quiet. These days I can get much more work done at home than I can here, in terms of designing. From about 1960 to the early 1980s our offices were in what was then the Girl Scouts of America Building at 830 Third Avenue and Fifty-First Street—on the second floor. During that time I used to occasionally rent a room around the corner at the Summit Hotel and spend two or three days working there because it gave me the time to actually concentrate on the thing and do it, which I could never do in the office. I would take the cheapest room available, as long as it had a desk, and I never stayed overnight.

The hotel was actually designed by Morris Lapidus, the famous architect of Miami Beach hotels including The Fontainbleau. If I recall, the Summit was mostly green and had a bit of that Miami look which made it a fish-out-of-water in the midst of New York City. Anyway, that's just me. I can't have music. I don't want any distractions. No kids, no nothing.

Technology

T/ I know that both of us believe strongly that drawing is really key. It's the language that we use. All of us always start out drawing. Once you have it, it quickly gets into the computer, but drawing is the shared language.

I/ I carry that to extremes by not touching any buttons. All I have are jars and jars of different weights of pencils and those "peelies" because their colors are strong. I don't even have a cell phone. Not because I want peace and quiet. I just don't like being the most incompetent person pressing buttons in the office. Young people are brought up that way. You can ask them something and you don't have to wait for the answer, and that's very efficient. Otherwise, pencils are fun.

T/ I actually use a computer all the time. I like to do that myself because Ivan is relying on the staff. Then he looks at it, it gets changed, and whatever comes out in the wash. It's just a different way of working.

Popular Opinion

T/ Knowing the audience is part of our research. We use our own sense by looking around and we ask also. It's not such a mystery. For the people we deal with, it's pretty clear and you don't get too involved with it. Up to a point you want to understand it, but that's it. We absolutely don't believe in focus groups, or any of that stuff. We've never found that helpful in any way because you're just getting people's opinions because they're forced to give an opinion on something.

I/ We like to know what the hell our clients are about. We like to get a big box of everything—all the pieces of paper and all the photographs and whatever it may be and find out who in their company we can go and talk to. We don't have any big attitudes about it until we have at least a feeling about where they want to go. Having built the company, the chief executives or whoever are usually pretty smart. We spend a lot of time listening, but not necessarily believing everything we hear as the absolute truth. After all, if they knew and were unprejudiced, they would do the jobs themselves and not hire anyone to help. I actually think this is why most things are crap—because they actually believe that they can do it themselves and that because they have an opinion and can get something put in front of them to which they say, "Ok, let's do that." That ability doesn't make for quality or growth or flexibility, which all may be required for the project.

Early Days

T/ I think everyone is really molded by their schooling and when they've come of age. When we first started, I think there were only three schools in the country that taught something called "graphic design." I was at the Rhode Island School of Design and there was no course in graphic design, only "advertising art," that was the closest thing. There was something in the wind about ideas because up to that time, other than the few practitioners like Paul Rand and Lester Beele, there were all these illustrators who did illustrations for the ladies magazines. It was all technique and style. For us and Alan Fletcher, with whom we were very friendly, it was much more about finding ideas and being open about how it looked. Take whatever is out there in the world to get across an idea. I think that has stayed with us.

I/ When we started, that was only the second year that Yale had the program because Alvin Eisenman, who was the head of that program, was interested in the whole subject. He would ask people who were really good like Lester Beele if they'd mind coming up to the school for a few days and talking to the students. There were only twelve of us in the class and nobody says no to Yale, so we had very good people who were coming in and out on a constant basis, which made it a very good place to go to school because you heard different voices—from Herbert Matter to Paul Rand.

T/ I think that we especially picked up a lot of the modernist and the European stuff. We certainly saw what was going on, but without all the theoretical backing and seriousness of it. I think that was an American thing. We always thought of the work we did as very American. We tried to have fun—we liked to do things that had a sense of humor and other kinds of things that I don't think you'd find in traditional Swiss work.

The Client

I/ In the early 1960s we did Chase and I think the only reason our work was approved was because it was given to David Rockefeller who was on the board at MoMA and he had an interest in art. Someone at Chase said, "David, you look after this thing," since he was familiar with modern art, modern communications, and that made a difference because people in that kind of position are often very conservative. It takes somebody with some power and guts to do things in a newer, simpler way and it worked out to our benefit, and theirs.

T/ It's a little fuzzy after all these years, but he [David Rockefeller] was very involved. The story we always tell is that there was the president and chairman, both of whom were above him. The president said, "Why can't it be a picture of our building?" The chairman said, "David, you make this decision, but let me tell you, I don't want to see it in my office. I don't want to see it on my letterhead. I don't want to see it. It doesn't mean anything to me." And six months later we ran into the chairman in the hallway wearing a tie with the Chase pattern on it, a Chase pin on his lapel, and the Chase cufflinks.

Influence

T/ I think something we've always said is that the whole world out there is important to us in terms of what we do here. We're very aware of books and film, and certainly what's going on in the world is very important.

I/ What I do is make collages and I can make collages because I find new connections between garbage. I pick up gloves because men drop one. They lose one and they throw the other away. At work sites, they're always flattened by trucks. Women drop pairs as they get out of taxis. Men's gloves are one of a kind. The hand is expressive without a hand in it so that's why I like that kind of thing. But I just like finding connections and collaging. I can do things very rapidly without interfering with the responsibility that I might have. I can do it between telephone calls. I end up looking at my collages, which start to pile up, and throw quite a few away, which nobody knows because I just tear them up and throw them in the wastebasket.

The best thing, in a way, is making new connections between things that are completely different. It means there are certain things that are portable and joinable. In my office I have two bags of pebbles because I walk on the beach. I always look for round pebbles that don't exist, because it's against nature to end up as a sphere. You might find a round flat one, but you'll never find a sphere. And that's interesting to look for. Making new connections is a big part of it.

Robert Brownjohn

I/ That poster over there, which was done by our partner when we started out—Robert Brownjohn—that's a remarkable poster he made in about thirty seconds. It's the ace of spades and it's spelled A-C-E and it's the last three letters of the word "peace," or isn't it? With the question mark, is it about war or peace or what? And after all that he signs it, "Love, BJ." That's not the normal way of signing a poster. So he's got the whole thing about connections and language, all done there in less than a minute.

T/ And as far as we know it was the last thing he did before he died, sort of mysteriously. That's the whole thing about ideas and that's what he was all about.

I/ He would put things together in odd ways too. He was an original guy. He was really quite an incisive character. Very funny and extremely smart and a heroin addict, which is not a good combination.

I'll tell you another thing about him because his name doesn't come up all the time since he's been gone since the 1960s. We were at a crosswalk and a cab comes and stops at the stoplight right in the middle of the crosswalk, almost straddling it, and there's an old couple sitting in the back of the cab.

T/ This is one of those old checker cabs with the big backseats—not like the cabs today.

I/ Right, and BJ starts walking across the crosswalk. He opens the door and crawls in, right over these two old people. He reaches over the woman and opens the door on the other side, gets out on the other side, and continues on his way. There are very few people you'll ever meet who would actually do that—but he was that kind of guy.

James Victore

December 11, 2014

Early Days

In coming to New York, I thought I was going to have a career like Tomi Ungerer—making graphic images, being a poster designer. I wanted to do what Ungerer and Milton Glaser and those guys did—and then the industry changed. Today there are very few people who have that level of talent who are allowed to make work at a very high level of creativity and enjoy the reward. Stefan Sagmeister has a little bit of it. I think Paul Sahre is a genius, and his work is so smart, but there's no fucking reward there. The really big paying jobs aren't coming to somebody like him, which is crazy. It's really hard to have a commercially viable gig and also be yourself.

Turning Point

When I was working with Paul Bacon, I was a book jacket designer. I was doing illustrated paintings. I'd stay up all night doing a painting of a church for a mystery novel. At the time, Paul was doing all of James Clavell and Robert Ludlum's covers. He was doing *The Bourne Identity* series—the original hardcovers. There was one that got sent back from Simon and Schuster, and the editor said the reason was the Ludlum thing was the big book look. So "Robert Ludlum" was the top third of the book. "The Bourne Identity" was the lower third of the book. Top half and bottom half, just massive words. In the middle would be a little symbol, a single little circle drawing about two inches wide. Paul did the drawing with gouache with this exquisite little brush. He made this beautiful image of a guy with a gun running across the White House lawn with helicopters. This big [holding thumb and pointer finger less than an inch apart] and it was exquisite. They sent it back and they said, "Paul, in the book the guy has a carbine and you've painted in a machine gun." I listened to that conversation and I said, "Okay, from this point on, I am an abstract expressionist. I'm never going to have that fucking conversation with anybody."

I switched my gears then, which gave me a lot of freedom. It gave me a lot of freedom to play. Even in the iterations, I don't like to work. I don't want it to feel like work.

What I'm trying to do—almost always—is something that I enjoy, make it look fresh, and also come at it from a place that hopefully nobody else would come at it from.

I always say there are jobs you do for God and there are jobs you do for money. I approach everything as an opportunity to do great work but when it starts being a money job, then I get it done. Get paid.

Making Work

These days I don't do as many iterations physically, because you do something long enough, you get good at it. There's so much of it that just happens in my head, that doesn't come out on paper. Or it's literally a sketchbook full of words, explaining to myself what it means.

One of the things I learned from Pierre Bernard and the Grapus guys a bunch of years ago—I asked him, "When you're doing your lettering, do you write it fifty times and then cut? Take the 'E' from here and put it here and fix it up?" He said, "No, we usually do it about two or three times, and we always choose the first." I know that's a lie, but it's a lie to illustrate the truth. And the truth is, the first one is always best because you're not thinking about it. If you start thinking about it too much, it just becomes a mess.

I've always said that going right to the computer is like going straight to C from A. Hand-eye coordination and teaching your hand is an extremely important part of what we do. People usually skip that part and go straight to the next step. I know that there are mistakes that happen on the computer, but not like what you get with a pen or a brush or scissors.

I don't really set-up parameters—in fact it might be the opposite. Instead of setting parameters, I open the work up to chance and mistakes, but I don't want to call them mistakes because they're beautiful—all the little hairy bits, all the splatters, and all the stuff. I am very open to seeing what can happen. Even if I use paint pens, markers, I go in with a blade and I cut up the tip so that it has almost an arthritic tip because I want to be open to it. I'm really not searching for perfection.

A bunch of years ago I used to hang out with Michael Kaye, who was a good pal of mine. We were both in the book jacket business. I went to his studio one night when he was at FSG [Farrar, Straus and Giroux]. I'm looking at his work on screen, and he hits F7, which then was "show guides" and I'm like, "Whoa! Did you purposefully put in all those guides?" He said, "Yeah, I have to know. I have to see the grid. I really have to understand." For me, the only grid I ever used was a quarter-inch margin all around. But we both ended up in the same place. We just did it differently.

On Perfection

The designer Henryk Tomaszewski would spend hours arranging and cutting and juggling on a page, to make it feel like it was just born there. You look at his work and wow. You can look at these pieces today, and they're timeless, completely appropriate today. But I know that it took a lot of work to make that.

On the other hand you have Massimo Vignelli who was all about perfection, "This is perfect, that isn't." I can't believe how people get all wet in the pants for his shit since perfect assumes a number of things. It assumes that you are right, that you have the answer, and that you're smarter than your audience because you have the rules. This is Massimo's work since it leaves no room for the audience to be involved. It's empirical.

I'm much more of the bloody, hairy Grapus-ian, Tomaszewski, Ungerer school. Where there's a level of humanity, not business. With that said, someday I will be 90 years old—it'll happen—and I hope I won't be like two of my heroes—Sam Peckinpah and A. M. Cassandre, who both died penniless.

Technology

People say they have a love-hate relationship with technology. I definitely do. I really don't trust it. Stephen Hawking came out and said recently that AI is going to be a major threat to human existence. That's fucking *Terminator* shit he's talking about—Skynet and consciousness. He got a new voice recognition system, and it is so much better at picking the words that he would say—it picks his words for him.

I did a talk recently with Bonnie Siegler and Ellen Lupton. They asked me to pick a project and show and talk about it. So I picked this project that was done for Mudac in Switzerland—an exhibition that we did all the stuff for—banners outside, posters, catalog. It was big Swiss-style silkscreen in fluorescent orange and black so you could see where the black went over and where the white showed through. I started the talk and I was showing the poster and I said, "Listen, technology sucks, because this poster, there's a pentimento, there's a feeling." And someone said, "Aw, technology doesn't suck!" And I'm like, "No, technology sucks because this, in real life, has an otherness to it, a beauty to it that you can't see. It's fluorescent orange, which you can't see on your fucking screen."

I'm not satisfied looking at stuff on a screen. I don't understand the headlong diving into the Kindle or whatever. I don't think it's because I'm 50. I think it's because I love what we do and I love touching things and using my hands. I also don't believe in having all of our eggs in one basket—and not a sturdy basket at that.

Gratification

Laura [Victore] and I took a Zen archery course a bunch of years ago with a master. In Zen archery, it's all [exhale]. It's all large beautiful sweeping movements you make with the bow. And hitting the target? Who the fuck cares? That's not important. That informs my work—it informs everything I do.

I never cared about the reward. I never cared about the target. I didn't do things for money. I turned Pentagram down twice. I made decisions because I wanted a life, and I wanted to make and have choices in my life.

It's not just about the work. It's a life thing. That's how it manifests itself in my work and life. I've said a million times, I'd rather die with the reputation I have now than fifty bucks more in my pocket.

Habit

I've always had a live-work situation with every studio I've had. For me it's terribly important, because first thing in the morning, before I actually start working, the table is a mess and things are all over the place and there are some clothes left from dragging myself home last night. I have to clear all that. All the jobs that I'm going to be working on today go in neat little piles, and I will put all the other stuff away. That is clearing my head. I'll push it all aside and concentrate.

I'm a huge list guy, and I actually save them all. That makes me happy—crossing shit out. I would put "take a dump" and "brush my teeth" just so I could cross them off. I learned when I was a kid that a good day starts the night before. So I always make a list before I go to bed.

I also like to be in the studio by myself. I'll have Merle Haggard going, and I will just whip things up. I go and go and go and go. I'll have a glass of wine and put that in the mix. I'm just trying to figure out how I can really tap into something human—simple marks on a page like that bass string that really reverberates inside somebody? I believe in that. That's why I think the computer is a lousy date.

Sign-off

I hope you got good stuff from me. I hope you're getting the stuff you want from other people. I hope they're being as honest and forthcoming as I tried to be.

I know that there are successful design studios that are basically run by MBAs who figure the business out. They add this "pentimento" of color and typography on top of their work and they can all rot in hell.

Objec
ts
Work
s
Studi
os

The space a designer works in, along with the objects, tools, and finished work they collect and display, are perhaps the most personal aspects of the process. Althought often of little worth, the true value of these materials is measured by total environment they create.

Plaster sculpture for a *New York Times* illustration

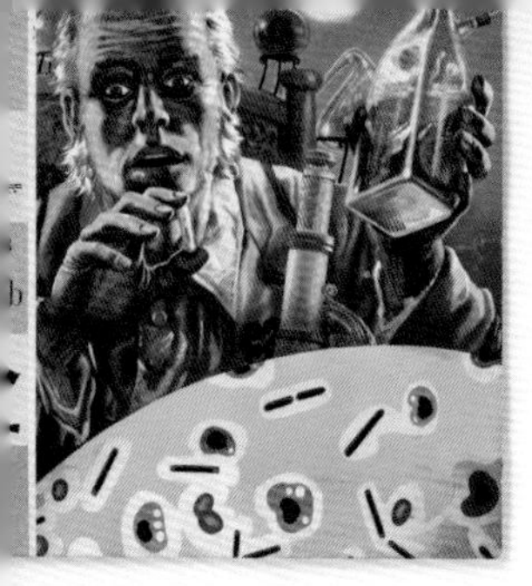

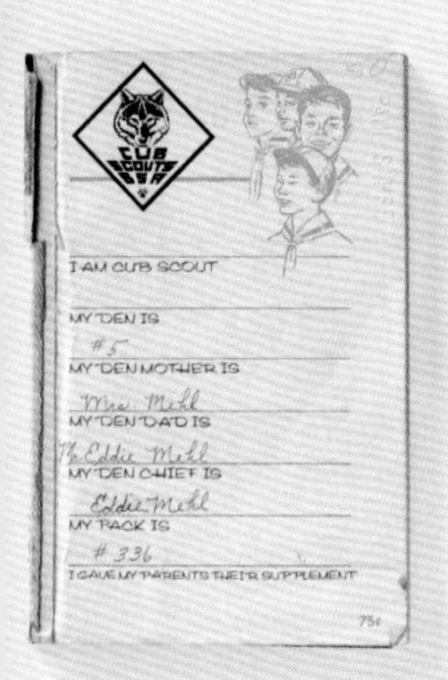

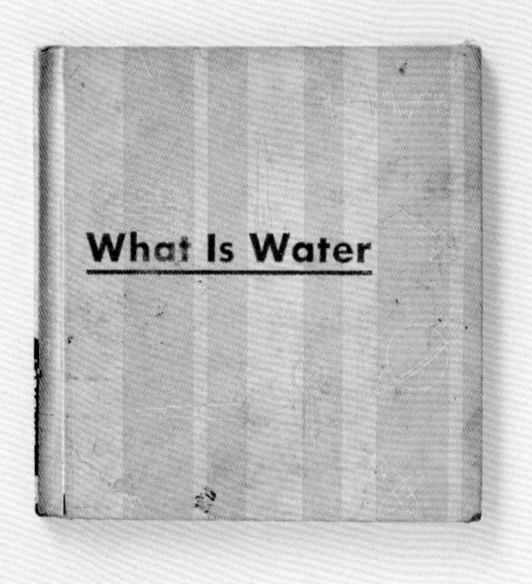

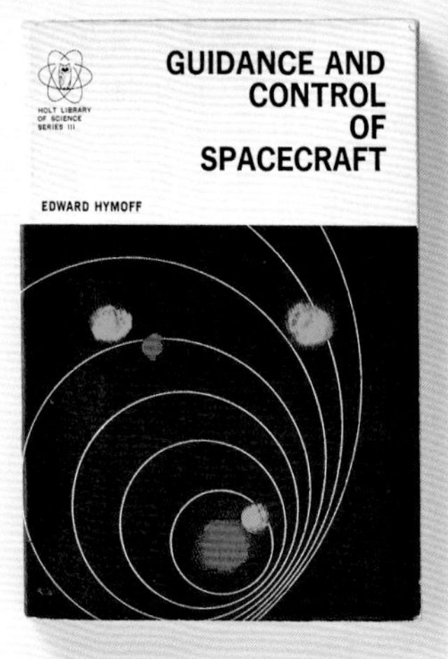

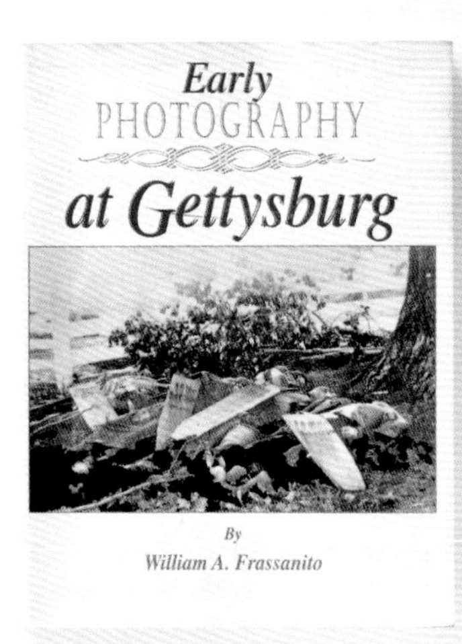

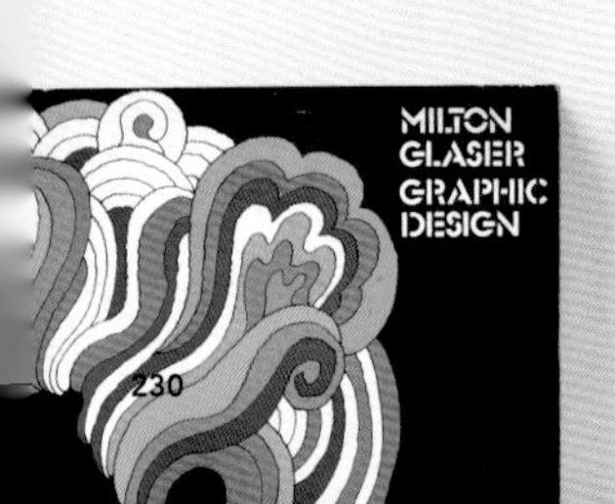

Books from studio library

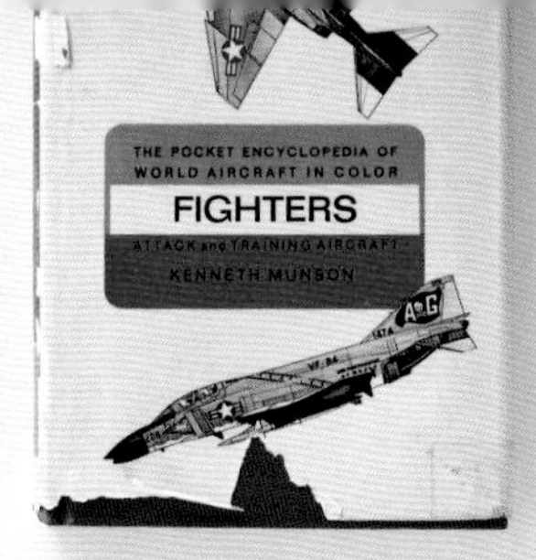
THE POCKET ENCYCLOPEDIA OF WORLD AIRCRAFT IN COLOR
FIGHTERS
ATTACK and TRAINING AIRCRAFT
KENNETH MUNSON
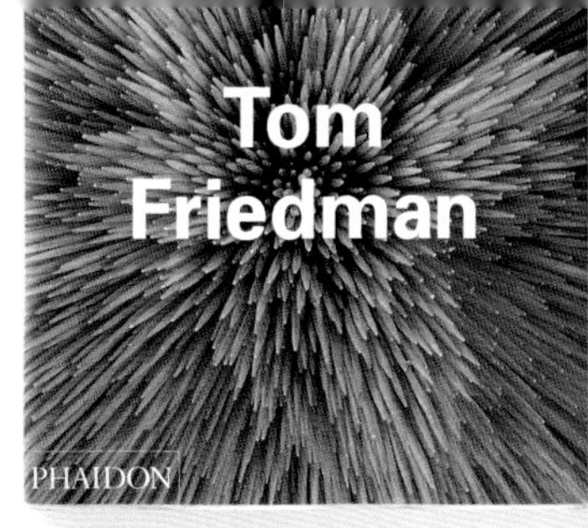
Tom Friedman
PHAIDON

ROCKIES
Crest of a Continent

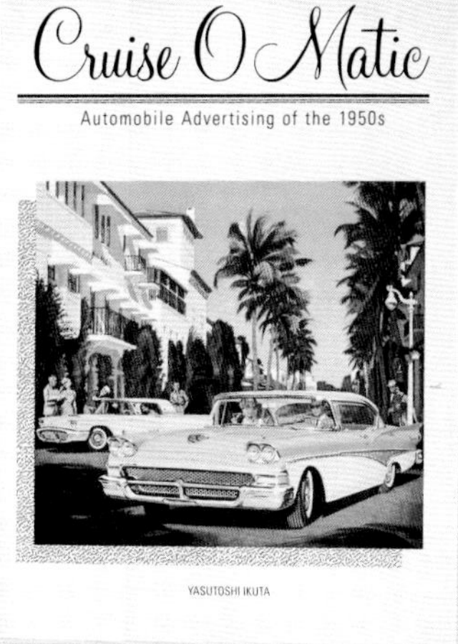
Cruise O Matic
Automobile Advertising of the 1950s
YASUTOSHI IKUTA

ideals

garcia
UPLAND GAME HUNTING
by FRANK WOOLNER

ROBERT WELLS

A SELECTION BY ANTHON BEEKE

NORMAN ROCKWELL'S
CHRISTMAS

TWO OR THREE THINGS I KNOW ABOUT PROVO. W139 AMSTERDAM

Two or Three Things I Know About Provo
A small, subjective (and ultimately incomplete) archive of the Provotarian movement in Amsterdam (1965–1967), as well as a selection of documents related to various post-Provo activities (most notably Aktiegroepen Nieuwmarkt, 1967–1975), with a particular focus on the role of activist and printer Rob Stolk (1946–2001).

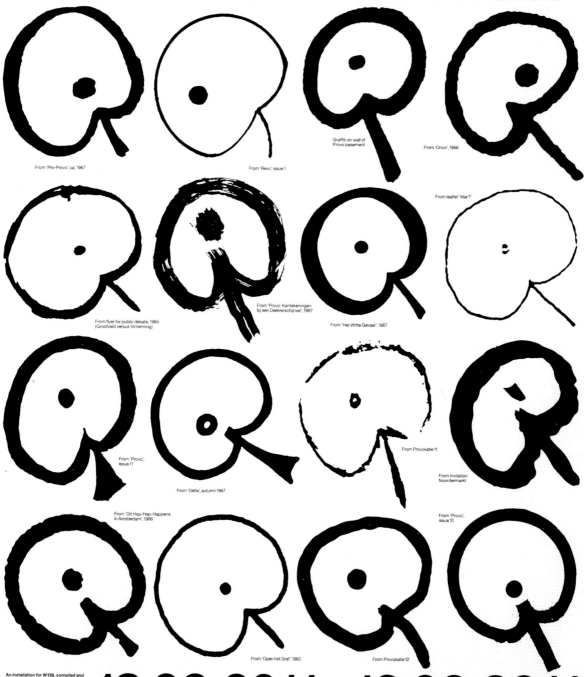

From 'Pro-Provo', ca. 1967

From 'Revo', issue 1

Graffiti on wall of Provo basement

From 'Orion', 1966

From leaflet 'War?'

From flyer for public debate, 1965 (Grootveld versus Vinkenoog)

From 'Provo: Kantekeningen bij een Deelverschijnsel', 1967

From 'Het Witte Gevaar', 1967

From 'Provo', issue 11

From Provokatie 11

From 'Delta', autumn 1967

From invitation Noordermarkt

From 'Dit Hap-Hap-Happens in Amsterdam', 1966

From 'Provo', issue 10

From 'Open het Graf', 1962

From Provokatie 12

An installation for W139, compiled and constructed by Experimental Jetset

Warmoesstraat 139, 1012 JB Amsterdam
www.w139.nl
www.experimentaljetset.nl/provo

Graphic design by Experimental Jetset
Poster printed by Drukkerij Atlantic

18.02.2011–13.03.2011

Two or Three Things I Know About Provo finished poster

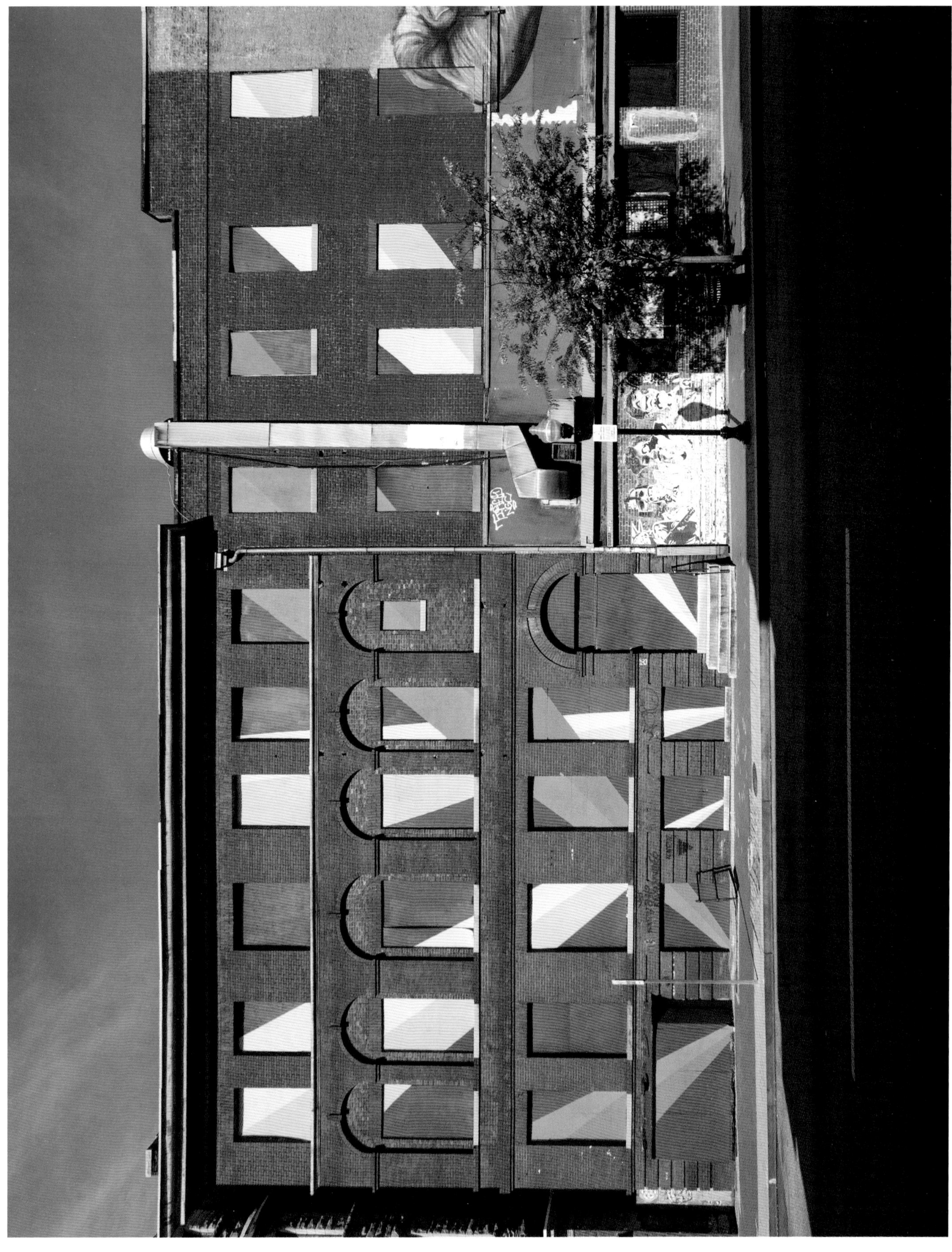

Parkway Film Center environmental graphics, Baltimore, Maryland

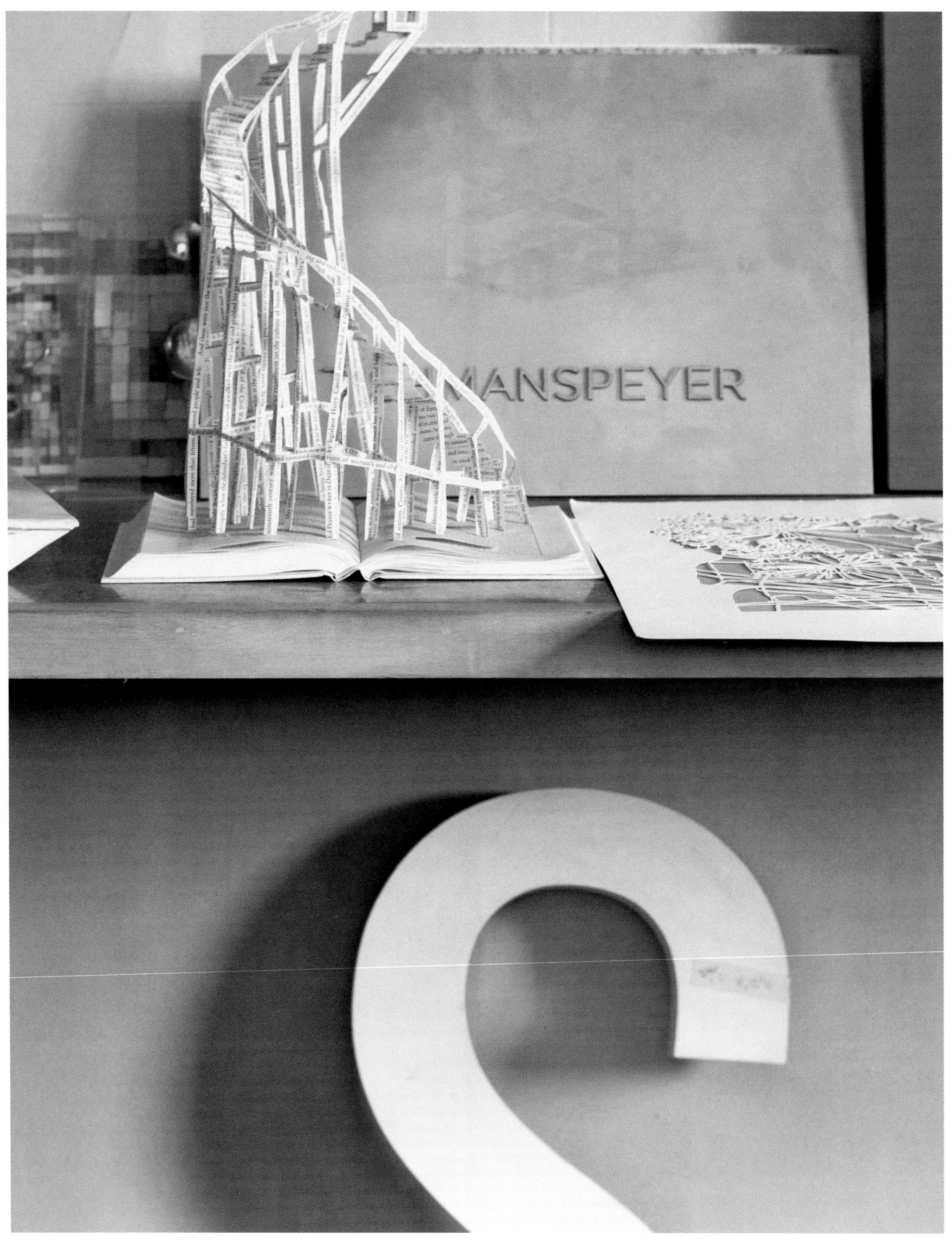

Detail of studio space

 Detail of studio space

Detail of studio space

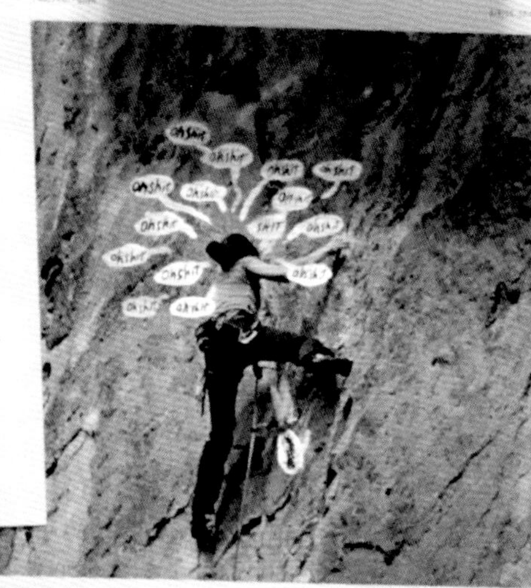

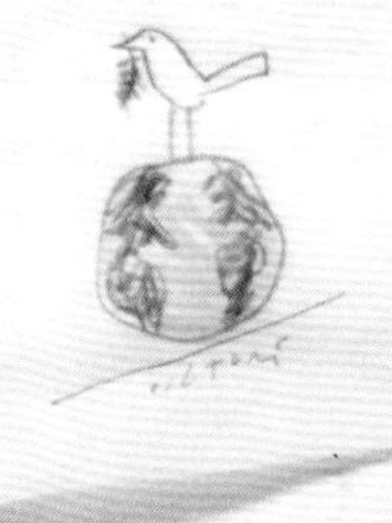

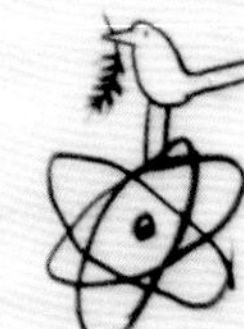

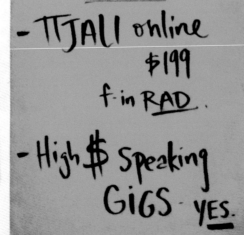

Detail of studio space

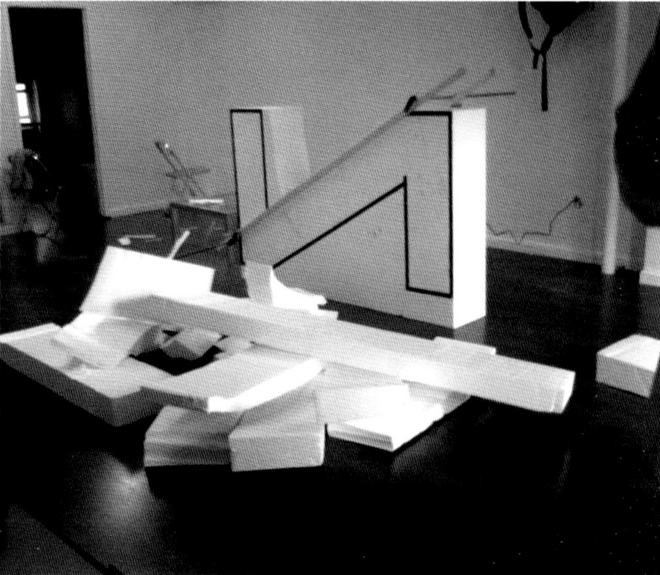

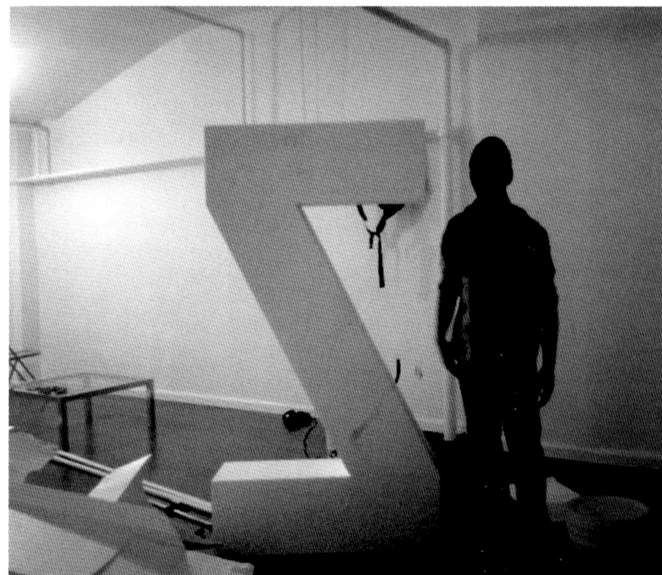

In-studio construction for self-promotional "Giant Z" project

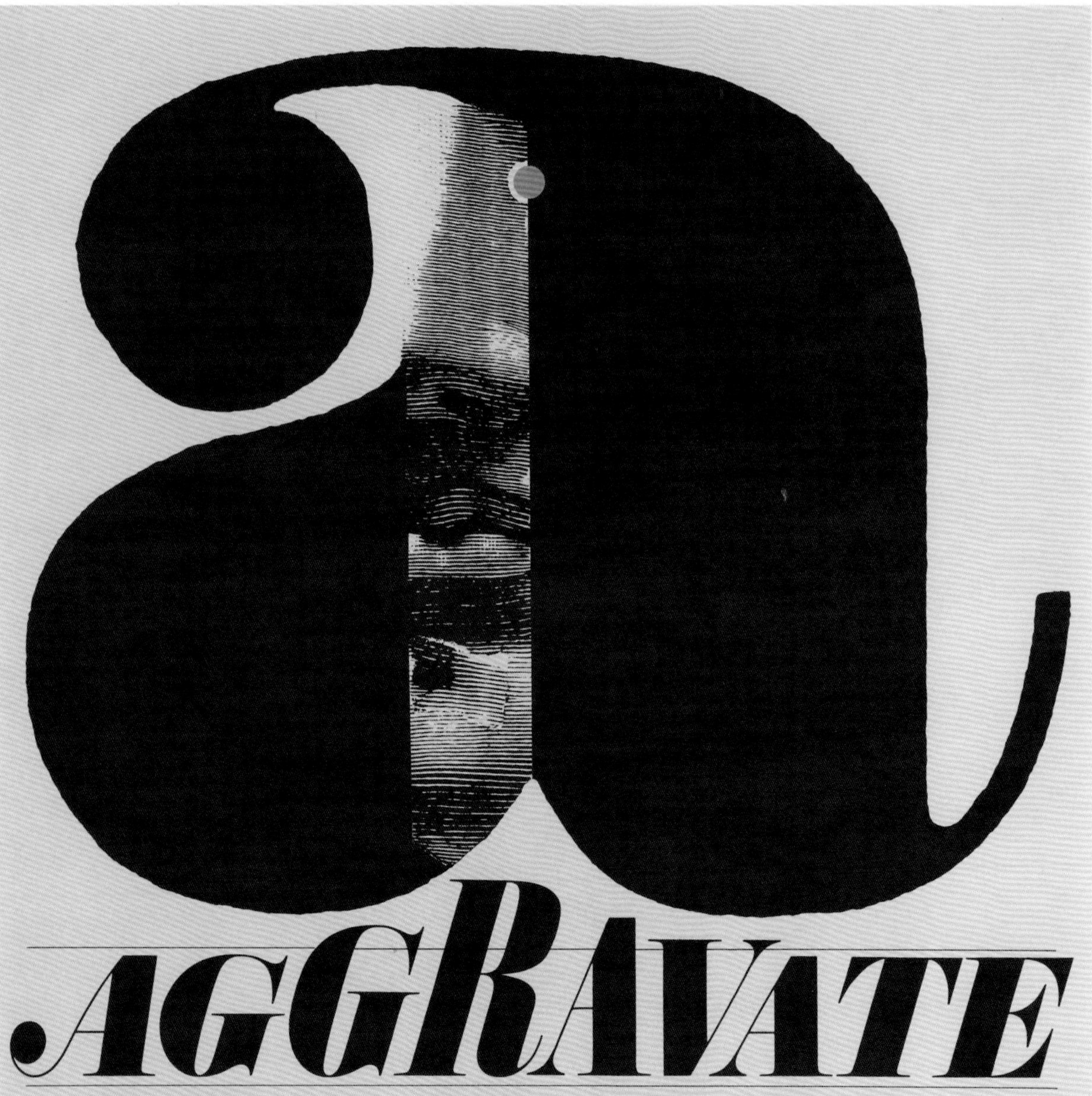

Finished "Fat Face" (Aggravate) poster, 1986

"Elegy for the Collapse of the Empire; Detroit Craft and Disintegration" installation, 2011

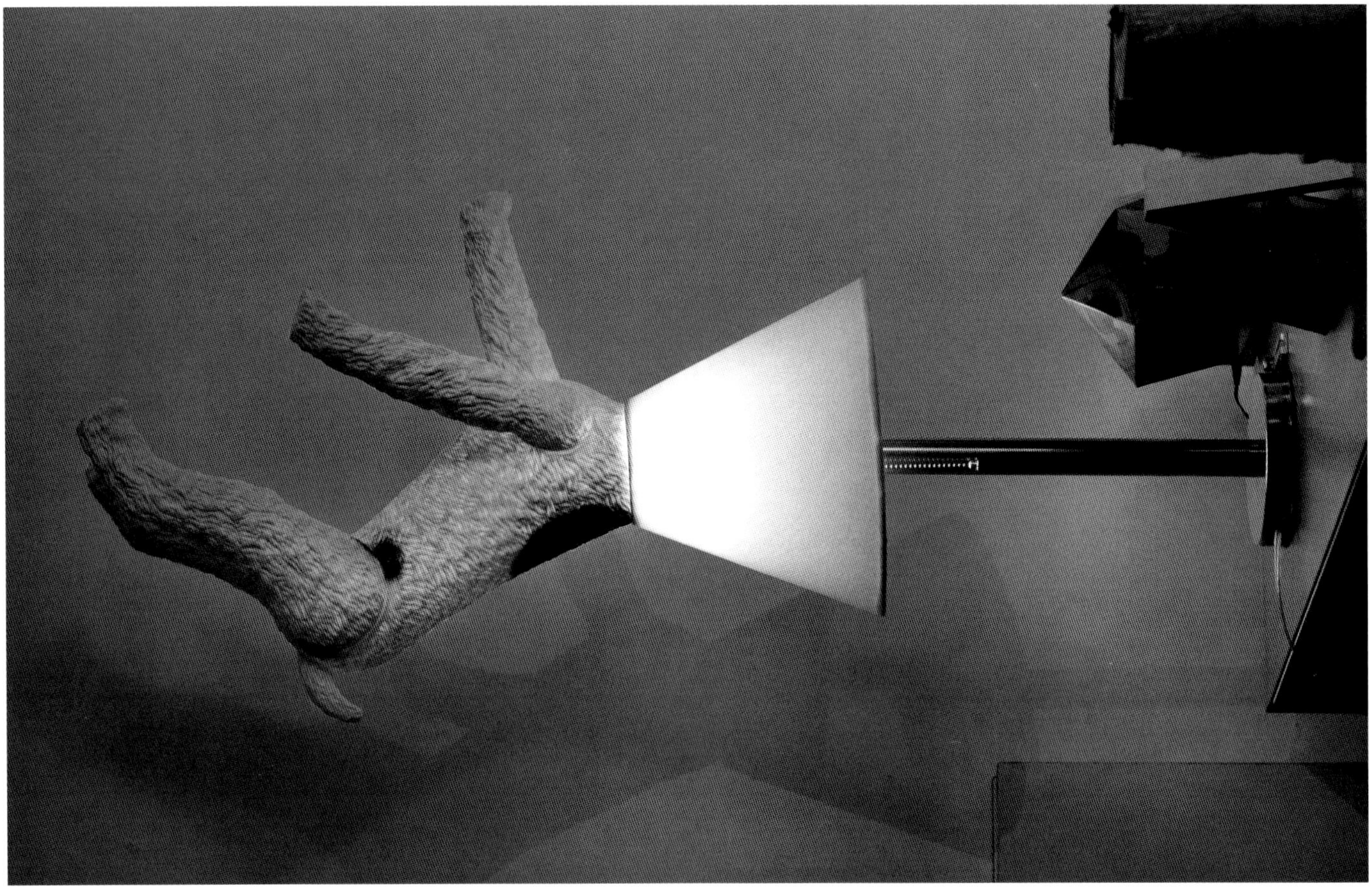

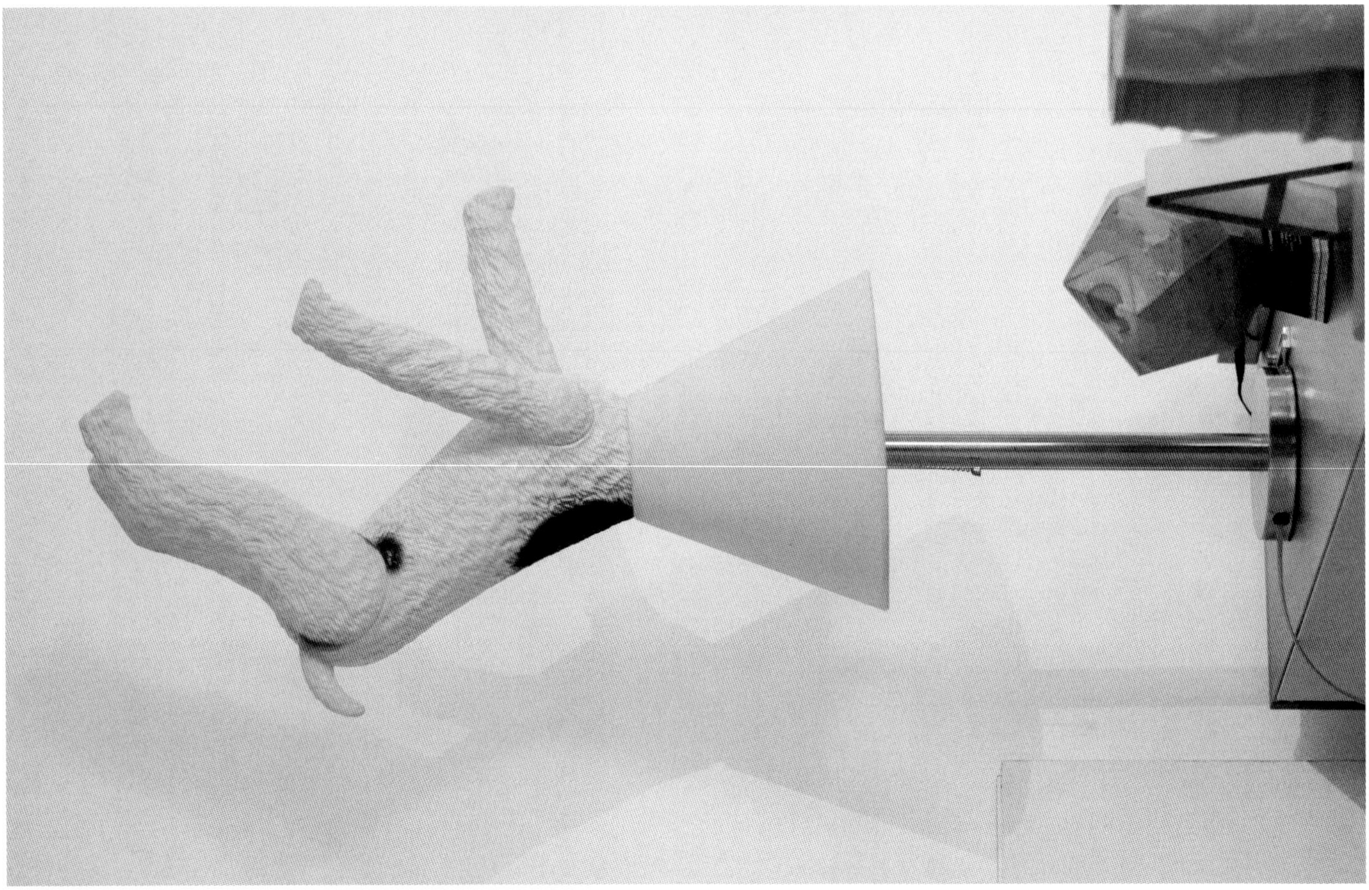

"Doglamp," 2012

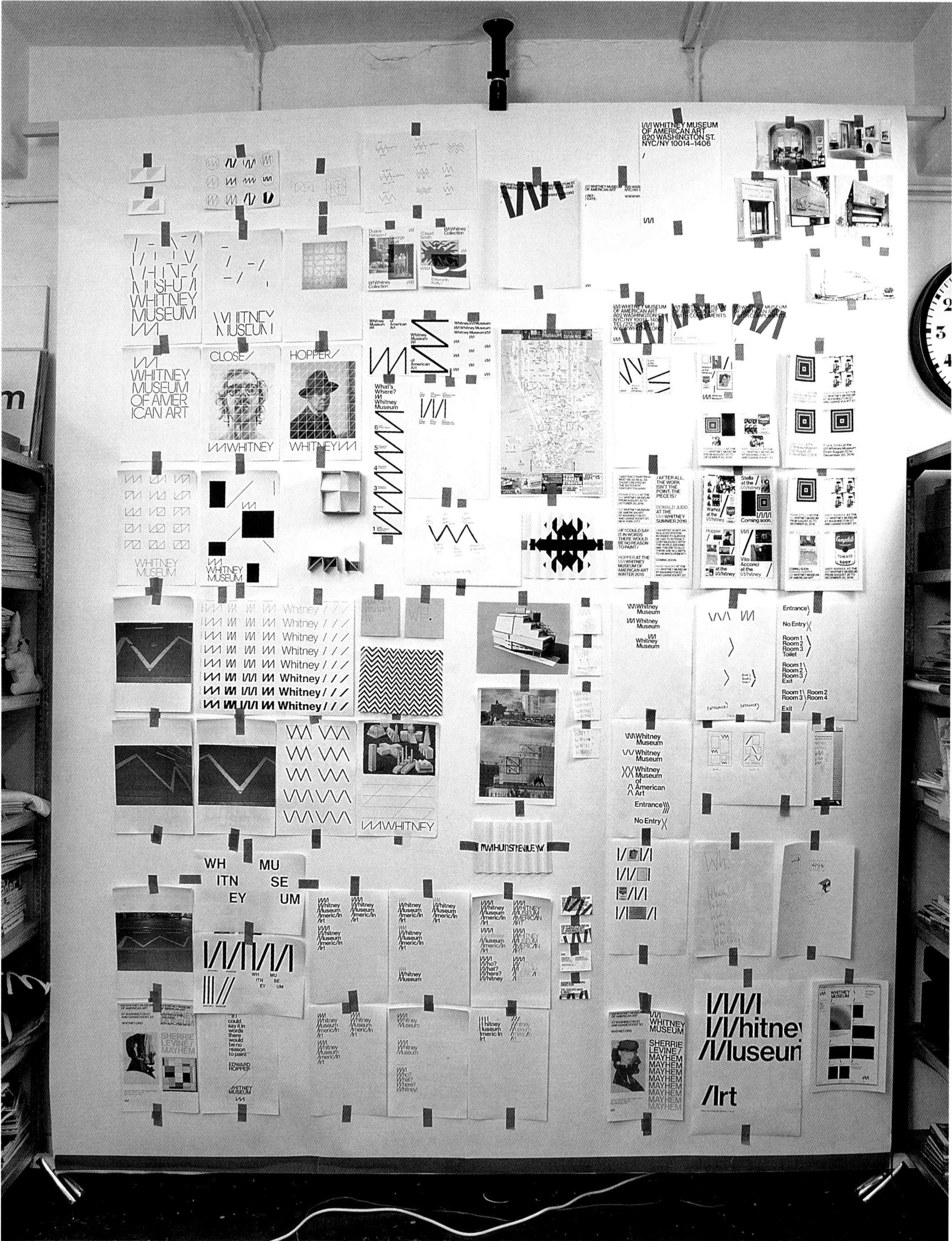

Studio wall with early sketches for Whitney Museum, mid-2011

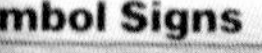

Finished "Celebrate Columbus" poster in Paul Sahre's studio

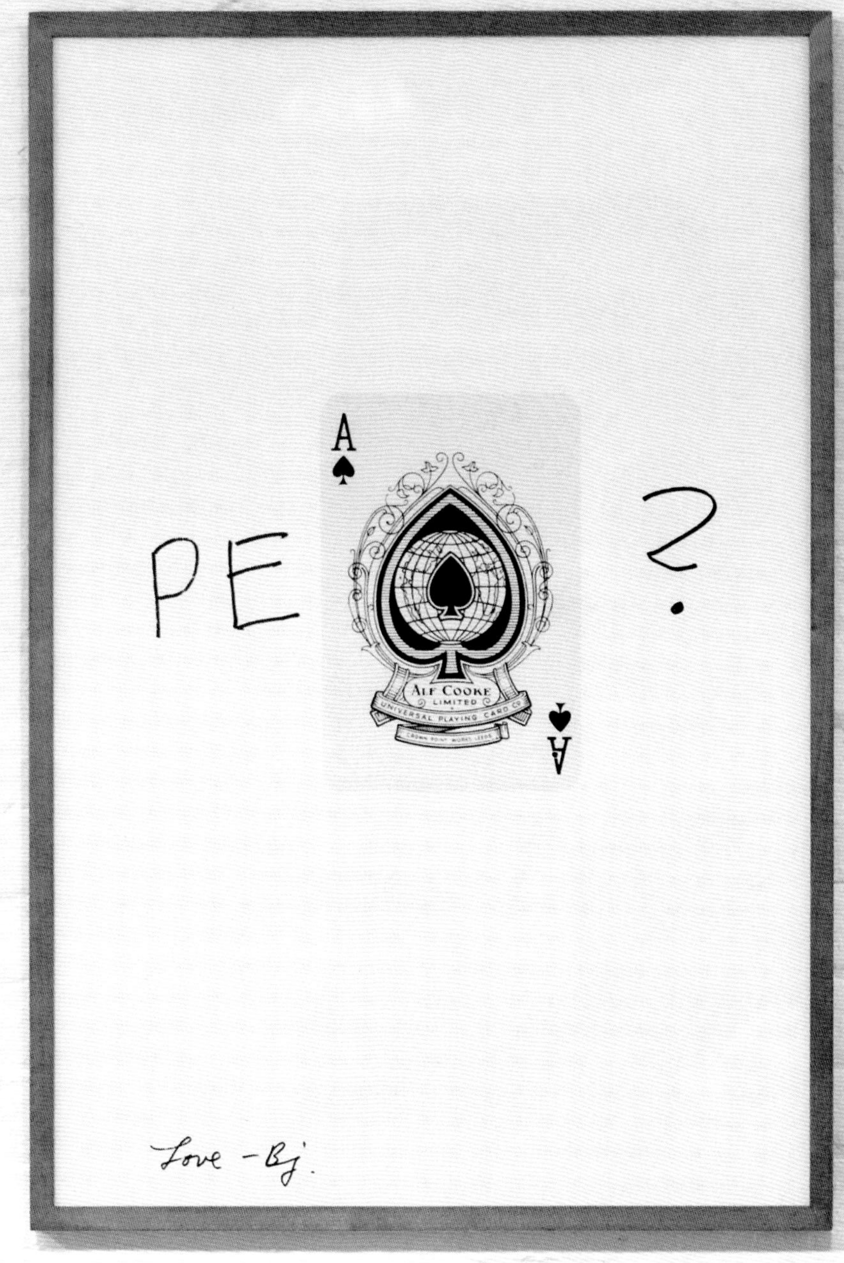

 Finished “Peace?” poster in Chermayeff & Geismar’s studio.

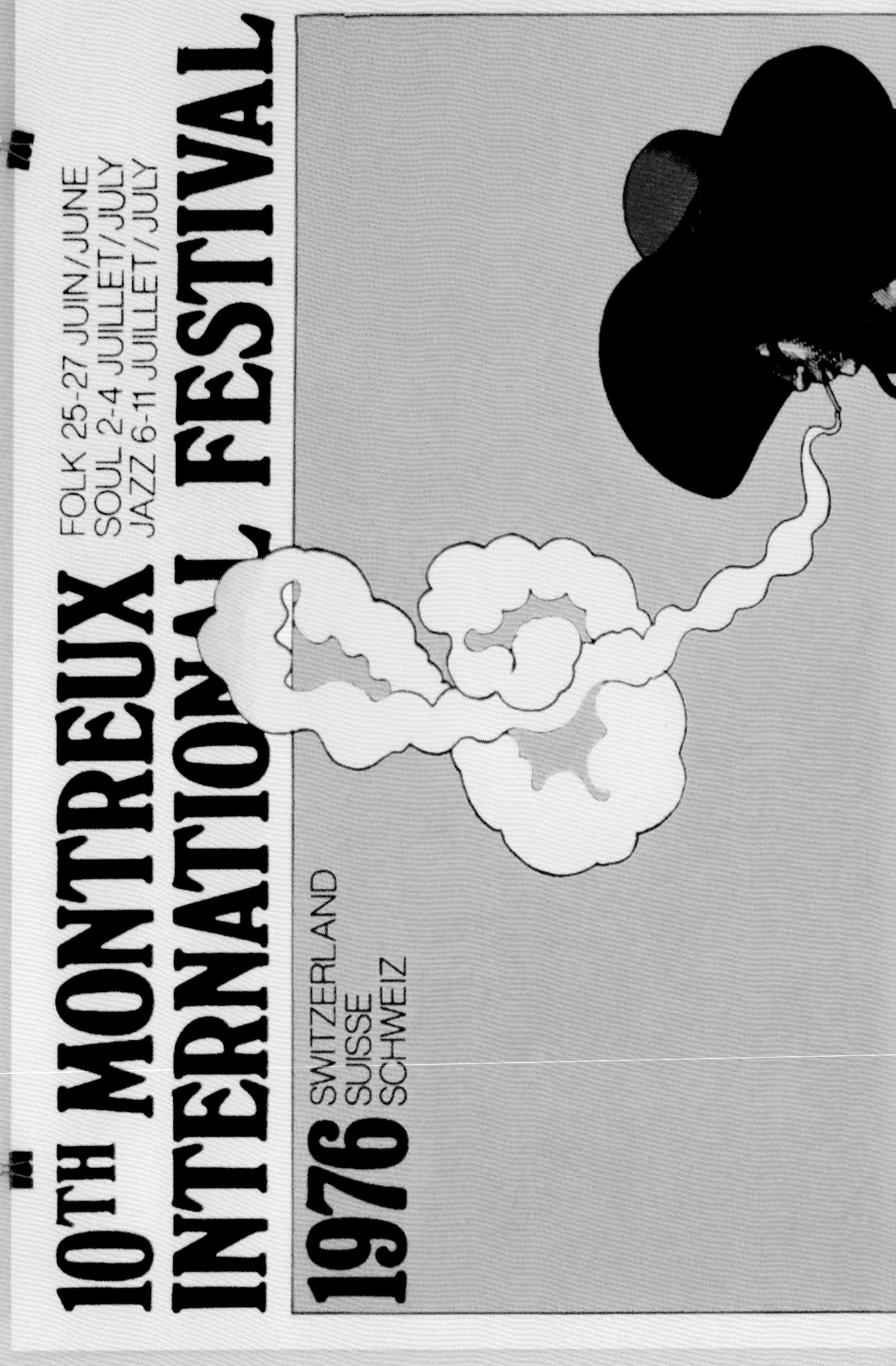

10TH MONTREUX
INTERNATIO
L FESTIVAL
FOLK 25-27 JUIN/JUNE
SOUL 2-4 JUILLET/JULY
JAZZ 6-11 JUILLET/JULY
1976
SWITZERLAND
SUISSE
SCHWEIZ

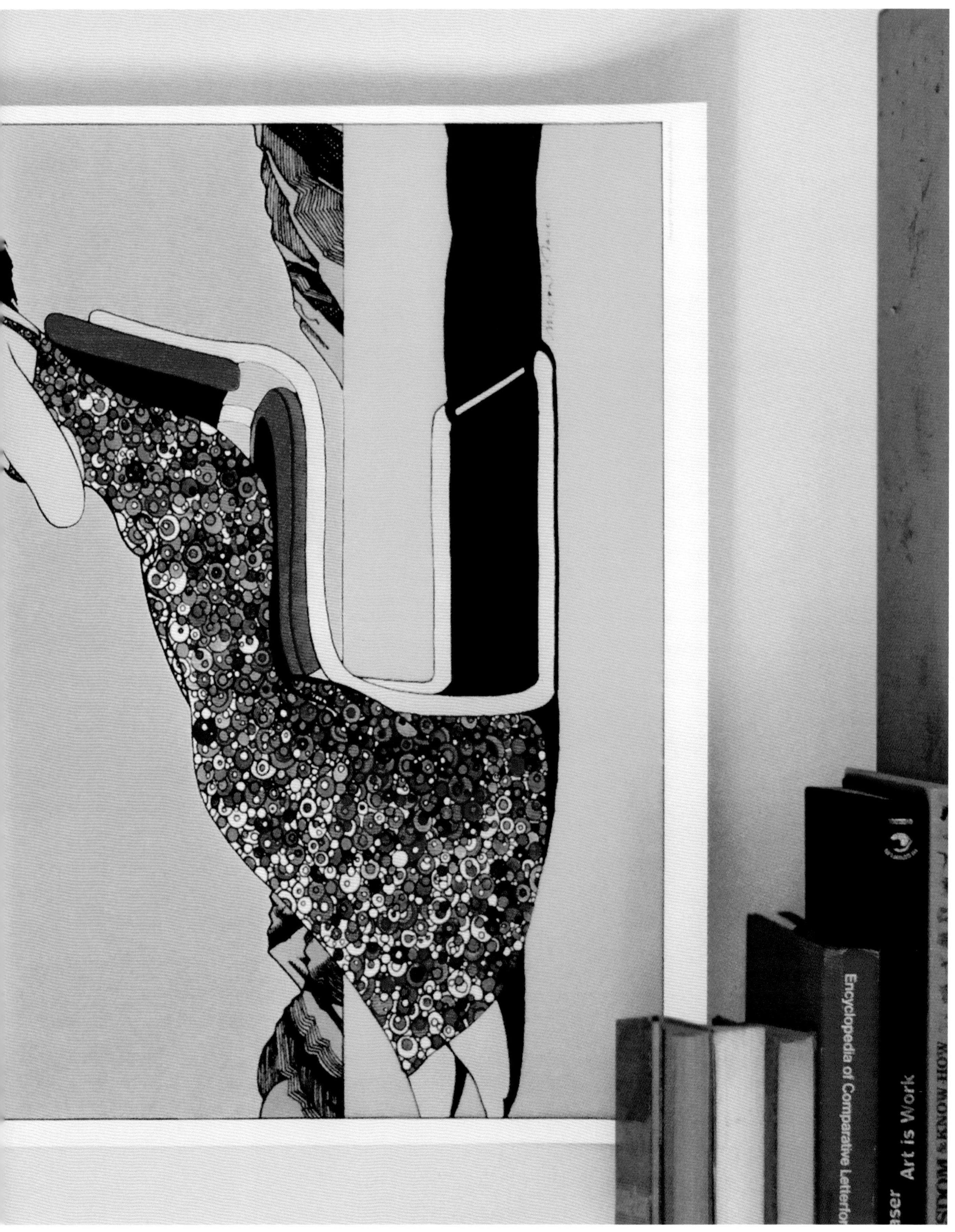

Finished Montreux Jazz Festival poster in Peter Ahlberg's studio

LUX
DOMENICA
5¢
INSECT
WIFFLE
school
LYON
HANDBOK
PARIS
CHICAGO
KEX
COLUMBIA PRESENTS
TURKISH SONGS

ARIEL
Dash
Silver Dust
new pink dreft
SOAP PADS
BONUX
RAPID'MAIN
sans frotter
SUPERIOR CUB
Poulet
22¢
BOSTON
5¢
6¢
noon
RULAV
Joy
baby soap
Milky
FAN
The Second Barbra Streisand Album
STEREO
THE FOX
Vivaldi
The Four Seasons
Leonard Bernstein
GUMMED PRICE LABELS
cubism
Olatz

SHOW CARD WRITING
CATALOG
F
N°5
CHANEL
PARIS
33
Mary Russel Wright
EASIER LIVING
TANCI

crafts

Studio wall

 POST TYPOGRAPHY (DOUBLE DAGGER) On stage

 ALAN FLETCHER Working on *The Art of Looking Sideways* book in his London studio

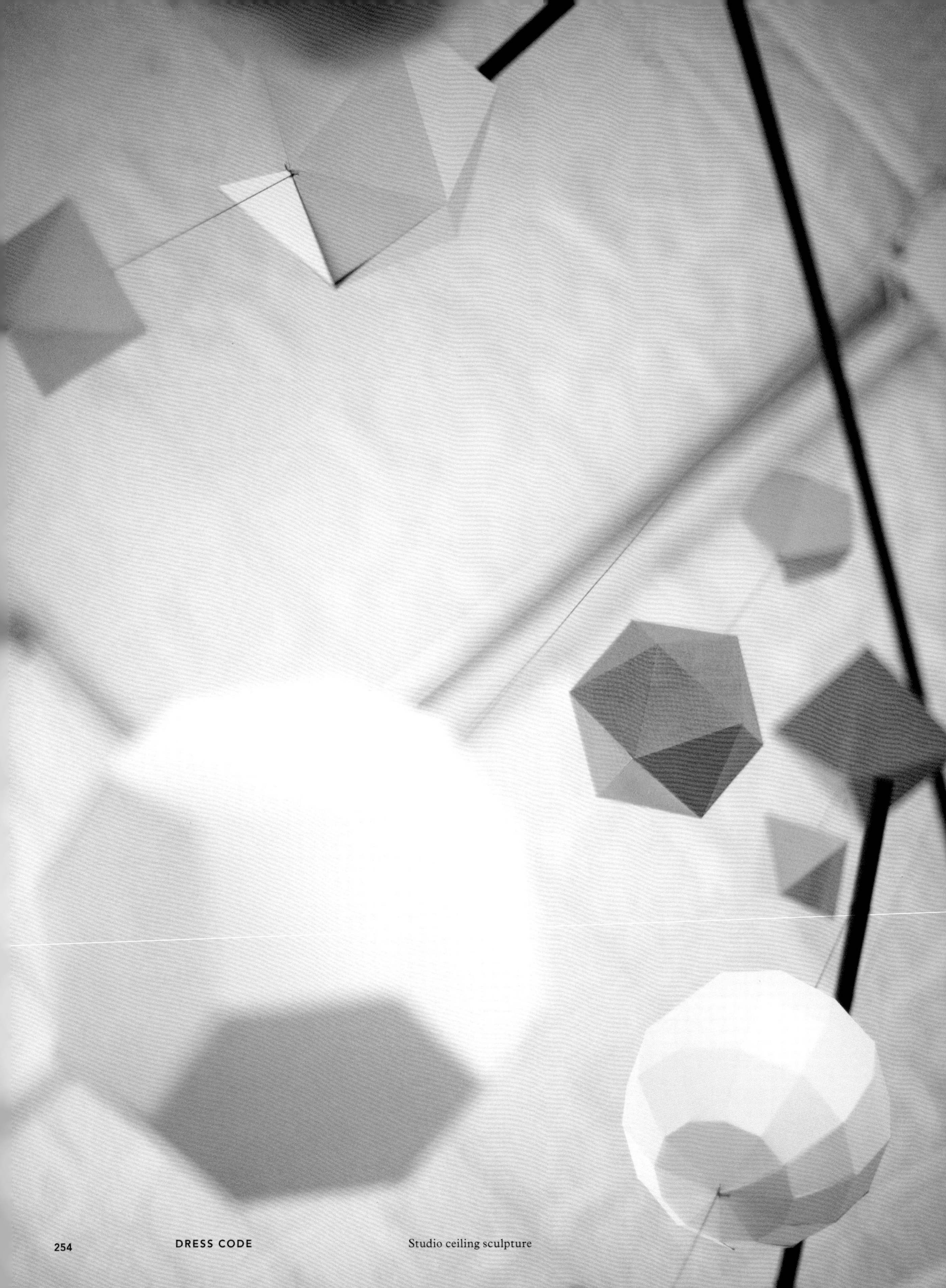

Studio ceiling sculpture

Shell imprint in petrified mud, from Ivan Chermayeff's collection

Paula Scher

March 5, 2015

Playing the Game

I think that we're essentially like baseball players. We have to be ready for the really good pitch because first you're going to be dealt and thrown a lot of crap. So you have to conserve your energy. In your twenties you think everything can be terrific and you work like a devil on all of it and you're always disappointed and frustrated.

It's usually a job you're doing for free, something nobody cares about, where you have an opportunity to invent language and make discoveries because, as long as you have the time to invest, you can do it there—nobody's going to tell you that you can't. I'll spend time on those jobs. Then there are jobs where the scale is there, where everyone is going to see it, and it's going to live. Those are the ones I become absolutely tenacious about—where scale and opportunity meet.

To manipulate craft against the opportunity for the scale. For example, I did this project for the Type Directors Club a few years ago. I made a kind of liquid identity. I wondered, "Can you recognize something if you use just colors and stripes and the form changes?" I was inspired by a graffiti artist from the West Coast named Barry McGee. He did a pile of work that was funny geometric shapes in a bad maroon color, and they were powerful. They weren't letterforms but they were geometric forms. I looked at them and I thought, "God, if they're typography, then you can actually make infinite logos for the same thing and just repeat it." There was a moment where it didn't connect. I had group of twelve people work on it with me and everybody on my team was making "T" "D" "C" letterforms. The rules were that the edges had to be straight. We found that if you curved them, you don't recognize it anymore. But there was a point where the question was, "How far can you push it?" We did all kinds of stuff with it and then we used it in a myriad of things—and that was pure experimental play.

Craft and Creativity

At Pentagram, I think all of us have superb craft. The craft skills are all we need. After ten years in the music industry, doing 150 record credits a year, I learned how to manage my craft—and that a lot of that sort of work is persuasive work. In other words, you're getting a group of people in a room to agree that they're going to do a specific thing for their company or product and then see to it that that happens.

The level of energy or creativity that it's going to need—you can gauge—it's like you know you're going to get a bad pitch. Don't swing at it—save your energy for the thing you're going to knock out of the ballpark. It's that kind of a judgment call that we make. It's not like we blow off our clients. I think that would be too cynical. It's more that you're making an assessment of what the right form is of both your personal engagement and the type of professional relationship that's being required of you at a given moment. The notion is to do that while keeping the quality up.

When you have the ability to persuade a group to behave because they're difficult to persuade to behave, that's one side of the work. Another part of work is the stuff where you're inventing form. They're both exciting. I think Michael [Bierut] would tell you he likes both equally. I probably don't. I like inventing form more, but I engage in the other. I enjoy the other. I see the value in it.

Outside the Studio

Painting changed my work. When I began making these illustrations, they were very small, and then I decided to make them huge. I was up at my weekend house with my husband Seymour Chwast, who works all the time. I don't have any kids and I'm in a house with a guy who's up in the attic drawing. So what do you do? I got a big piece of canvas and I pinned it up on the wall of the bedroom and I started painting it. That's why I'm a painter—I didn't have anything else to do.

The first painting, which was only five-by-eight feet, took me six months The next painting was ten-by-fourteen. They started to get really immense and when I realized I could do them, that was amazing. At that particular time, which was about 1998, I had spent a year doing Citibank and going to laborious meetings and making minor iterations to get this global buy-in on something. I felt at the end of the year that I didn't make anything. So I also started painting because I missed the actual craft of making. When I started out in the profession in the 1970s, I used to comp type by hand, so I felt like I had lost my handwork. Everything is done on the computer, so I felt like I hadn't touched anything. As a result I was making things like the Public Theater work in the 1990s, like for *Bring in da Noise, Bring in da Funk* and other things that were very intricate and obsessive—complicated typography that was done as a counterpoint to mind-numbing things like Citibank. I gave more value to that sort of Public Theater-ish thinking than to corporate logos.

After I started doing paintings, my work got very simple and it was because I had put that form of complication—that part of myself—somewhere else. I was doing something else with it, so I could do the High Line logo or the Criterion Collection logo—even the way I thought about the Windows logo. I'm very clear about it and I think they're opposites. The ability to do this one thing over here made me able to do this other thing.

I don't want to call myself a modernist—but it made me suddenly appreciate the minimalism. The maximalism led to the minimalism—which was very cool. Now I'm starting to miss the eccentricity. Nicholas Blechman gave me two *Book Review* covers just a couple of weeks ago and I happily started doing it again because I had missed it. I'm doing something like that right now, just because it's fun and I can.

The balance has to be there. It's all those things together and they all play off each other. All design plays off each other. A magazine teaches you how to do a building. A building teaches you how to design a package. Everything is connected.

I have to tell you that doing this art thing by yourself without any client in a room, taking up your time, committing to that, that's scarier than design—that's where you feel more naked. Design has a context, and you get paid for it.

Collaboration

At Pentagram I do little sketches of things and my team works them up. They see it through their eyes and so it's different. It's not the thing I drew anymore, it's this thing that has part of this other person in it and I get to use their eyes. So they are part of my process. It's like if you pick a color of paint and you mix it wrong but this other color is better than the one you thought you wanted. You've got this thing coming back to you that you didn't quite expect.

Suddenly it's something else and it's great. I have been doing that since 1994 but it changes because the kids change. It's never the same person. I've had better ones and worse ones, but it's always a new thing. What's great is when you have the new person, you get to see it a whole new way and then you're still playing—it's like teaching. You see how it works. That's one thing where the collaboration against the technology is great.

Technology

I have to confess and I don't know why—I think it has to do with longevity—but I have no interest in digital communication. I don't care if I never design an app. A website, it's nice—I know what it should look like. I guess I like it more now that the type is at least controllable because I hated working with some standardized crapola that you had to plug in. But I don't really care if I do that or not. I feel bad about it because I actually like to explore new areas and I love the three-dimensional thing. We're doing a tower—a sixty-foot-high typographic twisting tower in Florida and I'm dying, I love it. I'm learning new stuff and it's fun. But with digital technology, I just don't care about it, maybe because it goes away.

I remember this electronic publisher named Byram Price. He hired me in 1994 to do some packaging. He told that we were going to go out business because I couldn't get my head around CD-ROMs. I feel like I hear that every year.

Idea or Form or...

I don't really start with form or concept. I start with a sensibility. If I'm working for an organization or a corporation that is very much driven by a few things—what is that organization, what are they trying to achieve, and what does that have to express? Based on what they're describing and what the general milieu around them is—because, as I've said before, you can't force somebody to be the only one wearing a red dress when everyone's wearing black, but you can get them to wear a red belt!—so within the style of the times, how can you create an understandable aesthetic for that group that reflects where they are, what they make, how they fit into the marketplace, and who their audience is. Those considerations influence the design.

I knew when I was going to work with Tiffany [& Co] that what was wrong with their packaging was that the type was too big. It didn't look expensive enough. What looks expensive? Something that's withholding, something pulled back. Who wants it? Women who shop. What do they do? They go like this—they feel it. If you have a shiny, crappy piece of paper on the outside of your box that isn't making a beautiful pattern, get some expensive paper. It's goddamn Tiffany's. Don't have this crap stuff you can buy at a five-and-dime store. Dye the inside of the box. Make this stuff look like it's letterpressed. It's money, you're designing for money. I know I would feel that way if I got a crappy bag from them. When I saw their stuff I said, "Eww, this sort of feels tacky." You know that. You make those decisions.

Other People's Work

You can't not look at other design work or you'll lose your footing on what's going on. If you really, really hate something, you have to pay attention. If it's making you mad, it's cutting into something. Somebody made some discovery that you're ready to accept. That, you've got to work out.

Gratification

Nothing is ever finished. Nothing is ever right. Nothing is ever good enough. You're only as good as your last job. For every high, there's the smack in the face the next day. I've been practicing design for forty-five years. It's a long time, and what keeps it interesting is not fame, awards, money, but that you might see something in a new way. You might have one more "Aha!" moment where you really get it. Sometimes you get it in a new way and that is really great. If you're at that point in a job when you think, "This is going to be terrific, this is the best thing I've ever done. Oh, it's going to build a movement!," even if it sucks the next day and you say to yourself, "What have I been thinking?," it doesn't matter. That's great. That's the whole point.

Down Time

Walking down the street. Seeing every movie on the planet. Life. Going to Paris. Eating something great at a great restaurant. Having a terrific conversation. Getting mad in political discussions. All of it really.

I heard a terrific thing on NPR just yesterday that I thought was so true—that boredom really matters. If you're bored—meaning you're not really paying attention to anything—that's when all the great stuff happens. iPhones are bad because they take away your boredom. They involve you and then you don't have time to let your mind drift.

Dynamics

Now I have a coordinator come with me to meetings to take notes because at least she can find them. I never look at those notes because my takeaway from the meeting is better than any note because I've heard an inflection. When you look at the note, it neutralizes all the information. But I remember who said it. I remember where they were sitting at the table. I remember who had the power and whether it was some idiot with no power at the other side of the table who said something that doesn't matter, but it still got written on a piece of paper. It's not just the intake but also the dynamic of the room that matters.

The Process

The best explanation I could give of the process is that you have this part of your brain where your brain is your computer, you get a brief, meet the people, and do the research. Then over here is every movie you ever saw, every television show, every color that you like, all the artists you admire, all the countries you visited, your parents, every experience of your life. You're feeding this thing and it's rolling, like a slot machine. You're trying to get the cherries to line up and you're doing it unconsciously. You've actually made logical decisions along the way, so after you let the thing roll around and the cherries have come up, you've put together your thing, you go back, and you realize you made a connection between the brief and this one thing over here. There's another point here where I made a connection and another point over here. You lay that back out and you explain why it works. But it happens too fast because your unconsciousness is part of it. How can you put a timetable on that? You can't put it in order, so you have to make up the order.

The Bullshit in the Middle

If you're working for a client, none of the process has value to anyone but you.

Showing it is nice and you can talk about how you made all these great posters. But in fact they didn't happen because the other one, the one that got made, got made. The whole thing about it being a shame—no, it isn't a shame. The thing that you're doing is the end thing. It's not the stuff in the middle. The stuff in the middle is sometimes better than the end thing because there's a client that got in the way or the job itself isn't an interesting job to begin with. Sometimes the stuff in the middle is better than the stuff happening because you couldn't persuade the person to go in the middle, but none of that stuff counts—that's all your private closet. When I hear that, I get absolutely furious because the belief is that somehow there's this loss in that. The end is the goal. The other stuff is the process to the goal, but it's not the thing. It doesn't mean it's not interesting to look at or talk about, but that's not the thing you're making.

You start here and you end there. How you got there is how you got there, and that's your bullshit. Everything—it's just bullshit in the middle until you get to the end thing. That's why I would draw this diagram because I think it's more tied together. It's not like it's unraveled and it's perfect and linear. You have to actually cut the thing together to get that bullshit right. You know, there's work involved in getting your bullshit believable enough to do it. That's part of the process too. We're all doing that. That's the real thrill of it. If you want to have a process and show lots of wonderful things, there are lots of wonderful things that get made as a result of it but that's not the activity. That's for students and that's so important for them to understand. The idea that this thing results. The point is not that there's a heartbreak in the middle. It's all just a means to the end.

Stefan Sagmeister

January 28, 2015

180

I very much believed that the idea was everything when I was young and starting out, both as a student and then also when we had the studio. That came from the teacher that I had and the work that I admired at the time—1970s and '80s British *Vogue* magazine, Pentagram, and other solid idea-centric design, where the form was basically just a hand that made the idea, always subservient to it. It needed to be the right form for that idea, but not much more. As I have gotten older, I see this whole process completely differently. Now—while not quite a dime a dozen—I think that ideas are not that difficult to come by. It's the treatment of an idea—formally or stylistically—that is super important and might be its own thing or maybe even its own idea. If you remember the little sign we had in the studio in the beginning that said "style = fart," meaning style is hot air—that it means nothing—I couldn't be further away from that now.

I think that so much of what it means to be a designer right now is being able to make things happen. That ability is much wider than just having the idea or even being a form giver—it's the possibility or ability to actually make something real in a way that is in line with the project and your thinking and your abilities. In some ways, of course, I always knew this because I worked for Tibor [Kalman], who I thought was particularly fantastic at making things happen. Ultimately, he probably got so good at that that maybe he could get away with being weak in other areas. He had very good ideas but formally he was very weak. He employed people who were good, like Stephen Doyle, who were good students, but he prided himself on not quite knowing what Helvetica really looked like—which was not the truth—but he made a shtick out of it.

The point of view of our process is very different, where the process of coming up with something beautiful is somewhat different than coming up with a good concept. I find myself now almost having done a 180. I find that it's extremely difficult for us to hire somebody who can make things look beautiful while it's very easy to hire somebody with good ideas. I am baffled by—specifically with so-called high-end designers—this distancing of oneself from beauty, putting up a wall there, as if it's so common. I feel like everybody I talk to says, "Oh, we're not about making things look good."

Beauty

For one thing, it is extremely difficult, which might be one of the reasons why there is so little beauty around us—not just in design but in almost all fields. Architects don't talk about beauty, high-end designers don't talk about beauty, and contemporary artists don't talk about beauty—with very few exceptions. And even those few don't really address it straight out. They definitely avoid the terminology and I think it's a gigantic pity. Like so many of the world's ills, I blame this on the Bauhaus.

Many of the artists were part of World War I, which was an unbelievably bloody mess with supposedly civilized nations just slaughtering each other in the worst possible ways. The nineteenth century had been so beauty-obsessed that beauty became this crazy moral value—one which was totally different from other aesthetic qualities. It was different from structure, color, and so on. Beauty was up there with goodness. If it was beautiful, it was also good.

When those civilized nations and their morals proved to be so unreliable, beauty couldn't be taken seriously anymore. Max Ernst talked quite elaborately about how he couldn't do anything beautiful. Obviously, Duchamp's whole fountain thing was very much empty aesthetics. They're saying, "Let's talk about something other than beauty, let's get rid of that crap." But Duchamp's fountain is signed "R. Mutt, 1917"! We're approaching its centennial anniversary and we still think this stupid old shit is amazing. It's crazy that you can still make a career in art with a readymade. How is it that readymade has any meat left on the bone? That you are not called out as the unbelievable bore that you are is amazing to me. That you can somehow put the mantle of the avant-garde around your shoulders by quoting somebody who did this so long ago? What other field can you do that in? Which current car designer gets his technical specifications from a Model T Ford? The conservativism inherent in the supposedly avant-garde world is astounding to me.

There are exceptions though. Clearly someone like Jonathan Ive is interested in beauty even though he comes out of the avant-garde. And although it might be difficult to recognize at times, artists such as Ellsworth Kelly and James Turrell created work that came out of modernism but was also very much concerned with beauty.

By and large, I think that most of the modernists were wrong. Le Corbusier and Mies both had some serious issues, not to mention the later misinterpretations of their work. This insistence on making things straight has led us to an economic modernism where people say, "Let's make it as cheap as possible and it doesn't really matter what it looks like so long as it's functional." It's this guiding idea that has left us in a world that very few want to live in—one that has become unbelievably dysfunctional.

Approach

Ultimately you can get to good work with a myriad of processes. The whole design school mantra that I still hear all the time—a faculty member tells me proudly, "In the first year, we don't let them on the computer." That seems to be the thing because the thinking is, I guess, that if you start on the computer, only bad things can come out—and this isn't true. There's a whole generation out there that has been using dynamic things since they were very, very small. They're so fast that they are comparable to you with a pen. I also think that the "massaging" of something—as opposed to having an idea and then building it—is just as good and can create great results. More to that point, there are just a lot of different possibilities.

The New Dark Ages

Obviously the entire idea of commercial design is steeped in functionalism—where someone says, "I made something that works for you." Function is easier explained if you have an idea that directly relates or if you can show how the idea will take you from A to B. These days, I'm doubting even that.

If you compare a walk in the park, which is low function and high enjoyment, to a commute, which is high function and low enjoyment, very few people would say that they love their commute more than the walk in the park. Yes, the commute is necessary but there are aspects within communication and design where a strategy of very low function and high enjoyment might yield better results and ultimately a much greater functionality.

Look at what has happened to these high-rise "project" buildings that were meant to be highly functional by housing as many people as possible, as cheaply as possible. The result was that nobody wanted to live there and many of them have been demolished. Ultimately they had zero functionality—they didn't fulfill their only intended purpose. In the end you had no beauty and no function. They were a complete and utter disaster. Even if they had built something beautiful and housed only 10 percent of the people, it would have functioned much better. Let alone the delight and the wonderfulness and the humanity it could have achieved.

After having been in Rome for two months last summer, I now think our entire mindset is wrong. For six hundred of the last two thousand years it had been the most dominant city in the world. During those years the things that were made in Rome were the best in the world. The city attracted the best people to live and conduct business. Consider how that time was deeply informed by beauty and the main decisions were made in response to beauty and, ultimately, humanity. Contrast this against what we're doing—not just in the [United] States but worldwide, with this gigantic effort to build "non-spaces." A huge percentage of the areas that are developed for a functional purpose wind up not functioning at all, neither as a space to live nor as a place for humans to congregate. My guess is that we are—and have been for the last seventy years or so—living in an era that will be looked back upon in amazement, as a time where we lost the desire for beauty. I'm not frustrated about the times that I'm living in, but I think that in this respect, it will take on a bit of the Dark Ages.

Uniformity

We do not want everywhere we go to look the same. Time and again, in every psychological test conducted, it is shown that what we really love is variety. So this idea of an international style, where every building looks the same throughout the world, again, is an idea that came out of World War I after the slaughter, and has now been proven not to work. It's just stupid to build the same building in Iceland as in Brazil. It's not working for us on a human level. I've never heard anyone say, "I'm so glad that when I land in Osaka, the airport looks exactly like when I started in Istanbul." It would be nice, however, if the signage systems were the same—but those are actually all different. The one thing that would be lovely is if all the signs that tell you where to find Gate 15 were the same. Instead we have different signage systems everywhere, and everything else is exactly the same. It's completely fucked, everything is totally wrong.

Novelty

I am not particularly interested in the new for new's sake. There's clearly a functionality involved in "new," as in the strategy of surprise, which is a proper, very solid strategy if you're communicating something that needs it. Say, when the viewer has a ten- or twenty-second attention span. In that case, surprise is probably a more valid strategy than if you were designing a Zen Buddhist monastery, where you would have the attention of everybody for weeks on end. With that, novel things and newness play a bigger role than they play in other areas of the applied arts. Having said that, the big question is always, ultimately, is it justified? Do you have a reason for it? Is the newness working? Consider the difference between eating a dish made by Ferran Adria that is completely new and completely delicious, or eating a dish made by one of his many followers, which is also new, but not delicious. That gigantic difference is why that style of cooking has gotten such a bad reputation, because so many of the people who tried to do it couldn't make it delicious. It just wound up as gorgonzola and olive ice cream. If it's not delicious, it's not a good idea, it's just an idea.

As a young designer I used to try to create and develop a new direction for every project. Soon enough I realized that wasn't possible. I thought we just weren't good enough to do that. I later realized that it's not just me but that it's not humanly possible and that the only people who do that for prolonged stretches of time are stealing other people's stylistic and formal developments—historical or contemporary—and working in those for a while. Steven Meisel is a good example of someone who would pick and choose from the grab bag of photographic history. He did it at an extremely high level because he actually could do a lot of these things.

Earlier in my career I always preferred, in all of the arts, the changer-overs to the stay-the-samers. For example, Warhol over Lichtenstein. Warhol pursued several very strong directions for a very long time, but they were different directions. Lichtenstein, once he found his language, basically stuck to it. Now from my older point of view, I see that differently. There are a few people I'm very glad never changed. James Turrell would be one. It would have been a disaster if he'd said after three years, "Ok, I did that light thing, now let's move on to sound." It would have been a disaster for his career and for us as viewers.

I'm aware that this might be a bit self-serving, because as I grow older, I have much less of a desire and probably less of an ability to come up with new things. Like I said, I used to see this as a fault. I can remember discussions I had with other designers where we'd say that nobody over 60 has ever come up with something new in design that was relevant today—and we saw it then as a bad thing. I now believe that evolution designed us that way on purpose—that we have periods where we do come up with new things, where we have abilities, and the brain is new—probably around 30 years old. Then there are periods where we develop these things and really work on them and refine them and ultimately show other people how to do them. I think if we had newish, growing brains for the whole span of our lives, nobody would teach anything and nobody would refine anything. We'd constantly be reinventing the wheel.

Form

Karel Martens was a big influence. I came across his book and I was oddly attracted to the work but couldn't really explain what the attraction was because I thought of myself as an idea person and with him it's really about form. I think that I was also surprised by the attitude of someone his age because the people that I knew of that age were all idea people, specifically in the UK. I remember how he talked about this idea-work having very low revisitability because ultimately so much idea-work was a joke—a visual joke, a pun—and that might have worked fine for a magazine cover or a newspaper thing that you throw out, but it's not fine if it's something that you see time and time again, because then you're basically just looking at old jokes. It's actually conceptually bad, even though its whole reason for living is a concept.

It's conceptually bad to have a concept—a strong concept—if you want strong visibility. That's the reason why people prefer landscapes above their sofa to framed jokes. It's as simple as that. There's not a lot of idea in a landscape. But people like it so they choose that over framing a joke.

Technology

We—probably me much more so than others—pride ourselves in doing quite a lot of handmade things which is the reason why I use the crap around here that you might not see in the design studio next door. But at the same time, all of that stuff is really only properly doable with a lot of technology—where sometimes we choose to hide and sometimes we choose to be completely transparent about it.

We have also done many projects that couldn't have even been thought of if it weren't for the technology that could make it possible. For example, one of our friends knew about a smile-detection software, which allowed us to conceive of a little installation that changes color when you smile. That wasn't even an idea we could've talked about as little as seven years ago—the technology just didn't exist.

The Process

Personally, my design process is very much in my head. I avoid looking at things while I'm thinking about the project and it might be everything from losing myself, to taking a train ride, to coming up with a system where I have big lists. I write things down on index cards and then see if there is any correlation between all the cards and then try to forget about it and then hope that an idea comes from working on ideas that have nothing to do with the idea at hand.

On the other hand, Jessica [Walsh] comes up with ideas by putting together an unbelievable amount of images in one direction. I think because she puts in lots and lots of images, she avoids this trap that I would have always been afraid of, which is that if I look at stuff when I am thinking of ideas, I come upon something that's nice and do it, which, of course, is awful and deeply unsatisfying. Ultimately I think that the person who steals very rarely does something better than where he or she stole it from—you're the babysitter, not the dad. You're just not as careful with that idea or direction. I think Jessica looking at an incredible amount allows her to jump on things and really develop from there. It's a different version of my index cards, only my index cards stay in my head, while she does it through a web-based search.

I have also tried giving myself very tight limitations, saying, "I'm going to do this thing, but I have to be done in five minutes." Or, "I'm going to do this thing and I'm actually executing it, but I only have three hours," meaning I can only work with existing materials that we have in the studio.

Parameters

The self-imposing of limitations came later. It was not part of my education or early professional work. It was something I talked about with people I met. There is an artist named Allan Wexler who was influential for me and spoke very eloquently about the importance of limitations. He talks about how when working on a sculpture he would always look for the most difficult sites—the craziest, the steepest, but never the one down in the valley, because it's so much easier to work within the limitations of the site.

Brian Eno talked about how the guitar is the best and most dominant instrument because it's a stupid instrument that can do only a few things, but also allows the human spirit to go to the edge of possibility. I think that with most work there is a sweet spot, not so tight that you can't do anything, but also not open enough that you could do anything. Photoshop is a good example of this and explains why so many people do crappy work in Photoshop. It's too good of a tool, too sophisticated, and offers too many possibilities.

For me, in the beginning as a young designer, all of this was a big influence. It is also one of the reasons why we worked on *The Happy Film* in an open-ended way, without knowing what the end would be. It's something that made me extremely uncomfortable because my whole being wants to not work like that. My whole being wants to have a plan. For so long, even some of the most organic and free-form looking work I've made has been preceeded by careful planning and sketches. For the film, we worked and reworked our asses off to create a full-resolution sketch.

Time

Speed has never been a desire of the studio. Since the beginning, we've never really taken on clients who said they were in a hurry. I worked in Hong Kong for two years doing sixteen-hour, high-stress days and found it's not me, it's not what I enjoy, and if I keep on doing that I won't be a designer in a couple of years.

Having said that, I'm very aware of the wonderfulness of deadlines, having had a very movable deadline for our film, which I'm not sure was a good thing. It definitely didn't help my state of mind. We also have the system of sabbaticals every seven years, where we go away and have a year to work on stuff with no deadlines, just time to figure things out.

It was actually a little bit different in the two sabbaticals. The first, there was not any desire to finish anything, so it was literally just beginnings. If there was a "it's good enough," I thought to leave it, it's in the sketchbook, and maybe we can go back there at one time or another. The second sabbatical was a little bit more about completing things because part of what we did was furniture that definitely needed to be completed by a certain time because it was furniture for my apartment. As a result it definitely felt like a design studio again. I do feel that these sabbaticals were important for the studio and important for me and if I do another one it will probably be somewhere in between the two. You can think differently. If you have a year to think about something, the outcome is different from if you have a weekend.

Outside the Studio

I don't tend to have hobbies or be very secretive with projects. If I have an outside interest in something, we make a project out of it. I find that design is a very comfortable tool for me to explore a world.

List Making

I've always been a big list-maker and ultimately I find it satisfying, but as a deliverer of truth, quite disappointing.

I used to make a lot of pro and con lists for decision-making purposes in my diaries, so when I checked back on these lists, I found that they had surprisingly little longevity. When I made a list and went back and filled that same list out four years later from the current point of view, they were completely different outcomes to the same question. So my hope that they would somehow deliver rational decisions made over long periods of time, did not become true.

Gratification

I do find pleasure in the finished product. I think it's very central to design that it is so. I found the whole process-obsessed 1990s thing—that Tomato book *Process: A "Tomato" Project*—very curious, with designers proclaiming that the end result doesn't matter. It seemed a selfish stance toward the client and toward the public. It can't be all about, "I'm having a good time doing this one interesting journey and who gives a shit what comes out in the end." It just made little sense to me. I'm very traditional in that sense, meaning, if a project comes back here that we've worked on very hard and for a long time, it's a very satisfying feeling. It's very much a feeling of accomplishment. I'm not apologetic about that. I would think that many people feel that way.

Index

Pleas
Mak
Thi
Loo
Nic

I

J

K

L

M

N

P

Pleas
Mak
Th
Loc
Nic

This book would not have been possible with out the generosity, faith, and kindheartedness of many, many people.

My gratitude goes especially to: Brett Littman, Executive Director of The Drawing Center, for giving this project the chance to ever be more than a proposal; Caitlin Leffel, Senior Editor at Rizzoli, for sharing my earliest proposal with her colleagues; Charles Miers and Margaret Chace for seeing the potential of the project; Jessica Fuller, Senior Editor at Rizzoli, for keeping me on track with sage advice and patience; and Richard Wilde, Chair, BFA Advertising/Design Departments at the School of Visual Arts, for a seemingly endless supply of positivity, support, and encouragement.

My sincerest thanks go to those who were my earliest advisors and confidants: Ed Benguiat; Experimental Jetset [Erwin Brinkers, Danny van den Dungen, and Marieke Stolk]; John Gall; Bob Gill; Carin Goldberg; Yego Moravia; Paul Sahre; and Jan Wilker.

To those who offered archival expertise and assistance: Alexander Tochilovsky, Curator, Herb Lubalin Study Center of Design and Typography; Beth Kleber, Archivist, School of Visual Arts Archives / Milton Glaser Design Study Center and Archives; Zachary Sachs, Coordinator, School of Visual Arts Archives / Milton Glaser Design Study Center and Archives; Raffaella Fletcher, Sarah Copplestone Wood, and Ana Badescu, Alan Fletcher Archive.

To everyone I had the privilege of speaking with—on and off the record: Claudia de Almeida, Gail Anderson, Nicholas Blechman, Michael Bierut, Ken Carbone, Erik Carter, Chermayeff & Geismar [Ivan Chermayeff and Tom Geismar], Seymour Chwast, Stephen Doyle, Dress Code [Andre Andreev and Dan Covert], Elliott Earls, Experimental Jetset [Erwin Brinkers, Danny van den Dungen, and Marieke Stolk], Ed Fella, John Gall, Bob Gill, Joonmo Kang, Milton Glaser, Carin Goldberg, Natasha Jen, Maira Kalman, Karlssonwilker [Jan Wilker and Hjalti Karlsson], Ji Lee, Joe Marianek, Abbott Miller, Oliver Munday, Post Typography [Nolen Strals and Bruce Willen], Michael Rock, Stefan Sagmeister, Paul Sahre, Paula Scher, Sally Thurer, Michael Vanderbyl, Laura and James Victore, Jessica Walsh, Zut Alors! [Frank DeRose and Brendan Griffiths], along with many others.

To my good friends who to tolerated my ramblings and musings: Ian Allen, Dave Goldstein, AJ Mapes, Hal McCrory, and Nic Taylor.

Lastly, words cannot express my profound gratitude to my partner and wife Joanna Ahlberg for her tireless editing, re-editing, sound-boarding, re-re-editing, wordsmithing, and re-re-re-editing of all the texts included in this book. In addition, her endless excitement and encouragement, impromptu therapy sessions, and continual support were invaluable. I hope to someday return the favor.

All work © individual designer, studio, and/or archive.

Pages 18–19, 41, 46–47, 62–63, 70–71, 125, 178–179 Courtesy the Herb Lubalin Study Center of Design and Typography at The Cooper Union.

All photography and scanography © Peter Ahlberg unless noted otherwise:

Gail Anderson
Pages 68–69, 170

Dress Code
Pages 129, 138–139, 147, 155, 254

Elliott Earls
Page 241: "Elegy for the Collapse of the Empire; Detroit Craft and Disintegration" installation in the *No Object is an Island* exhibition at the Cranbook Art Museum, 2011

Experimental Jetset
Page 27: Book scan of *Magiër van een Nieuwe Tijd: Het Leven van Robert Jasper Grootveld* (roughly translates to *Magician of a New Era: The Life of Robert Jasper Grootveld*) written by Eric Duivenvoorden; published in 2009 by De Arbeiderspers, Amsterdam. Image caption in book reads: The 'Gnot'-sign, as presented by Bart Hughes and Robert Jasper Grootveld, during the 'Open the Graf' happening of 1962.
Page 232: *Two or Three Things I Know About Provo* / Amsterdam Edition (2011). A2-sized poster for *Two or Three Things*, an exhibition curated and designed by Experimental Jetset for exhibition space W139 (Amsterdam, NL).
Page 243: Whitney Museum graphic identity (2012). Chart ('periodic table') displaying a selection of possible variations of the 'Responsive W'.

Ed Fella
Pages 67, 84–85, 121, 185–187, 198–199, 240

Alan Fletcher Archives
Pages 102–104: Select sketchbook spreads for *Printed Pages: The It's Nice That Magazine.* Photographed by Benjamin Swanson, 2015.
Pages 105, 184
Page 253: Alan Fletcher working on *The Art of Looking Sideway* in his London studio. Photographed by Jan Baldwin, 2001.

John Gall
Page 92

Carin Goldberg
Pages 227, 248–249

Gottscho-Schleisner Collection
Library of Congress, Prints & Photographs Division [LC-G613-77360, LC-G613-78015]
Page 221

Natasha Jen
Page 133

Maira Kalman
Pages 100–101

Abbott Miller
Pages 180–181, 192–193

Post Typography
Pages 106–107, 167, 233

Stefan Sagmeister
Pages 54–57, 108–109

Paul Sahre
Pages 30

School of Visual Arts Archives / Milton Glaser Design Study Center and Archives:
Pages 58–59, 79–81, 152–153, 204–207

Josh Sisk
Page 252

Zut Alors!
Pages 134–135, 239

Design by: Peter Ahlberg
Cover design by: Peter Ahlberg, Claudine Eriksson
Edited by: Joanna Ahlberg
Transcriptions by: Meredith Ahlberg

Research & Design Assistant: Claudine Eriksson
Research & Design Interns: Ben Wittner; Michael Wong

First published in the United States of America in 2016 by

Skira Rizzoli Publications, Inc.
300 Park Avenue South
New York, NY 10010
www.rizzoliusa.com

2016 2017 2018 2019 2020 / 10 9 8 7 6 5 4 3 2 1

Printed in China

ISBN-13: 978-0-8478-4834-8
Library of Congress Control Number: 2015956764